P9-CJC-181

DATE DUE

Sale, Roger.

PN
1009   Fairy tales and
A1S24   after

RIVERSIDE CITY COLLEGE

LIBRARY

Riverside, California

APR   1980

Fairy Tales and After

Fairy Tales and After

FROM SNOW WHITE
TO E. B. WHITE

Roger Sale

Harvard University Press
Cambridge, Massachusetts
and London, England

Riverside Community College
Library
4800 Magnolia Avenue
Riverside, CA 92506

PN1009.A1 S24 1978
Sale, Roger.
Fairy tales and after : fro
Snow White to E. B. White

For Tim and Margaret

Copyright © 1978 by the President and Fellows of Harvard College
All rights reserved
Printed in the United States of America
Third printing 1979

Library of Congress Cataloging in Publication Data

Sale, Roger.
  Fairy tales and after: From Snow White to E. B. White.

  Bibliography: p.
  Includes index.
  CONTENTS: Fairy tales.—Written tales.—Animals.—
Lewis Carroll. [etc.]
  1. Children's literature—History and criticism.
I. Title.
PN1009.A1S24   809   78–18788
ISBN 0–674–29157–3

Acknowledgments

A quite different version of the concluding section of the introduction was given as a speech to the English Institute in September 1971 and subsequently published as "Child Reading and Man Reading: Oz, Babar, and Pooh," in *Children's Literature.* Somewhat different versions of "Fairy Tales" and "L. Frank Baum and Oz" appeared in *The Hudson Review.* I am grateful to the editors and publishers of these journals for permission to reprint these materials.

For permission to quote from currently copyrighted books, acknowledgment is given to the following: to Charles Scribner's Sons for *The Wind in the Willows;* to Harper & Row for *Charlotte's Web;* to Alfred A. Knopf for *Wiggins for President;* to Farrar, Straus and Giroux for Lore Segal's translations of "The Juniper Tree" and "Snow White"; to Pantheon Books for Velma Swanston Howard's translation of *The Wonderful Adventures of Nils;* to Dell Publishing Company for *The Animal Family.*

Most of the book was written during a sabbatical leave in 1976–77 from the University of Washington, and I am grateful for having had the opportunity to enjoy a long and unhurried time in which to do it.

All along the way I have received many helpful suggestions about what to read, how to read, and how to write better, which I have used in many ways; for all such favors, let me thank Jack Brenner, Tom Lockwood, Dorothy Sale, Tim Sale, and Ann Taylor. I am especially grateful to Tim Sale for the Kipling illustration.

But long before I contemplated this book, or imagined myself a writer at all, Dorothy Young was generating and sustaining my interest in children's books as interesting things to talk about for people who were no longer children. I was a self-important college lad when I first began courting her daughter, and she taught me much just by her quiet insistence that while yes, it was fun to argue about *Hamlet,* it was equally good to argue about *The Emerald City of Oz,* or hint my education might not be complete if I had not read the Bastable books or George MacDonald. In this way, as in many others, one of the joys of my marriage has been that she has become my mentor as well as my mother.

Contents

In order to have one last taste
Zephir bends his head, sticks out his tongue
and plouf - in he falls head first.
At this sound the chief cook looks around, and,
greatly annoyed, fishes him out by the tail.
The soup chef bursts out laughing. Arthur hides.
Poor little Zephir is a sight, all yellow and sticky.
Celeste scolds him and goes off to clean him up.

(1)　　　　　　　　　　Introduction:
　　　　　　　　　　　　　Child Reading
　　　　　　　　　and Man Reading

Everyone knows what children's literature is until asked to define it.
Is it literature read by or to people younger than some age—like the
Bible, *The Guinness Book of Records*, or a book I read over and over
between the ages of eight and ten called *Tour Book* (1930 edition),
though I did not know what a tour was? A child will listen to all
manner of words if they are well enough read, or pick up very odd
volumes indeed if nothing else is available. Is it literature intended
for children? That perhaps would get rid of the Bible, and *Tour Book*
certainly, but it would also throw out traditional fairy tales, *Kim*,
The Wind in the Willows, and *Peter Pan*, which is giving up too
much. Our best definition is going to be very loose and unhelpful,
or else cumbersomely long and unhelpful; we are better off saying
we all have a pretty good idea of what children's literature includes
and letting the matter rest there.

　For my purposes the important point is that children's literature
includes many books that older people, well past childhood, read and
enjoy even when they are not reading with or for children. Of course
many children like some books that most adults cannot stand; like
people of any age, children tend to enjoy a lot of junk. Most books
children like, though, are enjoyed by older people as well. The most
famous of all children's books, *Alice's Adventures in Wonderland*, is

more often enjoyed by older people than by children. Often, if far from always, adults are quite willing to say, or at least to admit, that they still enjoy very much this or that book they loved as children. Yet by and large adult people do not tend to write about children's books, or even to discuss them except very chattily; literary criticism of all but the most famous children's books is still in its infancy. To be sure, historians and folklorists have worked on fairy tales; librarians have written quasi-reference books or histories of children's literature; Lewis Carroll has long been the darling of some psychologists, philosophers, and mathematicians; many authors of children's books have been the subjects of some uncommonly good biographies. In recent years, when many more people have been "taking children's literature seriously," their published results have tended to be interested in "placing" the books and authors in some social and historical fashion or background. Literary commentary is still difficult to come by. Graham Greene wrote a brief appreciation of Beatrix Potter forty years ago that spoke of "the great Potter saga," her "great comedies" and "near tragedies," and Potter herself found it rather impertinent; it is hard, indeed, for anyone not to feel that Greene was mostly having a bit of fun.

There are two clear historical reasons for this neglect, one of long standing and the other more recent. First, although literary criticism is almost as old as literature, until well into this century it was usually written by people who also wrote poems, plays, and novels, and it usually concerned agreed-upon literary classics. If few people wrote about Potter or Kenneth Grahame, few people wrote about Trollope or Wilde or Chesterton, either. For obvious reasons, authors of children's books are among the last people who would want to write literary criticism themselves. English literature as a whole came into college curricula only within the last seventy-five years, so it is not surprising that only recently has "Children's Literature" been anything other than a branch of library science and, as a corollary, that literary criticism of children's books is in its infancy. Second, many people see no need for criticism of children's literature, since for them criticism is mostly explication, and children's literature demands little explicating. It is unfortunately true, especially in this country, that many feel that the justification of criticism is that it elucidates what would otherwise be obscure, and there is nothing obscure, nothing the least bit difficult, about *The Tale of Peter Rabbit* or *The Wizard of Oz*. Serious and presumably intelligent people clench their fists in baffled rage when asked to teach children's literature. Many of their students seem to agree with them when they sign up for such a course, anticipating that it will be easy because the reading is easy.

Yet the rage, bafflement, and consequent silence are irrelevant, or themselves impertinent. The most honored definition of the function of literature is that it gives profit and delight, and by this definition children's literature has given as much profit and delight as any other kind of literature. To be sure, children are impressionable creatures, accepting souls, and, when given a book, will derive from it as much profit and delight as they can. But millions of people have loved, say, *Peter Rabbit* simply because it is a very good book; it gives profit and delight because it can and should; it is one of the world's best known and best loved books because without it humanity would be the poorer. Of course its magic and power are not easy to describe, but that makes it all the more compelling as a subject for literary discussion and criticism.

It is in this spirit, the spirit of one wanting to write about very good books, that this book has been done. But my brief career as a person interested in writing about children's books did not begin with such a simple and worthy aim. I had taught and written for quite a few years about Shakespeare, George Eliot, D. H. Lawrence, and other "adult" authors before I found myself taking seriously the idea of literary criticism of children's books. Back in the first flush of pleasure at reading to our children, my wife and I discussed the possibility of writing a book like the present one, but, though we went on enjoying reading aloud for many more years, nothing ever happened to make the project real. It wasn't, indeed, until I found myself rereading the Oz books, ten years after I had first read them to my children and more than thirty years after they had first been read to me, that I realized that something so persistently profitable and delightful had to be accounted for. I am not sure if the experiment I then conducted on and for myself is one that any other adult reader of children's literature need go through, but it is one that undoubtedly many adults have experienced in a relatively unselfconscious fashion. What, I asked myself, is the role played by the child

I was in my adult reading of books I loved hearing and reading when I was young? In my own case at least, it became much easier for me to think and speak straightforwardly about all children's literature, to address myself to the ways in which some children's books offer great profit and delight, after I had conducted the experiment. My aim was not to lay ghosts to rest, exactly, because it wasn't really ghosts I was dealing with, but I have discovered that my own experience as a child reader came to seem less imposing or interfering after I deliberately went back to some books I had loved as a child and sought to learn the effects of that early love on my later reading of them. Thus, some of the books discussed in the following essays were favorites of mine as a child, while others definitely were not, and still others I did not know. But that fact, which once loomed large for me in the way I thought about these books, now seems not very important even to me. My favorite fairy tale as a child, "The Golden Bird," now is just one of many that I turn to; I discovered why I loved it when I went looking for it, and in the process of finding it I also discovered that there are quite a few fairy tales I would now more willingly reread or examine than "The Golden Bird."

Nonetheless that experiment still seems to me worth conducting, and, after making a few other introductory remarks, I would like to return to it and report briefly on it as a way of concluding this opening chapter. I can hope, however, that the way in which the rest of the book is "personal" is a way that could also be described as impersonal. I write as an adult, and for other adults; inevitably, and often regardless of any experience any of us had as children, I will look at these books in a way that some may find not just different from theirs, but alien as well. Here are these books, I want to say, good books, and we read them essentially as we read any book, left to right, top to bottom of the page, front to back. After reading them, we say what we have seen, felt, understood. But of course we don't see, feel, or understand the same things, and when we are dealing with very good books about which little has ever been written, we will diverge in method and disagree concerning emphasis and tone perhaps more than we would if the subject were, say, Shakespeare, about whom there is a long history of commentary and interpretation. If I can claim anything here, it is that if my criticism in the essays that follow seems personal, I doubt if I am much more personal when writing about "Snow White" than I am when writing about *Hamlet.*

Concerning my choices of books to discuss, I probably do not need to justify what I have included—they are all well agreed-upon classics—but perhaps might say something about why I have left out so many books obviously worthy of inclusion. Of course I could not possibly discuss all important books ever written for children and could not include even all that I know and like. It has, however, seemed important to concentrate on books with which I feel some marked imaginative sympathy. Though I have spoken of my aim as writing essays of literary criticism, and though a good deal of what follows includes assessments of weaknesses and limitations as well as praise and admiration of strengths, the spirit in which I write is essentially appreciative because, first and foremost, I am grateful that the books I write about exist. Thus, if there is some well-known children's classic that seems to be distinctly overrated—and I do believe there are many such books—I have chosen to ignore it rather than undertake the job of demolition that, under other circumstances, might seem necessary. There will be world enough and time, surely, for the undertaking of such tasks, but only if, as, and when the whole prospect of writing as an adult for other adults about children's books seems wider and more enticingly popular than it does now.

What is most needed, really, but what is most likely not to be undertaken until criticism of children's literature is well out of its infancy, is a good literary history. Almost as a matter of course I have arranged these essays in the chronological order of the books that are their subjects, and I have along the way suggested some historical pressures that worked to make certain books and authors as they are. Already a good deal has been uncovered concerning general trends, such as the shift during the nineteenth century from books that instructed to books that idealized children, or changes in the role played by illustration in the history of all literature, including children's books. The real problem of literary history, however, is always the matter of tradition, of the internal pressures of books on books within the realm of a given genre or language. Beatrix Potter influenced Alison Utley; Louisa May Alcott and Kenneth Grahame invented the collective hero; the publication of Kipling's *Stalky & Co.*

was followed by a spate of books about roguish schoolboys. Yes, that kind of information we have, because it is easily come by. But what has been the real importance of fairy tales for later children's literature? Who was the first parent who, in making up a story for his or her child, was aware, however unconsciously, of earlier parents telling stories to their children? When did the facts and problems of book publishing and production begin to play a major role in the way children's books were written and illustrated? When, asking the same questions, did child psychologists, teachers, and librarians become important, and with what effects? And, with all such questions, we need to know not just what and when, but how and why? Most of the important questions have not even been asked, and probably won't be, alas, until it is much more generally known that children's literature is one of the glories of our more recent literary heritage.

In the essays that follow I am aware of using at least three terms in ways that require some explanation here. The first, "latter-day," should become clear enough in the essays on fairy tales. Children's literature is a product of the latter days, of what until recently, at least, was called the modern world, which usually is understood to have begun in the seventeenth century and to have lasted well into our own. The term carries with it no necessary sense of value, though at the outset it may seem employed to describe something that was lost; I use it mostly to indicate the period after the invention of childhood, after books for children became printed and illustrated, after magic was generally discredited, all of which created opportunities and challenges for authors of children's books. The second term is "real" and its derivative, "realistic." I use these words as most latter-day people do, to refer to people and events easily seen in the world around us, or easily imagined to exist in places we don't know or in periods of history in which we do not live. *War and Peace* is "realistic," and "Kip the Enchanted Cat" is not, though no one now could empirically verify that statement. One wants to add that Kip, and other talking animals, may be more "vivid" or "lifelike" than many who are dumb and walk on four legs and use only their natural coats to keep them warm. But "vivid" or "lifelike" is not the same as "realistic"; the Cheshire Cat in Alice's Wonderland is more vivid and less realistic than her cat Dinah. Nor need the realistic be restricted to the frequent, the predictable, and the commonplace, though it must include these. When Dorothy Gale, in the opening pages of *The Road to Oz*, agrees to walk with the Shaggy Man to show him the way to Butterfield, she may be the first well-brought-up girl, in real or fictional Kansas, to undertake a journey with an adult man who looks like a vagabond or even a bum. It may be unlikely that this happens, but the event, to me, is realistic, as is her extraordinary conversation with Button-Bright a little later, and as the subsequent transformations in which the Shaggy Man is given the head of a donkey and Button-Bright the head of a fox are not.

As to what we are to call that which is not realistic, I think it is imperative not simply to call it the imaginary or the magical. Almost all the literature dealt with in this book is only intermittently realistic, but a great deal of it does not contain either deliberately or fully imagined alternative worlds or acts of magic, wizardry, or sorcery. Since a good deal of latter-day children's literature uses, as its major nonrealistic device, animals that talk or in other ways act like human beings, I have, as a bridge between the chapters on fairy tales and those on later children's literature, placed a chapter discussing some of the ways "talking animals" have been used. But there is nothing magical, except in a very loose sense of the term, about Peter Rabbit, or Grahame's Rat and Mole, or Kipling's Jungle animals, and since it seems to me important to specify in each case the precise effects of these nonrealistic creatures, I have avoided trying to find a catchall term to describe these effects, preferring to avoid any sense that the terminology we need in one case will help us much in dealing with the others.

We can see the need for such precision just from looking at the works of three authors who enchanted my youth (to come back to that), each of whom employs the nonrealistic in very different ways, each of whom is in many other ways different from the other two, each of whom seems to have contributed his bit to defining what I seemed to find most important in life, so that while their differences were, and are, manifestly apparent, they had something close to a single effect on me. What "I seemed to find most important in life" was not something I understood at all clearly when I began rereading these books, but, as I got further into the pilgrimage back to my childhood, I increasingly realized I was discovering something I might not have been able to discover had I tried to take more direct routes. It was not, perhaps, great personal riches that I uncovered, but something more like new bearings, and thereby new ways to see and understand what I have always tended to value deeply.

Dr. Seuss has been for some years the most popular author of children's books in America, mostly on the basis of his pleasant, rhyming books written to replace the moribund Dick-and-Jane primers. My impression is that the more popular Dr. Seuss has become, the less seriously he has been taken by those who take children's literature seriously, and it is true that his recent books seem to be rapidly written and increasingly inconsequential. But before *The Cat in the Hat* and the others came a long series of pleasant, rhyming books such as *Horton Hatches the Egg* and *How the Grinch Stole Christmas,* and even before that, back in the thirties, he wrote two major books of my youth, *The 500 Hats of Bartholomew Cubbins* and *The King's Stilts,* both pleasant, but in prose, and not really inconsequential either. There has always been a strain of bubbling whimsicality in Dr. Seuss; in these early books there is plenty of bubble, but the whimsicality is channeled by the tracing of unsentimental narrative propositions: the really hard thing about getting from one to five hundred is to get from one to two; a king who works and plays equally well is bound to earn someone's enmity.

It now seems to me that the second of these two propositions, the one that underlies *The King's Stilts,* is the stronger, but the other, for *The 500 Hats,* is the one that entranced me when I was young; so it is the one I need to concentrate on here:

> In the beginning Bartholomew Cubbins didn't have five hundred hats. He had only one hat. It was an old one that had belonged to his father and his father's father before him. It was probably the oldest and plainest hat in the whole Kingdom of Didd, where Bartholomew Cubbins lived. But Bartholomew liked it, especially because of the feather that always pointed straight up in the air.

A perfect opening, for me, at least. The name of the hero, the fact of the monarchy as well as a world where objects were handed down through the generations, all make it much unlike my world. Dr. Seuss, however, is clearly not trying to transport his reader to the

Other, the foreign, or magical, because he quite openly states the fact that what he seeks is a story, and a story that can get us from one hat to five hundred. Our concern is with hats. Dr. Seuss then shows us the grandeur of the Kingdom of Didd as seen from Bartholomew's hut, and the smallness of that hut when seen from the castle of King Derwin, and then sets us off, Bartholomew going to market at sunrise one Saturday morning.

Once in the city, Bartholomew hears a blare of horns, and the order for all hats to be removed: the king is coming. All the pictures are in black and white except for Bartholomew's red hat with the feather; so first the eye, and then the story, focuses on the hat, which thus is made more important than King Derwin, or even than Bartholomew's meeting him. The king rides by, hats come off, the king's carriage stops and backs up next to Bartholomew:

> The King leaned from his carriage window and fixed his eyes directly on Bartholomew Cubbins. "Well . . . ? Well . . . ?" he demanded.
>
> Bartholomew shook with fright. "I ought to say something," he thought to himself. But he could think of nothing to say.
>
> "Well?" demanded the King again. "Do you or do you *not* take off your hat before your King?"
>
> "Yes, indeed, Sire," answered Bartholomew, feeling greatly relieved. "I *do* take off my hat before my King."
>
> "Then take it off this very instant," commanded the King more loudly than before.
>
> "But, Sire, my hat *is* off," answered Bartholomew.

And there it is, in his hand. But the king insists Bartholomew is wearing his hat, so he reaches up "and touched a hat!"

There is the king, angrily pointing at Bartholomew's head, and on the head is a hat; there is Bartholomew, staring at his hand, and in the hand is a hat. The hats are red, and everything else is black and white. And the way you get from one hat to five hundred is first to get from one to two. This is not realistic, nor is it magic, and if one insists on asking what it is, Dr. Seuss will offer no answer except a story; soon there are not two hats but three, and soon the king is in a towering rage and orders Bartholomew off to the castle:

> *Flupp!* . . . the sharp wind whisked off Bartholomew's hat. *Flupp Flupp* . . . two more flew off. *Flupp Flupp Flupp* flew another . . . and another. "4 . . . 5 . . . 6 . . . 7 . . ." Bartholomew kept counting as the hats came faster and faster.

You get from one hat to five hundred by counting. One is released into the simplicity of getting from two hats to five hundred by just playing past the difficulty of getting from one to two, so that focusing on red hats and counting will carry us along. Bartholomew is taken to the castle, to the court, to the king's wise men and magicians, to the king's nephew who tries to shoot off Bartholomew's hat, and to the Yeoman of Bowman who has no more luck than the nephew. Finally the king orders Bartholomew to the dungeon of the executioner, but the executioner says the rule is that no one can be executed with his hat on. Bartholomew's hats, thus, level the court; he himself is not in the least raised up by all this, and no claims are offered for his pluck, cleverness, or courage, because he has these virtues only in ordinary quantities. Dr. Seuss's whimsical artistic skills are lavished on all the other characters, and their frustration offers one focus. Meanwhile Bartholomew remains small, wide-eyed, and counting, and he of course offers a second focus. But he and the others keep meeting on the hats. Dr. Seuss does not, as Hans Christian Andersen so often does, fire satiric shafts at monarchies, and he does not, as Milne does in the Christopher Robin books, imply extra points to readers who can count. Counting is the central activity in the book, the essential leveling activity, after we get from the first to the second hat, but the king has his own Keeper of the Records, Sir Alaric, to keep the official tally, and Alaric is baffled as much as anyone as he trails along after Bartholomew.

It all seems too simple, the sort of story that must please much more the first time one reads it than any subsequent time. Yet I have never tired of reading this story, and, so far as I can tell, my pleasure now is not only as great as it once was, but is pretty much the same, as Dr. Seuss continues his leveling by making the near forty years between my first and my most recent reading indistinguishable. I still stare at the hats, flying off the turrets of the castle with arrows in them, piling up around the startled, friendly executioner, lining the stairs to the tallest tower as Bartholomew tears hats off furiously because he is about to be shoved from the tower, hat and all. We know, as Bartholomew does not, that after he gets well past four hundred he is approaching a crisis, but Bartholomew knows he can think of nothing else to do except tear hats off. The story works, and keeps on working, because it insists on two apparently contrary feelings: first, we are in control here, well ahead of both Bartholomew and the court, because we know the book's essential journey is one hat to five hundred and no one in the story knows this; second, there is a problem, a mystery here, that will never be solved: how did all these hats get on Bartholomew's head? The effect of the two feelings on each other is to rob our control of complacence and to transform our sense of mystery into fun.

Following from all this, it is the last line that has always meant more to me than any other. After Bartholomew climbs the tower he takes off his five hundredth hat, and of course his life is saved because there isn't going to be a five hundreth and first hat, and so he can return home, happy and relieved to feel the breeze blowing in his hair at last:

> But neither Bartholomew Cubbins, nor King Derwin himself, nor anyone else in the Kingdom of Didd could ever explain how the strange thing had happened. They could only say it just "happened to happen" and was not very likely to happen again.

I carry that last line with me and use it often to "explain" strange events in this sublunary sphere. I do so not just because it is a good line, but because it is how Dr. Seuss slays the dragon of explanation: by walking between its legs. It isn't "once upon a time" at the start, and so it isn't "they lived happily ever after" at the end, but "it just happened to happen and is not very likely to happen again," as in a world, like mine, where the best that could be done was to get back alive to the point where I began. Not fairy, not heroic, but not antifairy or antiheroic either. How wonderful, when things just happened to happen, to get not only from one hat to two and thence to five hundred, but to get back home again, the only price exacted being the loss of one hat. It is more wonderful than I have ever been able to ask for or to expect, but not so wonderful I could not hope for it, and in this feeling the child I was and the man I am agree.

The story of *The 500 Hats* offers a narrative cradle, not for rocking one to sleep, but to encourage one with the knowledge that when one confronts angry kings and cavernous castles one goes on being oneself, taking one's hat off, and counting, and that all that one needs one also has. It was this rather than vivid or brilliant details that made this book alive and important to me; even as a child I could see how rudimentary Dr. Seuss's drawing is, how much every face resembles every other because, like me, Dr. Seuss has only one face he can draw. For sheer vividness in the memory there were frightening moments in other books and pictures that stayed with me longer than anything in *The 500 Hats,* compared to which this book has to seem rather tame. But as a whole, as an enterprise undertaken and completed, it offered and offers a residual sense of wonder and possibility that lies deeper than any single scary memory taken from other, "more powerful" books.

I want later to return to this deep residual feeling that this, and other very different books, gave me, but first I must look at some of those other very different books, the Babar stories of Jean de Brunhoff, which rightly rank with the Beatrix Potter books as the best ever made for very young children. Everyone who has read these books remembers two vivid moments in *The Story of Babar,* one in which Babar's mother is killed by a cruel hunter while Babar is riding on her back, the other in which the King of the Elephants eats a poisonous mushroom, turns green, and dies. Taken in isolation these moments seem like the piercing and frightening ones I just mentioned, and since many do thus isolate these moments, ignoring or forgetting de Brunhoff's context, it is perhaps better to begin with a somewhat quieter, though no less typical sequence, from *The Travels of Babar.* On their honeymoon, King Babar and Queen Celeste are rescued from a cannibals' island by a whale, who then puts them down on a reef, chases after some fish, and forgets to come back. They are rescued by a huge ocean liner, but the elephants' relief quickly turns to frustration and anger when the captain of the ship not only won't let them go ashore but puts them in the stables instead:

> "They have given us straw to sleep on," cried Babar in a rage. "And hay to eat as if we were donkeys! We are locked in! I won't have it; I'll smash everything to bits!"

Celeste then offers the advice often associated with the name of Uncle Tom: "It is the captain. Let us be good, and he may set us free." Babar, who could smash locks and tear the stables to bits quite easily, agrees, and on the next page we see only their large and seemingly defiant posteriors as they stand in the straw as though they were donkeys. But as reward for their acquiescence Babar and Celeste are sold to an animal trainer in a circus, which is just as humiliating as the stables, since of course they need no training and are no less smart and much more regal than the human beings who control them. But Celeste still counsels patience: "We won't stay in the circus long; we will get back to our own country and see Cornelius and little Arthur again." On the next page we are switched back to the elephant country where Arthur is exploding a firecracker on the tail of an old rhino, and Cornelius is unable to pacify the rhino, who then threatens war.

It is a sequence more somber than anything in Dr. Seuss, more destructive and apparently more cynical. Each of the rescues raises false hopes: the whale is pleasant but forgetful, the captain is greedy, the animal trainer is foolish and arrogant, Celeste is naive not to know these things, Babar is powerless while his country is getting ready for war. Every move that seems not to instruct us in cynicism is soon undercut. We do not need, thus, to dwell on the very troubling moments when Babar's mother is shot or when the king dies from eating a bad mushroom to see that de Brunhoff despairs that life is ever more than momentarily free of trouble, or that hoping does much good, or that, especially when dealing with people, we can ever know whom to trust or what to expect. He shows us misfortunes of a kind seldom found in children's books: betrayal, desertion, and cruelty, as we have seen, adventurousness and curiosity punished, capricious weather, house fires, nightmares, homesickness. De Brunhoff's tone in the presence of these events is impassive and accepting.

My rendering of de Brunhoff, however, falsifies the effect of his books. He does deal relentlessly with many unpleasant facts of life, but he is nowhere near as gloomy, or as gothic, or as like Edward Gorey, as I have implied. The major reason for this is that there is no register inside the stories to carry the burdens of the pain and sorrow, no invitation to imagine ourselves inside these terrible situations, though of course we must be very attentive to them from the outside. The impassivity that seems for a moment like indifference also assures us that this moment will pass, that there is nothing extraordinary about a cannibal attack, or a whale forgetting to come back after a meal of fish. When Babar returns home to lead the elephants in battle against the rhinoceroses, de Brunhoff says "King Babar was a great general" in exactly the same tone in which he says "It was a great misfortune" when Babar's predecessor eats the bad mushroom. As he uses them, words like "happy," "cruel," "great," "poison," "choke," "play," and "help" are all robbed of their capacity to excite or alarm. Nor do we have a narrative proposition to guide or offer power; de Brunhoff's stories are episodic, one thing after another, the task not being to get somewhere in particular, but to dwell slowly on a single moment, even to linger, and then to move on, thereby gaining all the equilibrium we need to juxtapose and eventually to reconcile disparate attitudes and possibilities.

All this, though, seems beyond even the instinctive comprehension of a child; at least none of this that I see now can I remember seeing forty years ago. I was, I know, almost totally absorbed with the pictures, which I stared at as I did no others. Part of their glory is that de Brunhoff thinks of so many wonderful things for elephants to do, especially with their trunks, that human beings can't do because they have no trunks, and that elephants don't do because they have no interest in playing tennis, watering flower beds, holding chalk, pulling naughty monkeys out of vats of vanilla cream. But there is more than that. I stared at that picture of the chef hauling the monkey Zephir out of the vanilla cream because, in effect, I was allowed to. There are V's drawn on the chef's brows to show his anger, but no one in the picture is frightened or even alarmed. Zephir is forlorn and a mess, no more, and the last sentence on the page has Celeste taking Zephir away to wash him. On the next page we are at a garden party at the Palace of Pleasure. The pictures don't register the feelings a reader of the text alone might be expected to have, so one is freed by de Brunhoff's somber equilibrium because it released him into playfulness in the pictures. If Dr. Seuss fights dragons by walking between their legs, de Brunhoff fights his by staring at them, by insisting he knows the limits of the dragons' power, since even the most shocking moments will last no longer than the most satisfying ones: both take no longer than two facing pages.

I could not say as a child how all this was done, but could receive "Look at the pictures" as the essential message of the text and not get the wrong message at all. It is no accident that my happiest moments of reading aloud to my children were with the Babar books. I could watch the child stare at the pictures, solemn but never frightened, amused but never laughing, and derive my own pleasure from the way the apparently skimpy text released us both into enjoying the pictures. De Brunhoff allies child and adult so that each can arrive at the same place by a somewhat different route. With Dr. Seuss my adult pleasure is only a replica of my childhood pleasure; with de Brunhoff the two pleasures are somewhat different, since I do see more in his books than I did as a child, but they are never in conflict with each other.

With A. A. Milne, on the other hand, I really am not able to read as I once could. I loved the Christopher Robin books, but find only intermittent pleasure in them now, and when they fail to cast their old magic spell, I am not just bored but offended. As a child listening to and staring at the Babar books, I trusted the relation I was enacting with the adult doing the reading, because the adult was not trying to ask me to respond any differently than I was. But the adult reader of Christopher Robin implicitly seeks more with the child being read to than that. The adult is explicitly put in the position of Milne himself, the child in the position of Christopher Robin: "you" and "I," the text says clearly. This might be all right, or even fun, except that Milne is always nudging Christopher Robin, instructing him, urging upon him good manners and good spelling and obedience, and this makes it hard on me as an adult reader. It may also explain why many children, after they become old enough to read to themselves, don't read these books, because so much in them depends on the relation of reader and read-to, adult and child.

Let me begin with a passage from *Winnie-the-Pooh* that shows Milne at close to his worst, being really quite offensive:

> "We are all going on an Expedition," said Christopher Robin, as he got up and brushed himself. "Thank you, Pooh."
>
> "Going on an Expotition?" said Pooh eagerly. "I don't think I've ever been on one of those. Where are we going to on this Expotition?"
>
> "Expedition, silly old Bear. It's got an 'x' in it."
>
> "Oh!" said Pooh, "I know." But he didn't really.

"We're going to discover the North Pole."

"Oh!" said Pooh again. "What *is* the North Pole?" he asked.

"It's just a thing you discover," said Christopher Robin carelessly, not being quite sure himself.

Here, as all too often in Milne, the essential action is to construct a hierarchy, to calculate one's superiority to someone else and then worry about who is superior to oneself. Pooh can't say or spell "expedition"; he knows it and Christopher Robin knows it, so Pooh is a "silly old Bear." Christopher Robin can say the word, can hear the "x" in it, but can't spell it, just as he can know the North Pole exists, and that people discover it, but nothing else about it. Milne forces his child reader or listener into one of two uncomfortable positions. If the child isn't old enough to spot the defects in Christopher Robin's learning, he can at least laugh at Pooh, since even a young child can hear the difference between "expotition" and "expedition." If the child can spot the defects in Christopher Robin's learning he can laugh at him as well. In either case he must agree that it is important to know how to spell "expedition," which it isn't, and to know a lot about the North Pole, which it isn't either, and to rank boys and bears according to how much they know, which is not only not important but fraudulent and shallow snobbery.

But we don't have to try to defend this shallow snobbery by calling its putative fun innocent; there is a lot that is real fun in the Pooh books. Whenever I've taught them to university undergraduates we have fought a good deal, because the students really like Milne. When I state my objections to him, they are offended: who would want to unload such heavy machinery on such sweet books? When we sort matters out, two facts emerge: they like these books better at twenty-odd than they did as children, and what they enjoy are the parts of the books that are most relaxed, lazy, and cozy, that is, Pooh's hums, especially "The more it snows, tiddely pom" and "I could spend a happy morning seeing Roo"; Pooh when he is alone with Piglet, and Piglet any time; the jokes against Owl; Eeyore's gloominess; and Poohsticks. To isolate these parts of the books as what one cares about is to treat the Forest as Utopia, so that someone speaking harshly about the books is put in the position of one who is announcing it is time to leave Utopia.

What my students see is really there and is really what is best about the books, but the Forest is no Utopia. The books are essentially about the fact that Christopher Robin is now too old to play with toy bears. He is given a world over which he has complete power, and if he is not very attractive as a deus-ex-machina in story after story, if he is never as interesting as the Pooh and Piglet to whom he condescends, the pleasures of his power are clear enough. Christopher Robin is now going to school, doing sums, spelling, worrying about not getting things right; he takes his fear of ridicule and his need to fit into a hierarchy and his schoolboy facts and imposes them on the animals in the Forest. Pooh is not, of course, a bear of very little brain, but Christopher Robin keeps putting him in situations where he will think he is, which is just what, one imagines, others are doing to Christopher Robin in his hours away from the Forest. Thus the alliance Milne seeks to create with Christopher Robin, whatever we may say of its entanglements otherwise, shrewdly seeks to console Christopher Robin for the pains of having had to leave the Forest. Children, certainly myself as a child, are much more interested than students of college age in learning about the ways it is sad, but all right, that we grow beyond early childhood, and even the snobbish Milne offers the assurance that we are growing toward something as well as growing away from something else.

Whatever of all this I may have understood as a child of Christopher Robin's age, I do know that Milne's most explicit statement of this theme, which comes in the closing sentences of *The House at Pooh Corner*, always moved me very much. It has come time for Christopher Robin to say good-bye to the Forest forever, and he takes Pooh up to the top of the Forest and dubs him Sir Pooh de Bear. Then:

> So they went off together. But wherever they go, and whatever happens to them on the way, in that enchanted place on the top of the Forest, a little boy and his Bear will always be playing.

I do not think it particularly sentimental of me that I still find it hard to say these words without beginning to cry, though I am aware that my tears are for the lost boy I was who also once wept over them. The lies they tell are known to be lies, and that saves everything. Pooh and Christopher Robin do not go away together, and we know it. The Forest is forever closed, except to the memory, and that is not a sentimental fact.

What I never saw as a child, but see in many places now, is that the Forest is becoming tainted long before it is closed by the alien values of Christopher Robin's and Milne's world. The animals are forever deferring and being asked to defer. Pooh and Piglet in clumsy ways, and Rabbit and Owl in more knowing and stupider ways, want to manage and control, to imitate Christopher Robin. That much is perhaps inevitable in most societies, but what makes it all painful is that Milne's view of schoolboy and adult life is so limited and empty, and his view of women, as seen in his digs at Kanga, is at the very least designed to foster the notion in Christopher Robin that one grows up by finding mothers silly and fussy. Even when Christopher Robin is at his best, as when he announces that the stick in Pooh's hand is the North Pole, he is still finding ways to control others by hiding his own ignorance. Candor is generally a fugitive and discardable virtue in the Forest, except, I must hasten to add, for Eeyore. He is, though not just for that reason, the one character I enjoy now even more than I did as a child, and his jibes at Rabbit at the end of the game of Poohsticks still make me want to clap, with surprise at Eeyore's sudden burst of healthy bad temper and with delight that the neofascist Rabbit is finally told off. But for the rest, the pleasures seem to me awfully thin, or else worse.

So I have three different authors of my youth, and three different responses to them as I compare my reading of them now with what I can recall of my reading of them as a child. I could, as an adult, proceed to accentuate these differences by calling Dr. Seuss American, Jean de Brunhoff French, and Milne English. Dr. Seuss's whimsical pragmatism, which says that the way to get from one plain hat to a second magical hat is to proceed on from two to five hundred, his guying at monarchies without ever taking them seriously or wishing them gone, his uninquisitive sense that evil is probably nothing more than someone acting like a naughty child—all this marks him as an American. De Brunhoff is even more distinctively French, impassive, civilized, both aware of the anthropomorphism implicit in racism and racist himself, never enjoying a plot and never likely to yield to the temptations of melodrama. It is no wonder that in extravagant moments I enjoy contending that de Brunhoff shares with Flaubert and Proust those qualities for which the more famous adult authors are admired, and if their display of these qualities is more copious than de Brunhoff's, it is no more pure. Then, just as de Brunhoff is witty but never funny, so A. A. Milne is often funny but never witty; de Brunhoff is a grown person and Milne is an arrested child; de Brunhoff is apparently able to include almost any aspect of life while Milne succeeds only when he excludes everything but snugness and whimsicality. Dr. Seuss believes Bartholomew Cubbins can take on the crowned heads of the Kingdom of Didd; de Brunhoff believes only in his own intelligence; Milne believes that if one learns how things are done, and named, and spelled, everything will turn out all right. American, French, English, and each a strikingly clear version of the national type.

But I knew nothing of that as a child, and it was not their differences but their similarity that allowed them to have such a strong impact on me. These are all accepting authors showing us the reassurances and even the pleasures that can follow if we accept. They celebrate the actual and possible in the midst of magic, confusion, loss, and lostness. I loved these books, apparently, because I was a willing candidate for their common imaginative dogma. With Dr. Seuss the truth is: accept whatever happens to happen and one will always get back alive and whole; with de Brunhoff, accept misfortune and the indifference of others, not only because one must, but because they are as transitory as the joys and peace that follow them; with Milne, accept the play of early childhood, for it is precious, accept that it is lost and then the schoolboy and adult world that replaces it will be more palatable and possible.

I cannot believe these writers taught me acceptance. The desire, and the beginnings of the capacity, to accept must have been present in me before I knew them, or else I would not have been so susceptible to their ways and means. But they could give me some of the terms of acceptance, the tone, manner, and the importance of so doing, and that was to give me a power that made other kinds of power seem less real or less important. Figures like King Arthur, or the boy David, or Superman, held me very little, because they could ignore or triumph over their situations, and for me the appeal of that had been preempted by the earlier and more appealing possibilities offered by Dr. Seuss, de Brunhoff, and Milne.

I was, apparently, a daylight reader, seeking to live in a daylight world. As a result, I can conclude from my relatively small childhood interest in fairy tales that I was unwilling, or, more likely, unable to touch down to my deepest wishes and fears in ways that some other children might be able to do. Perhaps I made a deal with life, that I would accept its pains and sorrows if I did not have to face what I feared and wished for most. In any event I think I can take what I learned about myself as a child from my rereading of Dr. Seuss, de Brunhoff, and Milne and see something about myself as a reader of adult literature. The authors who have proven themselves to be for me irreplaceable are Spenser, George Eliot, and the critic William Empson, all large and wise writers who seek to name and explore our possibilities only in consideration and acceptance of our common condition. Other writers, like Shakespeare and D. H. Lawrence, have often not only excited me more but have offered the terms of my speaking. The others, though, have seemed to reach deeper, to parts of me that are silent and that would, but for them, have perhaps remained unknown to me. In the present context I can say that Spenser began to be irreplaceable for me long before I had heard of him, when I first read Dr. Seuss and the Babar and Pooh books. The child is the father of the man in many ways, one of which is to create the imaginative terms of his knowing, and anyone with these books there to help create the terms cannot be said to have been abandoned in his early years.

As I said earlier, once I had undertaken this foray into autobiography I felt I had cut some real or imaginary umbilical cord, and I could then proceed more easily to read and write about children's literature without confusing it with myself as a child, or with the study of children's habits, tastes, or ways of thinking. Others who read this book may have read much more than I did as a child, while others still may have read almost no children's literature at all, and the impact of these various pasts on us is something I think we can discover, with little more than patience and willingness to explore. If what I or anyone else finds out is that there are some children's books that are hard to read freely and openly because of what they were for us when young, then so be it, and let it be openly acknowledged. But there is much that remains ahead of us, and the pages that follow are my effort to explore some of that territory.

THE ALMOND·TREE

"KYWITT, KYWITT, KYWITT, I CRY,
OH WHAT A BEAUTIFUL BIRD AM I!"

(2)   Fairy Tales

Fairy tale literature is one of the great kinds, a body of stories that do what no other literature does. They reach back into a dateless time, speak with grave assurance of wishes and fears, harbor no moralizing, no sense of "art," because their ways and means are varied, because there are so many stories to tell, so many ways to tell the "same" story. The term "fairy tale" is only a convenience since few stories we call by that name contain fairies, elves, leprechauns, or similar creatures. Yet everyone seems instinctively agreed on what the term includes and excludes, even though fairy tales blend easily into related kinds, like myths, legends, romances, realistic folk fables, and cautionary tales. "Cinderella," "Sinbad the Sailor," and "Hansel and Gretel" are fairy tales, while the stories of King Arthur, Pandora, Patient Griselda, and the Ancient Mariner are not. A nice borderline case is that of a Neapolitan tale that resembles many versions of "The Sleeping Beauty," but the king in this story, when he comes to the enchanted castle, rapes the sleeping princess. This is probably not what most people would call a fairy tale, even though the princess conceives and bears two children and eventually comes back to life, and other events as horrible as rape do take place in many fairy tales.

The existence of fairy tales is evidence of a cultural oneness throughout the Eurasian continent. Comparative folklorists have managed to uncover characters, events, and motifs that appear, often with only slight changes, in tales told in India, Japan, France, Germany, and Ireland. Each people gave the stories different twists and emphases, just as each people also developed distinctively native or local tales. The fairy tale book on which I was raised contains two Japanese stories, one of which, "The Tongue-Cut Sparrow," is similar to the Grimms' "The Fisherman and His Wife," while the other, "The Accomplished and Lucky Teakettle," is like no other story I am aware of. The best known stories in *The Thousand and One Nights* are distinctively "Arabian," but many of the lesser-known tales have much in common with some Indian and European ones. The various stories about Jack as the killer of giants belong strictly to the British Isles, while the English "Goldilocks and the Three Bears" resembles the Grimms' "Snow White" in its central episode. On the other hand, African and native American Indian stories belong to other families altogether from the fairy tales of Europe and Asia.

The stories we know derive from a relatively late period just before they began to be written down and collected, but are descendants of versions that go back into the mists of time, through centuries we can only sum up with the term "oral tradition." Furthermore, the stories themselves often reach back still further, to a time once upon a time; two thousand years ago, says the beginning of "The Juniper Tree," or when wishing still did some good, as the opening of "The Frog Prince" tells it. The versions we know were written, rewritten, and collected primarily in the two hundred years between Charles Perrault's *Histoires ou contes du temps passé* at the end of the seventeenth century and the *Fairy Books* of Andrew Lang at the end of the nineteenth. But all take us back to a world when only a handful of people outside the church were literate; what came before fairy tales, or the worlds they speak of, the teller knoweth not.

The ancientness of the tales, their curious persistence in so many different countries, their testimony to the strength of an oral tradition now all but gone, all serve to make them a literature that latter-day people need to treat with great care and respect if they are going to know them at all. The courtly French tellers around the end of the seventeenth century—Perrault, Countess d'Aulnoy, Madame de Villeneuve, Madame Le Prince de Beaumont—were given to making the tales wittier, more aristocratic, and sometimes more heart-piercing than they found them, and they often combined, within one story, elements they derived from their native oral tradition with others that had been part of a tradition of written tales almost as old. Clearly, however, the earlier the writer, or the closer the writers to the oral traditions, the better or less bruising the result. These first French written tales so closely resemble, and so fully respect, older traditions that few people know or care that "Puss in Boots" and "Beauty and the Beast" have actual authors. Hans Christian Andersen, writing more than a century later, had a more difficult time. He was raised in Odense, a Danish town where traditional stories were still told, but he spent his adult life in Copenhagen and became so imbued with a faint and faintly self-pitying Romanticism that even his best stories are distorted with authorial self-concern and flecked with satire and moralizing. But Andersen, troubled and vain though he was, was always essentially an oral teller; when we come down yet another century, to something like the fairy tales of C. S. Lewis, we see the damage caused when fairy stories are to be read from books. Lewis had a true and catholic love of older things, and a great longing to be part of their world, but the ear and instinct just weren't there, and the Narnia books, popular though they are with latter-day audiences, are brittle, mechanical, and naggingly preachy in ways older fairy tales never are.

Fairy tales may be irreplaceable, then, but whenever a tradition fades so it can be recovered only imperfectly, and only by isolated individuals, damage is inevitable, to the reader and to the tale. When many people shared the tradition, even in the latter days when it was more a written than an oral tradition, the sharing helped free the literature from being a matter of individual taste; so many stories were known that the intent of each individual tale could be felt and understood. This discouraged the distortion caused when fairy tale literature became thought of as children's literature; also it helped maintain the balance between wishes and fears that is the equi-librium of all fairy tales by keeping individual listeners and readers from being isolated from each other. That balance is often so delicate that any individual might well feel that fairy tales are mostly daydream wishes or nightmare fears, when in fact they are neither. Finally, in this century at least, so many people know fairy tales only through badly truncated and modernized versions that it is no longer really fairy tales they know.

The enemy, thus, is historical provincialism, the attitude that pretends one's native latter-day eyes and instincts are bound to be enough to gain an understanding of fairy tale literature. Of course our eyes and instincts are all we have to work with, but they can become more alert and better attuned just by reading many fairy tales, from many different places, with as much slowness and patience as can be mustered. Some sense of historical change can help a great deal here. The crucial point about fairy tales is that they *became* children's literature but were nothing of the sort for most of their long years of existence. Indeed, fairy tales could not have been children's literature originally, because, at least in our sense, children and childhood did not exist until recent centuries. To begin to contemplate the importance of that is to begin not only to understand what fairy tales are not, but to glimpse what we can best presume they once were.

Childhood was invented, and when it was, children's literature followed quite naturally. As for what was before the invention of childhood, here is a summary offered by Philip Ariès at the end of his long and painstaking work on the subject, *Centuries of Childhood:* "In the Middle Ages, at the beginning of modern times, and for a long time after that in the lower class, children were mixed with adults as soon as they were considered capable of doing without their mothers or nannies, not long after a tardy weaning (in other words, at about the age of seven). They immediately went straight into the great community of men, sharing in the work and play of their companions, old and young alike." Ariès is describing a world that lived with the most rudimentary—as we might think of it—conception of maturity as a physical matter. If there were stages in the growth of children, they were simply before and after infancy. This is easily seen in medieval and early Renaissance depictions of the Seven Ages of Man and in portraits of royal and noble children in that period. There are no children there, at least not as we think of them, but babes in arms, the putti that surround the madonnas, and then people of varying sizes all of whom have adult faces. People we think of as children look like what we call midgets.

Since children were either nursing infants or small adults, families did not have the importance they later came to have in a more bourgeois society: "The family fulfilled a function; it ensured the transmission of life, property, and names; but it did not penetrate very far into human sensibility. Myths such as courtly and precious love denigrated marriage, while realities such as the apprenticeship of children loosened the emotional bond between parents and children . . . New sciences such as psychoanalysis, pediatrics, and psychology devote themselves to the problems of childhood, and their findings are transmitted to parents by way of a mass of popular literature. Our world is obsessed by the physical, moral, and sexual problems of childhood."

Before this conclusion Ariès has offered a great deal of evidence concerning clothing, games, the construction of domestic dwellings, and, above all, schools to show how "the child" was brought into existence during the seventeenth century and, at most levels of society, during the eighteenth and nineteenth centuries. If, with this in mind, we then think of the relations between parents and children as seen in fairy tales, we may be less surprised at how straightforward, unanguished, and even businesslike they usually seem. The parents in "Hop o' My Thumb" and "Hansel and Gretel" must abandon their children, the king in "The Frog Prince" tells his daughter she must go to bed with the frog if she said she would, the miller in "Rumpelstiltskin" sells his daughter because he has boasted about her, Laidronette in "Green Snake" is told to live apart from her family because she is ugly, and at no point do any of these children protest or show so much as momentary resentment at their treatment. This is not easy for latter-day people to understand, but it does help to know that the basic sense of the relations of members of a family to each other has changed since fairy tales were commonly being told.

We can also learn something from this about both the tellers of the tales and the audience for them. First, the teller is never self-conscious, never calls attention to himself or herself, seldom calls attention to particular details or offers to interpret them; never, as we say in this century, apologizes and never explains. The tone is always assured without any accompanying sense that that tone has been adopted; such assurance comes with the territory. Second, the audience is not a restricted group in any way we can recognize; except in the literal sense in which a told tale probably must have an audience, we can learn almost nothing about it from the tales themselves. Ariès speaks of children, at about age seven, moving into "the great community of men," but this was not, as we might call it, the human community or the family of man, but, rather, all the rest of us. For most people the community consisted of groups that ranged from thirty or forty to as many as a hundred or more people, but no group ever would mistake itself, no matter how isolated it was, for the whole world. Other communities existed relatively nearby, itinerants traveled easily between them, and not very far away would be a church, a castle, a town, where one might go upon good occasion, where life was lived differently but in ways one learned or was told about. Presumably both the passing of time and the intervention of people from the outside would alter the way a story might be told, but would not, therefore, alter the fundamentally anonymous tone of the teller speaking to this little segment of "the great community of men." Variations on stories could come and go, travel around, develop still further variations until one story began to seem like two or three somewhat different ones, without any alteration of the relation of teller to tale. No one in particular had to say anything, no one in particular had to learn anything, everyone anticipated certain motifs or characters or events without ever insisting that one way of telling a story was the only way or the right way. The property that was the tales was truly communal, both within the smallish group (but much larger than a family) that was hearing a particular telling of a particular tale and within the much larger group (impossible to define or delimit) that could be presumed to listen to fairy tales.

We are apt to want to know what something means, but we are self-conscious and inquisitive people, liable to a fear of ignorance or stupidity. We are also apt to imagine that there is some implicit schedule in human life, so that we can imagine something especially interesting to people of a certain age, or something that is "too much" for a child, or something we are "too old for." We select our audiences and often tell our tales with a precise sense of a particular audience. Parents pick particular books for particular children and particular ages and adjust their stories so they can be more easily understood or so they can seem more grown-up or up-to-date. There is no trace of anything like this self-consciousness, this selectivity, this careful choosing of words, in fairy tale literature. What was was, and was equally for everyone. What we now call "French," "Scottish," or "German" fairy tales did not exist, because the community's sense of itself was not national and because so many variations existed in the languages we now call by these names.

A girl is in a wood. Give her a brother and one has "Hansel and Gretel," give her many brothers and sisters and one has "Hop o' My Thumb," send the girl to dwarves and one has "Snow White," to bears and one has "Goldilocks," to grandmother and one has "Little Red Riding Hood." Make the girl a boy and one might have Jack, either the one who climbs beanstalks or the one who kills giants; make her a man and one has "The Wonderful Musician"; give her three drops of blood and a servant and one has "The Goose Girl." Probably no one teller at any one time or place ever had all these variations available, to say nothing of a sense of these as variations, but something like this sense of variety and possibility all, clearly or vaguely, intersected by one or more familiar motifs or events. Now suppose that we ask, in our latter-day fashion, what is the wood? Does it mean anything, symbolize anything, suggest anything? Of course, because in a wood one can get lost, or encounter known, suspected, or unknown dangers; almost no one in fairy tale literature goes into the woods to play, or to meet someone as in an assignation. What happens in woods in fairy tales happens so often that one begins to make easy associations, so that when these associations are denied or ignored, as in "The Wonderful Musician," one is quickly aware of it. But forests in fairy tales are so frequent, their associations so obvious, that they come to seem a given, not unlike an opening chord in a piece of music that can be played loudly or softly, by this or that instrument, and go on to this or that among countless melodies. The wood is important, thus, because the story cannot proceed without it—no wood, no seven dwarves—but the last thing one needs to do is to ponder what it means, since what it means will be what is made of it in this telling of this tale. By itself the wood is nothing; combined with other things it can direct a tale, be a place where princes never live but often visit, where woodcutters can be found, and wolves, and witches.

The more we sense the community of fairy tales and fairy tale tellers, the more we can get rid of our latter-day sense of community associations of family and nation, the more we can rid our sense of literary kind, or genre, of association with convention, narrative stance, and tone, the better we can glimpse these tales, tellers, and their audiences. We love to say that the *meaning* of something *is* that something; here we get a real chance to practice what we claim. This does not mean we are to be struck dumb by fairy tales, or that we should never ask questions, or never interpret, but that we can gain a great deal from the stories if first we read, and read a lot, and watch, with patience and a love of slowness, and then, when we come to speak, do so with the tentativeness that all older things deserve. Above all, we need to adjust or even temporarily to abolish our sense of older and younger, parent and child, and let the tales give us their sense of these people and these relations. This can be hard, as reading about courtly love or kingship can be hard, since we think we know about these things already, and it is much easier to learn a truly foreign language than it is to readjust the meanings and emphases of one's own. But if we look at just one kind of mistake of this sort we can perhaps be more aware of how easy it is to make such mistakes.

During the first century and a half of children's literature, from roughly 1700 to 1850, a long battle was fought to expunge fairy tales on grounds that they were about what the Houyhnhnm master calls "the thing which was not" and could not therefore teach anything. It was, however, assumed that the danger they posed was for children, since presumably no parent or adult would want to read a fairy tale. Part of this battle is a work called *The Parental Instructor,* which can best be found today in an interesting collection of early English children's literature edited by Leonard de Vries and called *Flowers of Delight.* Charles and Mary Elliott have asked their father to tell them a fairy tale, "Cinderella, Ass-skin, Tom Thumb, or Bluebeard," all Perrault stories, one notes, as if "childish" fairy tales were made worse by having been imported from wicked France. Their father reproves them: " 'What!' said Mr. Elliott, 'at your age— would you wish me to relate stories which have not even the shadow of common sense in them? It would be ridiculous to see a great big boy of ten and a young lady of nine, listening, with open mouths, to the adventures of an ogre who ate little children, or the Little Gentleman with his Seven League boots; I could only pardon it in a child, who requires to be rocked asleep by his nurse.' "

Mr. Elliott is, we say, wrong, wrong about fairy tales, wrong about children; it is not required that all literature pass literal-minded utilitarian tests, especially not required that the imagination of children be stifled and channeled so as to exclude everything not realistic, sensible, educational. But, in my experience, whenever I have asked someone to state the objections to Mr. Elliott, he or she has always begun by saying Mr. Elliott is repressing the natural and normal instincts of his children. That, apparently, is what we find most objectionable about him. The counterargument to his, however, tends to have some assumptions buried in it which are fatal to any decent understanding of fairy tales. Children need to be imaginative, need to learn about that which is not, need to discover and explore their own fantasies and those of others. Thus they need fairy tales. That is, say, the counterargument offered by Bruno Bettelheim in *The Uses of Enchantment.*

Both Mr. Elliott's argument and the counterargument offered by Bettelheim and others suffer because they are based on a sense of children rather than an understanding of fairy tales, and because they draw a clear distinction between the real and the magical that fairy tales do not make and presumably their tellers did not make. Fairy tales are no more "for" children than they are "not for" children, and no fairy tale I know distinguishes real from unreal, to say nothing of fantasy from fact. About children I agree with Bettelheim and disagree with Mr. Elliott, but that is irrelevant to fairy tales themselves. Mr. Elliott wants to say fairy tales are at best stories for the nursery, worthless for lads and lasses of nine or ten; Bettelheim wants to say they are good for children of nine and ten because they are about maturing processes children are frightened of and yet must go through. Both are really psychologists, putting fairy tales into some prearranged idea of growth.

Their mistake, as I have said, is all the more difficult to correct because it is, in the latter days, so hard to spot in the first place. Correction begins with a slow reading of many tales, done with as few prearranged ideas as possible; a full reading of tales from one country followed by a sampling from a number of others is a good way to begin. Take, as one does this, a motif or event, and see what happens to it in various tales, something more articulated than a girl in a wood, like births. In "Snow White" a queen pricks her finger and wishes for a child, who soon is born; in "Rapunzel" a couple vainly wishes for a child until a witch from whom the husband has stolen rampion announces a child will be born; in "The Sleeping Beauty" a frog announces to the wife while she is bathing that she will become pregnant; "The Goose Girl," on the other hand, opens with a child and mother, and the mother bequeaths three drops of blood to the daughter as she sets out to find her prince. All these are German stories, to be found in Grimm. Countess d'Aulnoy's "The White Deer" opens with a wife being told by a shrimp that she will have a child, and the shrimp then turns into a handsome old woman; the Russian tale "Kip, the Enchanted Cat" starts with a queen and a cat, and the cat has a kitten before she tells the queen she too will have a baby.

We have, thus, a motif or a scene that seems to know no national boundaries, at least in Europe. A couple, but especially the wife, wants a child, and something must happen, blood must flow, an enchanted animal must make an announcement, before the wish can be granted. If we ask why this should be such a common motif, we probably need to know little more than that women of much earlier times, especially women not of the nobility, came to puberty much later than women in latter days and also tended to marry much younger than women do now. Thus many couples could have been married some years before they could have had a child; the period we know as adolescence hadn't been invented yet, of course. Beyond that we need not inquire, I suspect. Nor need we be surprised that this motif invariably comes at the beginning of stories, nor that, for the most part, the child that is born will turn out to be much more important in the story than either parent. The woman often died in childbirth, the man tended to remain faceless. But each use of this motif is somewhat different from the others, so that we can easily imagine the tellers of a particular tale shaping the episode of the annunciation and birth to fit the child to come and perhaps even the story to come. Here the basic wish, for the child, and the basic fear, that there will be no child, meet so simply and obviously that nothing need be made clear except whatever is required by the particular story being told.

And so we come to our first significant example, the opening of "The Juniper Tree," a story told by the Grimms, sometimes called "The Almond Tree," and here translated by Lore Segal in *The Juniper Tree and Other Tales*:

> It is a long time ago now, as much as two thousand years maybe, that there was a rich man and he had a wife and she was beautiful and good, and they loved each other very much but they had no children even though they wanted some so much, the wife prayed and prayed for one both day and night, and still they did not and they did not get one. In front of their house was a yard and in the yard stood a juniper tree. Once, in wintertime, the woman stood under the tree and peeled herself an apple, and as she was peeling she cut her finger and the blood fell on the snow, "Ah," said the woman and sighed a deep sigh, and she looked at the blood before her and her heart ached. "If only I had a child as red as blood and as white as snow." And as she said it, it made her feel very happy, as if it really were going to happen. And so she went into the house, and a month went by, the snow was gone; and two months, and everything was green; and three months, and the flowers came up out of the ground; and four months, and all the trees in the woods sprouted and the green branches grew dense and tangled with one another and the little birds sang so the woods echoed, and the blossoms fell from the trees; and so five months were gone, and she stood under the juniper tree and it smelled so sweet her heart leaped and she fell

on her knees and was beside herself with happiness; and when six months had gone by, the fruit grew round and heavy and she was very still; and seven months, and she snatched the juniper berries and ate them so greedily she became sad and ill; and so the eighth month went by, and she called her husband and cried, "When I die, bury me under the juniper." And she was comforted and felt happy, but when the nine months were gone, she had a child as white as snow and as red as blood and when she saw it she was so happy that she died.

Nothing here is unfamiliar, yet it is all put together to make something unique, which is true at least of all major tales. J. R. R. Tolkien calls this opening "exquisite and tragic," which it certainly is, and of all the stories that begin with childless couples and the birth of children, this is the only one that can properly be called that.

The cues that highlight this story in contrast to all the others which involve the birth of a child come early: the wife is both beautiful and good, the couple love each other, the wife prays—each detail softens the wife and makes her more than an incidental figure. The pricking of the finger is almost identical to the one in "Snow White," but the similarity only serves to set off differences; in "Snow White" the husband is barely mentioned, and, more strikingly, there is no tree, no incantatory rolling out of spring, summer, and harvest to follow. Indeed, "The Juniper Tree" is exquisite and tragic because the natural cycle enfolds the wife and fulfills her thereby within one turn of the seasons. She is but a flower that glides, and we feel this not because of what the wife here shares with childless wives in other stories but because of those emphases that set this story apart from others similar to it. If we speak of the power of the blood, the power of the tree, or the power of the natural cycle, we are really speaking of the literary power of the storyteller, who takes material common to all stories with childless couples and develops it in a distinctive way. Out of the great reservoir of possibilities for such an opening, a reservoir known not just to the teller but to many listeners, attention to these outstanding details is commanded.

After the death of the wife, "The Juniper Tree" seems to change direction, and the tone is decidedly different. The child is a boy, for one distinctive fact, and after the father remarries and the stepmother becomes threatening, she succeeds, for the only time in fairy tale literature I am aware of, in consummating her hatred and murdering the child. Unlike the stepmother's in "Snow White," the woman's motives here are muffled, obscure, assumed, perhaps, but not explained. More striking still, the stepmother is both a blunderer and guilt-ridden. She scurries around after the murder, puts the boy's head back on his shoulders, places the blame on her own daughter, whom she loves, and serves the boy to his father in a stew. All this contrasts very sharply with the exquisite and tragic beginning—it is the sharpest I know in fairy tales—and also with the cleverer and more demonic stepmothers and wicked fairies of other stories. This stepmother is brutal and callous, but haunted, too, and pathetic in her ineptitude. Oddly, the effect of both these contrasts is to show us how the story continues to be about the juniper tree. The boy is just a boy, the stepmother blunders in a recognizably ordinary household, and his facelessness and her clumsiness keep them from having anything like the stature of Snow White and her stepmother.

Thus, when the daughter places the boy's bones under the juniper, and her heart feels suddenly happy, and out flies a bird, we notice how the daughter's actions parallel those of the first wife, and how the tree has changed its powers from natural to extranatural without changing itself; the bird "is" the boy, but that seems no more magical or miraculous than the first wife's becoming happy and pregnant after wishing in front of the tree. The bird/boy flies around the village, cheerfully singing a song about its own murder, bargaining for objects with which to console and reward the father and daughter and to punish the stepmother. It sings its final song from the branches of the juniper tree, then leaves the tree aflame and becomes the boy again. The juniper tree is not Yeats's great-rooted blossomer, and in this story body is consistently bruised to pleasure soul, but the power of the human beings is sufficiently limited and that of the tree held sufficiently mysterious that it is and becomes both the dancer and the dance.

To say even that much, though, may make the tree "mean" too much, "symbolize" too much; there aren't more than a handful of sentences about it in the entire tale, and all speak of it in perfectly flat, straightforward language and tone. The storyteller does not meditate on the tree or encourage our doing so. But knowing all we do of other fairy tales that begin with a childless couple, we will see that this juniper tree is more than just another announcer of a pregnancy. So we attend to it every time it appears, and our attentiveness gives it its central location and strength. But the tree remains a tree, though the most powerful one in fairy tale literature, and out of it come juniper berries, and a bird, and alongside it a child is conceived, a girl's heart is made happy, and a boy is resurrected. For such wonders "symbol" is as clumsy a term as "magical," or "natural," or "religious." And, to say it once more, our sense of these wonders increases as we are made aware of the stories this is not, an awareness we gain simultaneously as we learn about the story this is.

The procedure I am speaking for can hardly strike anyone as being sophisticated, but it has the advantage of being simple more than naïve, and of not being something other than literary. If one reads many fairy tales, one sees along the way that there are many things to interest the folklorist, the psychologist, the cultural anthropologist, but since their professions are all distinctly modern and fairy tales are all distinctly old, the evidence they look for and find is probably never the most distinctive evidence in the tale, that which sets one story, or even one version of the same story, apart from another. We have to believe, however, that simple collecting and comparing of similar characters and motifs in a variety of tales is something any hearer of tales could easily have done in the former days. That which made one story, or one version, popular with a community need have been nothing more than the skillful development of certain familiar motifs to suit the shapings in this rather than that direction. Furthermore, when one gets used to watching for themes and variations, one can turn to English or Russian or Indian fairy tales and invariably see how tellers make one particular story distinctive by turning familiar material one way rather than another, or sooner rather than later. For instance, there is a fine Russian story, "Go I Know Not Whither, Bring Back I Know Not What," in which, in the second paragraph, an enchanted dove is turned into a beautiful woman, just as so often happens only at the end of other fairy tales. One notes it, finds it odd, right away. But that is not so odd in Russian tales, which often concern themselves with life after a marriage rather than before. Still, having the marriage begin with a broken enchantment is unusual even here, and throughout the long tale which follows, the wife remains mysteriously formidable, and it is not surprising that she can turn herself back into a dove, as she does at one point to escape from a king who wants to marry her even though she is married. Having such a conception of a woman, and a wife, it suits the storyteller beautifully to make her her own enchanter and disenchanter.

Bearing all this in mind, I think we can then face more directly the central magical issue of fairy tales, their wishes and fears. If one asks what is the characteristic mold of any fairy tale, the most obvious answer is that they begin "Once upon a time" and end "they lived happily ever after." In fact quite a few tales do not begin just this way and well more than half do not end just this way, but we all know and recognize the formulas. A great many people seem then to conclude, since from the beginning the tale is avowedly imagined and since, at the end, "things turn out right" that fairy tales are optimistic and even happy. They note beautiful women, often princesses, marrying handsome, brave, or clever men, often princes, and use that as evidence that in fairy tales everything, or everything essential, is cast in an unreal, golden mold. To "have a fairy tale ending" is to have an unusually surprising and happy ending, in our common speech. But then, when given, say, "The Frog Prince," which does begin "Once upon a time" and which does end with a princess marrying a prince and living happily ever after, the general response is often a kind of outcry: why should a princess who seems petulant and spoiled, who doesn't want to keep her end of a bargain, be rewarded precisely at the moment when she is being most petulant and insistently breaking her bargain, when she picks up the frog and smashes him into the wall? It is unfair, surely, thus to reward princesses.

"The Frog Prince" is indeed a very unfair story, and in this respect may be more strikingly so than many others, but not essentially different from them. The rewards are clearly in excess of the princess's deserts; she *deserves* a spanking, if you like. But the strain in the story that creates this sense of unfairness is exactly what is required to overcome the fear of the repulsive object that has come to eat and sleep with the princess. The child playing with her ball has made her bargain with the frog, hardly thinking what she is getting herself into. Her father, when the frog comes calling, insists she keep it. But keeping bargains doesn't rid her of her fear and revulsion as the frog's moves become increasingly intimate. Thinking of it that way—as the story of a girl forced by her father and her own past consent to let a repulsive creature come to her bed, as the story of a girl gripped by a fear that is understandable and stronger than any bargain—one finds a fear one sympathizes with as it becomes more unreasoning. To overcome such a fear requires a wish every bit as deep, demanding, and unreasoning. The wish is not that the frog will go away but that it will be transformed into a handsome prince such as any princess might want to accept beside her at table and in bed. The fear is not a fear of intimacy or of sex, but of ugliness and revulsion. The nakedness of both the fear and the wish is precisely what leads to such a strong sense of its unfairness if we consider only bargains and rewards. We might have been alerted to all this by the opening phrases, "In the old days, when wishing still did some good," the acknowledgment right there that the wishes involved must be great because the fears are also. Neither nightmare nor daydream, but both, with the two facing each other. Seeing this, we can perhaps also see why magic in fairy tales is seldom elaborate or even remarkable. It is used only to create the fear and to grant the wish, and these, not the magic, are always what is most important.

The fears and wishes themselves are never extraordinary, but what animates a good tale and distinguishes it from other similar ones is a precision about them. The stepmother in "The Juniper Tree" is frightening because she is *not* demonic but driven, out of control; the frog is repulsive because it is a frog, but frightening because it insists on everyone's playing fair when a feeling deeper than fairness is in question. In this context, one of the greatest tales, "Snow White," is great because it is so very precise about both its fears and its wishes. Furthermore, it is helpful because two eminent critics have recently discussed it in ways that can help us sharpen our sense of method or procedure in working with fairy tales, and because it offers clear insight into some historical conditions of the periods when fairy tales were still being told.

The point about "Snow White," in contrast to "The Juniper Tree" and to many other similar tales, is that the relation of the older to the younger woman is central. Just as the opening of "The Juniper Tree" makes us note the importance of the wife, the tree, and the seasons, so in "Snow White" we first note the distinctive details of the stepmother's mirror and the announcement that Snow White begins to be the stepmother's rival when she reaches the age of seven. This makes the stepmother important, makes her relation to Snow White important, and diminishes everything else in the tale. The first wife disappears very quickly and unremarkably, and the king-father is barely mentioned. In *The Uses of Enchantment* Bruno Bettelheim discusses this tale and seems to want to ignore these facts, as follows: "A weak father is as little use to Snow White as he was to Hansel and Gretel. The frequent appearance of such figures in fairy tales suggests that wife-dominated husbands are not exactly new to this world. More to the point, it is such fathers who either create unmanageable difficulties in the child or else fail to help him solve them. This is another example of the important messages fairy tales contain for parents." Out of context, one would hardly know what "weak father" Bettelheim is talking about, since the father in this tale is just not in evidence. In fact Bettelheim is referring to the huntsman sent to kill Snow White. It seems clear, though, that because Bettelheim is determined to make most fairy tales concern relations between parents and children—to move them down a few centuries to a time when a strong sense of family prevailed—he is forced to invent parents when they can't be found. The huntsman, after all, can hardly be said to have created Snow White's "unmanageable difficulties," and if he does not help her "solve" them, he does the essential thing in sparing her life.

Nor, when Bettelheim turns to the impressive queen, does his sense of the story become any more precise: "Now if the queen's purpose was to kill Snow White, she could easily have done so at this moment [when she laces Snow White and suffocates her]. But if the queen's goal was to prevent her daughter from surpassing her, reducing her to immobility is sufficient for a time. The queen, then, stands for a parent who temporarily succeeds in maintaining his dominance by arresting his child's development." Again Bettelheim is both distorting the text and partially rewriting it so as to be able to wrench these ancient characters into his latter-day developmental patterns. If the tale is momentarily silent on the queen's intentions as she laces Snow White, she has already eaten what she took to be the lungs and liver of Snow White, and with the poisoned comb and apple that follow the intention is clearly not just to "arrest his child's development." The pity is that Bettelheim is right to say that the queen's aim is not simply murderous, though in desperation she is quite willing to murder Snow White in order to be rid of the fairest in the land; in a sense the most important quality of the queen's passion is that it is impersonal, aimed at anyone the mirror might name as her rival. But such an impersonal passion is hard to see when one is bent on making all relations in this and other tales depend on parents and children.

It is also hard to see when one is interested in something that might be called a generic strait jacket. In a review of *The Uses of Enchantment*, Harold Bloom shows clearly how Bettelheim's training has betrayed him as a reader of "Snow White," but his own training obtrudes when he comes to offer a counterreading:

> What kind of story is "Snow White," when an adult encounters it in a good translation of the Grimms? It is about as uncanny as Coleridge's "Christabel," would be an accurate answer, and it is hardly a paradigm for the process of maturing beyond Oedipal conflicts, as Bettelheim wants it to be. Snow White's mother, like Christabel's, dies in childbirth. The relations between her wicked and disguised stepmother and Snow White, during the three attempts to murder the girl, are about as equivocal as the Sapphic encounters between Geraldine and Christabel. Trying to kill by successively tight-lacing her, combing her hair with a poisoned comb, and sharing a partly poisoned apple with her—all these testify to a mutual sexual attraction between Snow White and her stepmother. The stepmother's desire to devour the liver and lungs of Snow White is demonic

in itself, but takes on a particularly uncanny luster in the primal narcissism of a tale dominated by mirrors. When the tale ends, the wicked stepmother, dressed in her most beautiful clothes, has danced herself to death in red-hot slippers at the wedding feast of Snow White, a horror that is an expressive emblem of her frustrated desires.

Bloom does go to precisely those points in this story where an experienced reader of fairy tales has noted distinctive details: the mirror, the eating of the lungs and liver, the three "temptations," and the red-hot shoes at the end. But he is much too determined to make "Snow White" be like "Christabel."

Let's start with the mirror, mirror on the wall, because that shows at every point that this is a story about the desire to be the fairest of them all. The term "narcissism" seems altogether too slippery to be the only one we want here. There is, for instance, no suggestion that the queen's absorption in her beauty ever gives her pleasure, or that the desire for power through sexual attractiveness is itself a sexual feeling. What is stressed is the anger and fear that attend the queen's realization that as she and Snow White both get older, she must lose. This is why the major feeling involved is not jealousy but envy: to make beauty that important is to reduce the world to one in which only two people count. But none of this makes "Christabel" a relevant analogue. The queen's desire to eat Snow White's lungs and liver implies only her desire to include Snow White's beauty and power within herself, and whatever sexual feeling is involved in that is included in the original passion to be fairest.

Then we come to the three temptations, where Snow White is at last able to choose. On the first visit: "Snow White hadn't the least suspicion, and let the old woman lace her up with new laces"; on the second visit: "It looked so nice to the child she let herself be fooled, and opened the door . . . Poor Snow White, who didn't suspect anything, and let the old woman do as she pleased." Whatever we might say the stepmother wants, it is clear that what Snow White wants is to be laced, to have her hair combed, and finally to eat the poisoned apple. Her attention is directed toward what will make her beautiful, what will make her sexual even, and that desire need carry with it no suggestion of any desire for the disguised old woman or the wicked stepmother. Against the charm of what she is offered, Snow White is defenseless, not so much because she is innocent as because she is charmed. It seems equally distorting to say the stepmother is attracted to Snow White. What she wants is what Snow White has, the beauty of a young woman, but her intensity is more eerie if it isn't tilted from the desire for Snow White's beauty toward the desire for Snow White herself: " 'Are you afraid of poison?' said the old woman. 'Look, I'll cut the apple in two halves, you eat the red cheek and I'll eat the white.' But the apple was so cunningly made that only the red part was poisoned. Snow White longed for the lovely apple, and when she saw that the old woman was eating it, she couldn't resist it any longer, put out her hand, and took the poisoned half." Snow White wants, and is afraid of, the sexuality implicit in the red of the apple without wanting the one who gives her the apple. Thus Snow White's desire is the same as the queen's; it is for beauty and sexual power as goals in themselves. It is not a demonic desire as we see it in Snow White, though we know it is a fearful wish indeed, laden with danger and the potentiality of becoming like the queen.

The fear here is not of the wish for beauty, but of the power of that wish when separated and isolated from love, from handsome princes; the wish is that beauty will not be thus isolated. Which makes it a good deal more grim than Bettelheim's tale of growing up, and a good deal less gaudy and more earthbound than Bloom's Sapphic romance. It offers one of the best and starkest views of the world in which fairy tales were made that we can find. As we have seen, in fairy tales the primary task for women is bearing children, and childbearing was often fatal; whatever other power women had lay in youth and beauty. After a brief blossoming—shortly after the age of seven in Snow White's case, so we need not automatically associate it with puberty—people grew old rather quickly, and most of the palliatives against a grim and crimped existence were controlled by men. Older men in fairy tales usually are dutiful, stolid people, restricted to work, food, and small pleasures. But because their power was not primarily a sexual power, men in fairy tales seldom develop an envious murderous passion against younger men, because whatever power men have does not erode with time. On this score the evidence of fairy tales, taken from almost every country, presents a nearly unanimous view, and so what we see must be a clear reflection of what was.

Snow White's stepmother, thus, is involved in a struggle she must lose, to Snow White, but primarily to the passage of time. Her passion is frightening because the passion to be fairest seeks no value beyond itself; the queen doesn't want anything, or anyone, to be fairest with, except her mirror. She has been given only one power, and that one very briefly, and contrary to all our latter-day desires and hopes that sexuality can mature as youth goes and beauty fades, in the world of fairy tales sex is always allied with youth and beauty. For an older woman to fight against these facts and values made her frightening, and no fairy tale can imagine defeating such a woman without also destroying her. The more maternal passion of the witch in "Rapunzel" can be more easily excused because she only longs for a child of her own. Of course there is the countering wish, that men and women can find mates with whom they can live happily ever after, but when the tales focus on grown people they tend to give us stolid, ineffective men (or else tyrant kings) and frightened and frightening women. Of course, then, Snow White and the queen are locked in a terrible likeness, because they are the same person at two different stages of life.

For confirmation of this we can note the existence, in many fairy tales, especially those crucially shaped in the earliest of the latter days, of a third figure, the thirteenth Wise Woman in the Grimms' "Sleeping Beauty," the fairy godmother in Perrault's "Cinderella" and the Lilac Fairy in his "Donkey-Skin," the woman who gives raspberries to Lisa in Andersen's "The Wild Swans," and whose voice tells her how to un-enchant her brothers. These figures are substitutes for the good mother who has died bearing children, and in effect they pass on the hopes attendant upon birth or puberty. That the Grimms, who were telling stories straight from the oral tradition, do not have such a figure in their Cinderella story, or in their version of "The Wild Swans" called "The Six Swans," hints that these frankly magical and benign women were, in earlier times, too much even to wish for. Even these good mothers or their surrogates, however, work to reinforce the overwhelming sense that women had to struggle against women, and the wish they represent says no more than the wish that this struggle will not corrupt.

In his essay "On Fairy Stories," in *Tree and Leaf*, Tolkien says "They are now *old*, and antiquity has an appeal in itself." That is one tug on one's feelings which I, along with Tolkien and many others, have felt, but when I think of the world out of which "Snow White," "The Juniper Tree," "The Goose Girl," "Hansel and Gretel," and many others came, I shudder and am grateful I am not asked to be good, to be me, to be alive, in that world. Bruno Bettelheim wants to imagine that his psychological machinery can bridge the gap over the centuries between the former and the latter days, and I not only think he cannot safely build such a bridge, but am relieved the gap is there. Of course, to say antiquity does not have, in itself, an appeal is not to deny that it does, in itself, have an interest, a commanding power to make us ponder. It seems easier to me to respond to the purity of fairy tales, to the brightness of their sense of beauty and good, to the darkness of their sense of envy and unrequited desire, when one knows that one's own world is more impure, and the fates are not so inevitable and decisive. Look at the three men in "Rumpelstiltskin," for instance. It is not the miller who boastingly vaunts his daughter into peril, or the avaricious, cruel king who marries her, but the little man who helps her and wants only a child for himself who is singled out for punishment. As I think about the wishes and fears that went into the making of that story, I feel warm to remember I do not much participate in them. The story has its hateful power, to be sure, but it is the power of the alien insistence that the king must always be accepted, and even married, no matter how dreadful, and that the little man in the woods must always be thwarted, no matter how sympathetic. I always dreaded "Rumpelstiltskin" as a child, and I am glad I now know why.

This sense of chill is not my only response. If it were I would never go back to fairy tales again and again as I do. I can begin to describe it by referring to Tolkien's statement in *Tree and Leaf* that these "stories have now a mythical or total (unanalysable) effect . . . they open a door on Other Time, and if we pass through, though only for a moment, we stand outside our own time, outside Time Itself maybe." Let me add to this a similar statement made by Elizabeth Cook: "There is another door that can be opened by reading legends and fairy tales, and for some children, at the present time, there may be no other key to it. *Religio,* in one Latin sense of the word, implies a sense of the strange, the numinous, the totally Other, of what lies quite beyond human personality and cannot be found in any human relationships. This kind of 'religion' is an indestructible part of the experience of many human minds, even though the temper of a secular society does not encourage it, and the whole movement of modern theology runs counter to it." I am not sure how much of what Tolkien and Cook are referring to lies within my actual experience with fairy tales. I think I wanted them to have this effect on me more than they actually did, or now have. Both Tolkien and Cook speak of a door fairy tales open, on to Other Time or the "strange, the numinous, the totally Other," and I think I understand that, sympathize strongly with its longings and possibilities, and find myself looking through this door but only at some distance from it. Fairy tales survived through centuries and through transport to many different countries, and the storytellers seem to know this, to feel the strength of the great tree as they are speaking of what happened on one small branch. In one sense it matters which version or which translation of a story we read, but in another it barely matters at all, because each is its own tale, and there is never a "true" version of any one. All this bespeaks a power that has been lost or debased in the latter days, a power of sharing, of teller and hearer both knowing that each cue, each twist in the tale, is notable because so many other stories are about the events that are not in this particular one. In literature or other "high" arts we call this sharing a matter of conventions, but that is too conscious, too heavy a term for the sharing of fairy tales. On this side of the door, I feel I can understand something of this power as I glimpse it, "studying" fairy tales as I do, and I can see that some analogous power is often at work within the story as well, and these powers can make me still, even as I move no closer to the door.

That stillness is perhaps enough, since it makes the apparent arbitrariness and obscurity of events in fairy tales an integral part of their appeal and sense of wonder, and arbitrariness and obscurity are what most frequently lie in the path to our coming to any understanding of them. When I am thus still, I hear testimony in a story or a collection of tales, and a voice is speaking across a large abyss. But it is only a voice, or some voices, not something beyond human personality, not something beyond human relationships. It lies before human personality as we know it, before human relationships as we normally experience them, but the abyss between me and most tales is not as wide as that between me and *The Iliad* or the books of Joshua and Judges. My feeling gives me a position between that described by Elizabeth Cook and Tolkien—where one is stilled when confronted with the totally other—and that of a scholar, whose search for evidence is totally secular. My way to that feeling I call literary, because it seeks to honor the particular events of particular tales and to honor the surfaces of all tales, and to do this by reading many tales. The result is a kind of historical sense, a grasping of ways in which Then is not Now; that often is enough to create the feeling of stillness of which I am speaking. But when I come to speak about an individual tale, I am aware that my description ends up at times looking very much like a plot summary; and while I of course want more than that, I think I am still and wondering enough to settle for that if it is all I can get.

There is a fable in the Grimms' collection, a *hausmärchen*, called "The Death of the Hen." It runs only a few hundred words, and within that span the story is remarkable for seeming to change itself half a dozen times or more, seeming at one moment like a cautionary "Chicken Little" story, at another like "The Old Women and the Pig," at a third like a version of "The Friendly Beasts" that came to Jesus' manger. It is too solemn and bewildering ever to be a joke, yet the tone is at times so detached as to seem deadpan and amused. In Lucy Crane's translation, the last lines are:

> So the cock was left all alone with the dead hen, and he digged a grave and laid her in it, and he raised a mound above her, and sat himself down and lamented so sore that at last he died. And so they were all dead together.

I feel here almost like shouting that there is nothing like this in the world, never before and never again. Wordsworth's great phrase about Michael, "And never lifted up a single stone," seems practically sweaty in its reaching for poetic effect beside the last line of this story. We are back at the foot of the great narrative tree, where stories can, as if by a kind of natural magic, go anywhere, because life, crimped and fearful though it be, is wondrous and full and one must accept it all. One minds mortality less when remembering that we will all be dead together, along with the hen and the cock and the teller of that tale.

(3)

Written Tales: Perrault to Andersen

In 1697 Charles Perrault had published eight stories under the title *Histoires ou contes du temps passé*, a volume often better known by its subtitle, *Contes de ma mère l'oye*, or *Mother Goose Tales*. Perrault is usually and properly given credit for having written the first children's book, and while there is not all that much that is original in his achievement, there is great convenience for using him, his book, and that date as a point of origin and change.

In our reverence for fairy tales of the oral tradition, we must not think that written fairy tales are any less old. A written version of "Sleeping Beauty" can be found in the Twentieth Dynasty in Egypt, a number of written tales can be found in the Sanskrit *Panchatantra* of the fifth century, and written versions of some of the *Thousand and One Nights* were made hundreds of years before they were imported into Europe in the eighteenth century. Perrault's "Puss in Boots" is really only a reworking of a tale he found in Giovanni Francesco Straparola's *Le tredici piacevoli notti*, a collection from the mid-sixteenth century, and a work that was the apparent source for some stories now known as being "by" Countess d'Aulnoy and Madame de Villeneuve. Written fairy tales in their older forms are usually found in collections that include beast fables, legends, myths of religion and metamorphosis, cautionary tales, fabliaux, and ballads, which is to say almost any kind of traditional narrative except perhaps the epic. Chaucer and Boccaccio did not put fairy tales into their collections, but they quite easily could have.

Nonetheless, Perrault's *Histoires* stands out, for two reasons. First, his was a pivotal period in the history of the invention of childhood, and thus of children's literature, when traditions of both oral and written tales were taking a turning. Second, of all the many collections of fairy tales that were written and collected in France around the turn of the seventeenth century, Perrault's were the ones most clearly designed to be read to children. The tales of Countess d'Aulnoy, and of her daughter, Madame de Heere, of Mlle de la Force and Madame de Murat were all part of a rampaging fashion for *contes de fées,* but these stories are long and intricate and are not designed for children, though they were told to young as well as old. Perrault's stories are relatively short, because he had "children" as an audience expressly in mind, so that when, after him, fairy tales became nursery tales, his were the versions of the stories he told that latter-day people came to know. One has to search quite hard to find some of Countess d'Aulnoy's most brilliant stories—the last edition of her tales in English came late in the last century—and even the best known, like "The Blue Bird" and "Green Snake," can be found only in an occasional anthology. But "Cinderella" and "Little Red Riding Hood" are known in some version or other by millions who have never heard of Perrault.

In dealing with written tales, one has at the outset an understandable desire to find those versions which are "closer" to oral tales, which are less sophisticated and self-conscious, which have the least air of a teller calling attention to himself or herself. We prefer, thus, the writer who learned tales from a nanny to the writer who learned them from a book. There can, however, be something self-defeating about this desire, since written tales clearly played a major part in the wide transmission of tales and of characters and motifs within tales; if the nannies did not read written tales, written tales played a role in giving the nannies the stories they knew. This is more demonstrably the case in countries like France, Spain, and Italy than it is in Germany, England, and Scandinavia, where all people, and not just the peasants, were more isolated and more reliant on local tales. Within France, the Bretons, who were Celts, were more immune to influences from the Mediterranean than were the Provençal. But that does not make northern stories better than southern ones. Those who learn "Cinderella" from Perrault's written version rather than from the Grimms' "Aschenputel" are not therefore more deprived.

In the last chapter I mentioned a Neapolitan version of "The Sleeping Beauty" in which the king, coming on the beautiful princess in the castle, rapes her. I also mentioned "Rumpelstiltskin," in which a miller sells his daughter to a king and the king threatens to kill her if she does not spin straw into gold. The events in both stories are harsh and repellent, and were I ever interested in shielding the young from the darker and more malicious aspects of human nature and history, I would be hard pressed to include either story in my collection of acceptable tales. There is, though, a real difference between the stories, and one that would be hard to eradicate in any retelling. The rape is a climactic event, and so we are forced to think about rape as a means of impregnating, and then awakening, sleeping beauties. By comparison the selling of the daughter and the king's threats in "Rumpelstiltskin" are machinery in the background, assumed ingredients in the story, not its point. We can overlook the aristocratic barbarity of the king in "Rumpelstiltskin" much more easily than that of the king in the Neapolitan "Sleeping Beauty." The wish of the woman in "Rumpelstiltskin"—to escape the threats of her husband and to keep her child—is not morally an acceptable wish since it involves being cruel to the one person who has been kind to her, but it is a wantable wish nonetheless. It is hard to see, however, how any outside a tiny minority could wish to be raped in order to be awakened or could wish to rape in order to awaken. That is, the written Neapolitan story seems shaped by the desire to tell a story in a bizarre way, while the motive in "Rumpelstiltskin" is the great traditional motive of fairy tales, to triumph over our deepest fears with our deepest wishes.

This distinction, which is clear enough, would be difficult to maintain in any absolute sense in order to differentiate oral from written tales; it is nonetheless useful when we look at the great proliferation of written tales at the outset of children's literature. Perrault's stories, since they are short and confine their more sophisticated gestures to shadings of speech and narrative tone, are not quite as central here as those of Countess d'Aulnoy, next to whose stories Perrault's stand as a beautifully pruned bush beside a jungle of overgrown vines. Both writers were responding to what was for them primarily a fashion which was also a change in attitude toward fairy tales, a change perhaps most clearly articulated in this passage from Madame de Murat:

> The old fairies, your predecessors, now seem very frivolous creatures compared to your modern fairies. Their occupations were menial and childish, and could amuse only servant-girls and nannies. Their only interest was in sweeping out the house, putting on the stew, doing the washing, rocking the children and sending them to sleep, milking the cows, churning the butter, and a thousand other trivialities of that kind . . . That is why nothing remains to us today of their activities but fairy-tales . . . They were nothing but beggar-girls . . . But you, my ladies, have taken a new road. You busy yourselves only with great things, of which the least important are to give wit to those who have none, beauty to the ugly, eloquence to the ignorant, and wealth to the poor.

Madame de Murat and presumably all the other tellers of *contes de fées* were improving oral, "old-fashioned," servant-told fairy stories. Ennoble the tellers and raise the aims of the tales.

Countess d'Aulnoy reveals this fashion and this shift in attitude much more clearly than does Perrault. Reading her tales, which are never as short as his and are often more than ten times as long, one is aware of many borrowings and adaptations, only one source of which is traditional oral fairy tales. Her transformations seem closer to Ovid's *Metamorphoses* than to "The Frog Prince," her narrative weavings and digressions seem more like Ariosto than anything in folk literature. She delights in profusion, in odd and striking combinings, in elevating, as she would have thought of it, traditional fairy tale materials to romance. Andrew Lang accuses her of confounding various tales and cites her mixing of "Hop o' My Thumb" and "Cinderella" in her "Finette Cedron" as though she did not know what she was doing, when obviously she wanted to see what would happen if she wove two very different stories together. In her version of "Beauty and the Beast," called "The Ram," the ram dies untransformed and the princess dies of grief at having caused his death. In "The Pigeon and the Dove," the prince and princess, having been transformed into birds, decide they would prefer to stay that way, and do.

All this must seem anathema to the purists; these tales are not the real thing, as the Neapolitan "Sleeping Beauty" is not. With a writer this elegant, this devoted to an aristocratic knowingness about narrative, one is bound to be aware of the writer, and the great strength of the oral teller, the anonymous narration of wishes and fears, is twisted in a somewhat different direction, so that we become aware of narrative pointing, of goodness seen as a moral antidote to evil, of characters able to change their feelings, of a story that seeks to be wise. " 'The good one does is never lost' is a truth known only to fairies, the poor, and distressed animals," she says in one tale. "It is difficult to love much, and not to fear what we love," she comments in another. "I do not accuse you of my misfortunes, but if you do not wish to add to them, receive my son kindly, for he is the strongest here and can work you terrible mischief," cautions a character in a third. D'Aulnoy thus can remind us in many ways that she was writing at the end of a century two of whose major figures were Corneille and Monteverdi, and she willingly deprives herself of that timeless quality we rightly admire in oral tales. "There was once upon a time a king and a queen who managed their affairs very badly," begins one tale; "There was a king who for a long time had been engaged in a war with his neighbors," opens another, and, rather than look to see if older tales have such beginnings, we can do better by remembering that she wrote after Louis XIV had been king for fifty years.

So d'Aulnoy was not writing down traditional oral tale materials, and she was not writing children's literature either, though most of her stories fit well enough into latter-day tale collections for children. But she is a powerful writer nonetheless, because her sense of improvement and elevation of fairy tales does not in any effective way deride her predecessors in the written fairy tale tradition. The story that reveals this best is "The Golden Branch," but that tale of stunning beauty and intricacy is so little known and so difficult to find that a more familiar one will probably prove more helpful. "Green Snake" can be found, adapted but still vital, in Marie Ponsot's *Fairy Tale Book* and some other collections.

"Green Snake" opens, as quite a few of her tales do, with a version of "Sleeping Beauty," involving twelve fairies invited to a christening and a powerful uninvited thirteenth fairy full of wrath. The twist here is that there are two princesses rather than one, and the ugly thirteenth fairy strikes one of the girls fearfully ugly and leaves the other alone. Like most *contes de fées*, the tone is social, the matter a matter of manners:

> The queen shivered at the sight, fearing some disaster, as she had not invited her to the entertainment; but, carefully concealing her uneasiness, she placed, herself, an arm-chair for the fairy, which was covered with green velvet embroidered with sapphires. As Magotine was the eldest of the fairies, all the rest made way for her to pass, and whispered to each other "Let us hasten, sister, to endow the little princesses, so that we may be beforehand with Magotine." When the arm-chair was placed for her she rudely said she would not have it, and that she was big enough to eat standing. But she made a mistake, for the table being rather a high one, she was not tall enough even to see over it; and this annoyance increased her ill-humour.

Given this opening tone, it is not surprising that the king and queen, after Magotine has uglified one of their daughters, want somehow not to repudiate the unfortuate Laidronette, though they of course prefer the beautiful Belotte. Nor should it be surprising that Laidronette grows up to be a princess of great considerateness, who, when she becomes twelve, asks her parents to let her shut herself up in a distant castle so she won't inflict her ugliness on anyone else.

All this bespeaks a self-justifying courtliness that is seldom found in oral fairy tales, where the value of being royal and beautiful is assumed rather than discussed, and the pain of ugliness is diminished because it is seldom self-conscious. When an ugly green snake appears to Laidronette in a forest, she is horrified. When the snake offers to help her when she is caught in a storm in a boat, she answers, "Death strikes less terror to my heart than you do, and if you want to do me a favor, never show yourself in my sight." The effect of this emphasis on the horror of ugliness is to make **Laidro-nette's** plight more pitiable than a sleeping beauty's could ever **be.** Knowing how ugly she is herself, she becomes an expert on how revolting ugliness is, so her scorn of the snake seems beautifully futile rather than mocking or nasty. Perhaps physical ugliness and deformity are sufficiently rare in the industrial democracies in this century for us to pretend to feel superior to d'Aulnoy's emphasis, but it is not at all hard to see through that pretense, to recognize how shy any fear of ugliness makes one, how easy it must be for the ugly one to accept the judgment of others.

Laidronette falls asleep in the boat, expecting to drown, but instead she wakes up in a beautiful palace where, in an interlude that resembles first "Beauty and the Beast" and then "Cupid and Psyche," she is given everything she wishes, including "books, serious, amusing, and historical," so that the days pass like minutes, even though she never sees the owner of the place. At night, though, she is visited and wooed by an invisible king she finds it difficult not to respond to:

> "Although," said the princess, "I have resolved never to love, and have every reason to defend my heart against an attachment which could only be fatal to it, I nevertheless confess to you that I should much like to behold a king who has so strange a taste; for if it be true that you love me, you are perhaps the only being in the world who could be guilty of such a weakness for a person so ugly as I am." "Think of me whatever you please, adorable princess," replied the voice, "I find in your merit a sufficient justification for my passion; nor is it from singularity of taste that I conceal myself. I have motives so melancholy, that if you knew them you could not refrain from pitying me."

Older fairy tales know little of this beautiful mournfulness, because they never dwell on what it is like to live under the spell of wicked enchantments, and because they never allow manners to matter as they do here, where it is only the way Laidronette and the invisible king speak which can acknowledge the burden of ugliness and thereby keep that burden from crushing them.

Laidronette cannot at this point pretend to love the voice, because it is only a voice and because she cannot trust herself to be loved. She does, however, agree to marry the king and to wait patiently for the two years remaining on his term of enchanted servitude. When she tells her parents, though, that she is married, they insist on visiting her, and then on knowing where her husband is:

> "Oh, unfortunate creature!" exclaimed the queen. "How gross is the snare they have laid for thee! Is it possible that thou couldst have listened with such extreme simplicity to such fables? Thy husband is a monster; and how could it be otherwise, for all the pagodas, of whom he is king, are downright monkeys." "I believe, rather," replied Laidronette, "that he is the God of Love himself." "What a delusion!" cried Queen Bellotte. "They told Psyche that she had married a monster, and she discovered that it was Cupid. You are positive that Cupid is your husband, and to a certainty he is a monster!"

This is rather like Chauntecleer and Pertelote arguing about the validity of dreams, but it is all played in d'Aulnoy's insistent minor key, so that the fact of ugliness as a wicked enchantment permeates the entire tale and becomes so powerful that Laidronette gives in to the temptation to see her husband, who, of course, is the horrible Green Snake who now must endure a new seven-year punishment.

We are concerned here with goodness, with its frailty in a world of enchantments, with the need to endure with a steadfastness we know is well outside our ordinary mortal power. We may see this absorption in the state of enchantment as a distortion or even a corruption of the harder, more firmly outlined, oral tale; we may feel d'Aulnoy's emphasis on the extraordinary and the exemplary takes fairy tales away from wishes and fears and moves them to a beautiful, sad, remote world. But d'Aulnoy's equipoise is admirable, itself pure if we think for a moment of the more truly tortured grotesqueries into which such stories were transformed by Romantic writers a century or so later: "How she reproached herself for the affliction she had brought upon her husband! She loved him tenderly, but she was horrified at his form, and would have cheerfully given half the remainder of her days never to have seen him!" "She would have given half the remainder of her days"—that is just right. Once she wished to die because she is ugly, and now, loving and being loved but guilty and in terrible circumstances, she wishes with only half herself to give up. This is what it is like to be entwined in a d'Aulnoy story and to feel its narrative intricacies.

Green Snake has gone, far away, to endure his new punishment, and Laidronette is alone when Magotine comes to inflict new tortures on her. She is set traditional impossible tasks—to spin a cobweb into beautiful hair, to spin the hair into fishnets strong enough to catch salmon, to climb a mountain with her feet encased in tiny iron shoes and a millstone around her neck, to find there a four-leaf clover so she can go into a valley and fill a pitcher full of holes with the water of discretion—and at each point she is helped by a fairy protectress, and, at the end, when she washes in the water, she is made beautiful at last. But one of the potential virtues of such long tales is that they need not hurry, and neither discretion nor beauty is powerful enough to bring back Green Snake from Hades, from Proserpina, to whom Magotine has sent him. But by this point Laidronette, or Queen Discreet as she has become, has lost all sense of her own needs, has become stronger in her love by her beauty, and so she can make iron tears run down Pluto's cheek and make Hell grant what Love did seek. The strength of the allegory lies in its ability to emerge delicately, or, we may say, the strength of the myth is such that Laidronette can become Discreet, Psyche can become Orpheus, without the tales pausing on its determined path. We can even, at the end, have the wisdom distilled into the ditty of a quatrain:

> Gladly beat our hearts united
> Fearlessly in Hades' shades;
> Joyous love by love requited;
> Forever vanquished, terror fades.

Masquelike and courtly, it is far from the huts and castles in which fairy tales were told of old, but "Green Snake" is a beautiful tale, and d'Aulnoy has eight or ten in her collection of twenty-two that are its equal.

The world in which such a story was made was fading almost as surely as was that of the tales of the oral tradition, and it was, even more than the French Revolution, the coming of children's literature which was responsible. The profusions for which d'Aulnoy is most remarkable soon became, in the hands of her contemporaries and followers, excesses. In 1740 Madame de Villeneuve concocted a "Beauty and the Beast" over three hundred pages long, puffed out with invention and decoration, and so the fashion soon changed. Since, furthermore, it was as children's literature that all fairy tales were to survive, it was Perrault's *contes* rather than the grand and serpentine efforts of the ladies which effected the transition, and d'Aulnoy's stories had to be retold, to remain hers only in name and outline, before they could be handed on. Inevitably her stories lost something in the pruning, and some of her best tales proved so hard to prune they were ignored and were only very infrequently re-published as fairy tales for children.

The best known of d'Aulnoy's kind of tale had a more fortunate fate than any of hers has ever enjoyed. After Madame de Villeneuve's mammoth version of "Beauty and the Beast," it had to undergo immediate surgery if it was to survive at all, and, fortunately, a woman named Madame Le Prince de Beaumont was at hand to do the job. Le Prince de Beaumont was not a grand lady of Versailles but a governess living in England, and she was concerned primarily with laying down her ideas of the best ways to educate the young. She thus wrote, among a total of seventy books, treatises called *Instruction pour les jeune dames, Le Mentor moderne,* and *Manuel de la jeunesse.* She flourished in the middle of the eighteenth century and so was a contemporary of Madame de Genlis, who also wrote instructive books for children, and of John Newbery, the London publisher whose little books, like *Little Goody Two Shoes,* were attempting to extricate children from the clutches of fairy tales and the French fantastic. As a result, while Le Prince de Beaumont saved "Beauty and the Beast" for later generations, she also gave it an earnestness—rather than a seriousness, which it should have—and a perkiness—rather than a sense of life's possible pleasures, which it should also have—that are always slightly unfortunate. Madame de

Villeneuve's version opens with the merchant with six children when he needs only one; describes gardens and furnishings as though a handbook for landscape design and interior decoration; adds a whole series of visits in Beauty's dreams by Beast-as-handsome prince; and succeeds in making Beauty seem awfully dense. This will never do by itself, but can serve as an element in an amalgam of her version's and Le Prince de Beaumont's, the story as it "should be," slightly longer, slower, and less pointed than Le Prince de Beaumont's. It is a great story, yet no one ever reads it in the best of all possible versions.

For the most part Le Prince de Beaumont's is quite good enough. Its simplicity of outline makes it seem as close to "Snow White" as to "Green Snake," but the appearance is deceiving. Its ways and means are spare, but they are in important respects very different from those of the oral tradition, and it is this story, perhaps more than any other, that announces that the next, the nineteenth-century, form of the fairy tale will be the ballet. Its understanding of its materials is so secure it seems able to illuminate and interpret itself, so that by saying what happens in the story one is almost saying what the story means. By comparison, most oral fairy tales seem primitive, and most earlier written tales seem clumsily long-winded. For instance, when the merchant is about to leave Beast's palace for his home, he picks a rose in Beast's garden, and Beast accuses him of insulting his hospitality. A number of things happen at once, lines are drawn, and meanings emerge. "Perhaps you'll bring me a rose," Beauty had said when her father left, "I can't seem to grow them here." Now:

> As he passed under a trellis heavy with roses he thought of Beauty's wish, and picked a rose for her. Just then there was a terrible roar, and a monstrous beast rushed up. "I saved your life, and you show your thanks by stealing my precious roses. You'll die for this. Say your prayers, for in ten minutes I'll kill you." "Majesty, forgive me," begged the trader. "I took the rose for one of my daughters. She asked me to bring her one."

Instantly a role is established for the father to play with his daughter, a role different from his bringing home presents. It is sexual, because he wants to give Beauty what she needs and Beast has, but the father is not implicated in the sexuality. But, since the episode works primarily as a pivot for the plot, whatever we might call suggestive or symbolic about the action is apprehended simply as a matter of narrative, unlike, say, the many pricked fingers in oral fairy tales where the isolation or unconnectedness of the episode calls attention to itself.

Or, for instance, the moment when Beauty first comes to Beast's palace. In de Villeneuve's version this takes pages; the trees, birds, and insects all offer their welcomes, and Beauty goes through many rooms before she finally comes to one marked "Beauty's Apartment." Le Prince de Beaumont's version prunes all that away and insists that Beauty's fear of Beast's intentions is balanced by her sense of wonder at his delicate silence and considerateness; she doesn't need finery, or entertainment, or congenial surroundings, so much as a room of her own. Beauty slowly learns about her lover with every move she makes, and attention is drawn away from the architecture and toward the architect, the unseen figure who has brooded about what she most needs. By comparison, when the third son in d'Aulnoy's "The White Cat" is brought into the White Cat's castle, the welcome is ambassadorial, not personal; by comparison, Snow White's coming to the house of the dwarves is incidental to her ultimate fate. Here, unlike most stories in the oral tradition, we feel that the relation between the young couple is not assumed, but taken seriously.

But Beast is ugly. Oral fairy tales seldom concern themselves with ugliness as such, "The Frog Prince" being an exception rather than the rule. The written romances of the great Italian and English Renaissance writers also have little to do with ugliness. But Madame de Murat's "modern fairies" care about ugliness, and Countess d'Aulnoy scarcely has a story in which it does not play a major part. Being both profuse and knowing, d'Aulnoy knows many things about ugliness: it can make the ugly one envious and spiteful; it is the worst infliction of a wicked fairy; it is intolerable in a mate, even if the ugly one in other respects is superbly endowed. Le Prince de Beaumont, with characteristic simplicity, goes to the heart of our fear about ugliness: it matters more than it should. Beauty, a girl recently removed from the protection of her father, is at first merely frightened of Beast and obedient to him because of his power. The moment he grants her a choice, however, it is his ugliness that pre-occupies them both:

> "Tell me, do you find me very ugly?"
> "Yes," said Beauty, "I can't lie. But I believe you are also very good."
> "Yes," said Beast. "But I'm still an ugly, stupid Beast."
> "Not stupid," smiled Beauty. "Stupid folk don't know they're stupid."

And then later:

> Beauty had almost forgotten to be afraid of the monster, when he said, "Beauty, will you marry me?"
> Beauty was silent. At last she said, honestly and simply, "No, Beast."
> Beast gave a mighty sigh. "Good night, Beauty," he said, and left.

Ugliness puts Beast in the position of having to act as though his goodness were no real compensation; Beauty is forced to reject what she otherwise might be eager to accept.

As Beauty falls in love with Beast's love of her in those months where he calls every night, she is being weaned from the love of her father; yet when she sees her father lying ill in her magic mirror, she insists she'll die if she can't go home. So she returns and is tempted by her sisters to stay longer than she promised, because she cannot learn by herself that she no longer belongs at home and that she must now go where her heart leads her, even if it is to the ugly beautiful Beast. The princess in "The Frog Prince" discovers only that all will be well if she does as she is told, and once upon a time that much was all a young woman may have needed to know. But Beauty, by comparison a latter-day heroine though she lived a long time ago, needs to learn more than this: there is love deeper than kindness, and in that love, kindness is more important than ugliness:

"What if I've killed him?" thought Beauty. She looked everywhere for Beast. Then she ran into the garden, remembering her dream. There lay Beast, quite still. Beauty bent over him, quite forgetting his ugliness. His heart still beat faintly. She ran for water, and dashed it on him.

Beast opened his eyes. He whispered, "I couldn't live without you. I'll die happy, now that you're here."

"No, Beast, You mustn't die. Live, and let me be your wife. I thought we were only friends. But I couldn't bear to lose you. I love you, Beast."

In Madame de Villeneuve's version there is something that more closely resembles real conversation, which allows Beast a more courtly doubting and acceptance. Le Prince de Beaumont wanted to say to the young women in her charge that they could be sexually happy if they could believe in sexual happiness and could thereby transform the beast in every man into a young prince. Should we ask for proof, we must go elsewhere—the more prolonged and painful trials of d'Aulnoy's tales, perhaps—because this story wishes only for the evolution of a love that can overcome the fear of ugliness. The logic of an older tale like "The Frog Prince" may be more awful, because it denies the young woman any goodness and gives her only fear, but the logic of "Beauty and the Beast" is more stern, because it gives the young woman more frightening and lonely tasks. The "wicked fairy" who doomed Beast is really Beauty, so that she who enchants can disenchant, and make real, the burden of sexual love.

Of course the ideal shown us by Le Prince de Beaumont is not our ideal. It is quite defensible to say that Beast creates Beauty's love of him by his care of her, and to add that both her father and Beast cast Beauty in the role of rescuer and nurse—"I'll die without you" is the cry and implied threat of both males at crucial moments. Love is conceived of as a range of emotions from pity to fondness, and Beast's kindness and mournfulness wear Beauty down as much as they interest or excite her. Again here, then, as with d'Aulnoy, we are coming on something that makes the story datable. We can say that "The Frog Prince" is definitely an earlier story than "Beauty and the Beast" and that the era in which the ideal of women's love as a redeeming force is now an era past, or passing. But as a statement of that ideal this story has a grace and power that, for me at least, *Jane Eyre* and *Idylls of the King* do not have and that is totally beyond the reach of Andersen in "The Snow Queen."

"Beauty and the Beast" is almost the last story in the canon of what is now known as children's literature that does not deny a central role for romance and sexuality. No one, in all the stories we will consider later in this book, will fall in love. Childhood was becoming a stage of life, and Madame Le Prince de Beaumont was, as a governess and an author, responding to that fact, but the materials of her tales were still the ancient materials, and shortly after this the implicit sexuality of children could not be made explicit enough to guide the direction of a story, and adult people, increasingly, could not be central figures in "children's literature." As a result, as I have indicated, the true heirs of the tellers and writers of fairy tales wrote poems, composed operas, and choreographed ballets. For their part, the writers of children's literature had to turn away from fairy tales and to point children toward adult enlightenment and education, not adult romance and sexuality.

A century after the French writers we have been considering, Hans Christian Andersen wrote what he called fairy tales, what were accepted by his audience as fairy tales, but which show on almost every page how much a break had been made, with the oral as well as the written tradition. The voice of Andersen is the voice of a teller, but Andersen was a writer, a writer of the Romantic period, and so he tries to put his personal stamp on his tales, even the ancient ones he only retold, and he always considered himself his own major resource, his own necessary and sufficient inspiration. Many of his openings reveal this all too clearly:

> The Emperor of China is a Chinese, as of course you know, and the people he has about him are Chinese too.
>
> ["The Nightingale"]

Not just a joke, but a bad one; and if not that, pretty vividness:

> Far out at sea the water is as blue as the bluest cornflower, and as clear as the clearest glass; but it is very deep, deeper than any anchor cable can fathom.
>
> ["The Little Mermaid"]

And, if not vividness, remarks about storytelling:

> Listen! Now we are going to begin. When the story has
> ended, we shall know a lot more than we do now.
>
> ["The Snow Queen"]

He aims satiric shafts, he points his morals and adorns his tales. Of all the major reputations among authors of children's literature, Andersen's is much the hardest to understand or justify. Yet for precisely these reasons he is useful here, as a way to mark the transition from fairy tales to later children's literature, because what is wrong with his work is, almost without exception, what is wrong with all inferior children's literature and what mars even some of the masterpieces.

Since children's literature is written by adults and "for" children, authors of children's books can be strongly tempted to make the central relation be between the teller and the audience rather than the teller and the tale. The older authors of fairy tales, as we have seen, know their audience very well, but never alter anything in the tale to suit or please the audience; their respect for their materials is too great. But when children's literature was invented, the adults who wrote the tales often started contemplating the children who were to hear and read them, and they tended to get lost, because they became involved in what was essentially a false rhetoric. "The Emperor of China is a Chinese" is such a silly thing to say that it must express an essentially patronizing attitude toward the audience. The teller has an idea of a child in his head, he acts as though he knows "what children like" or "how children think," and the moment he does that his language becomes false. The tellers of fairy tales before this never thought their audience was any different from themselves, never thought of themselves as authors forced to conceive a relation to an audience. But after childhood was invented, adults inevitably began thinking about what language, what stance or tone, what materials were appropriate for children, and so we get something like the large and often subtle machinery of the Pooh books in which A. A. Milne guides his son toward an acceptance of the loss of early childhood. Even in many books which idealize children, the implicit rhetoric insists it is better to be an adult, and thereby be able to do this idealizing, than it is to be a child, who doesn't know any better than not to know that his or hers is the ideal time of life. Of course, anyone who writes a book for children will make some adjustments, but when the writer is really concerned with the tale and not the audience, the adjustments are easily made, since they will concern themselves with a simplification of vocabulary and the avoidance of prolonged abstract argument and discourse.

Andersen had certain initial advantages as a teller of fairy tales. He was born in Odense, a small town, the son of a cobbler and a peasant; he learned Danish folk tales from his mother and grandmother; his father, who was literate and a rationalist, read to him from *The Thousand and One Nights* and the *Fables* of La Fontaine. He was an only child, smaller and slighter than the others in his school, and his response to feeling an ugly duckling was to create his own small worlds, with dolls, puppets, songs, and retold stories; he became famous in Odense as a gifted lad who gave charming performances. The results of these beginnings can be seen in his lifelong love of the theatre, in his continual stance as a performer, in his love of pathos, in his evocations of the outcast who longs to be different or in a different place. Clearly, too, this early success failed to satisfy for very long. He hated Odense, for all it gave him the setting and imagery for many of his tales, and he was in Copenhagen before he was fifteen, trying to be an actor. All his apparent advantages, then, were something he wanted to exploit, to use as food for his inventiveness, his powers of mimicry, his theatricality, his desire not to be an ugly duckling. He wanted to be latter-day, to be famous as a writer and actor, but his shyness and sense of personal inadequacy kept throwing him back on his origins, on his loneliness, on his incurably provincial sense that life was better where the lights were brighter.

So Andersen is the soldier as well as the cobbler's boy in "The Tinder Box," he is the little mermaid, the mole in "Thumbelina," the steadfast tin soldier. Women could only admire and pity him, and their rejection in turn intensified his sense of himself as an outcast, with pathos and spurts of satiric revenge his only weapons.

His stories of the figures he made out of himself gained him fame greater than any Danish writer, before or since, has achieved, and during the last thirty years of his life he could travel anywhere he wished, meet anyone he chose, and be adored. But a writer who uses personal unhappiness as an exploitable resource is artistically as well as humanly engaged in civil war, since what succeeds is also what makes miserable. Especially in his earlier years Andersen was stubborn in his belief in his talent, but there was always something compulsive about this belief, because it was designed to take him away from who and where he had been as much as to take him any place he wished to go. The result was, on the one hand, great creative energies. He wrote many plays, novels, poems, and travel books in addition to the fairy tales for which he is still known, and the complete tales make a volume of half a million words. But on the other hand he wrote quickly, even slapdash, and counted on his assumed talent to carry him through. The result is not just a good deal of inconsequential work, but many stories whose confusions and contradictions reveal his civil war, often in embarrassing ways.

"The Little Mermaid," for instance, is one of Andersen's most popular tales, which means its pathos has found a responsive echo in many who feel they are little mermaids. But it really is a chaotic, desperate piece of work, very much out of touch with itself. "You are to keep your gliding motion, no dancer will be as able to move as gracefully," the sea-witch tells the mermaid who wants to become a human being, "but at every step it will feel you are treading on a sharp-edged knife." Andersen, himself willing to suffer great pain to be near the woman he loved, apparently never saw the trouble he entailed the moment he made the mermaid want to become a human being and established conditions for her transformation. D'Aulnoy and many other writers of fairy tales have characters willing to suffer for the sake of their beloved. In most of these cases, a transformation is involved, one that assumes the natural state of the lover is human, and the unnatural state is the green snake, the white deer, or the ram. In "The Little Mermaid," Andersen is driven to making the mermaid naturally inferior to the prince as a way of expressing his own sense of his social or sexual inferiority. If she is going to step "up" to the prince's class, she must no longer be a mermaid. To complicate the issue still further, since Andersen was also resentful of those who rejected him, he makes all the mermaids beautiful and the beloved prince a dense and careless man, so that one cannot imagine where the "natural" inferiority of the mermaid lies, and it seems like lunacy to suffer as she does in order to be able to dance before the prince.

All these difficulties would tear away at the story even if the prince finally were to love the mermaid, but Andersen felt driven, in addition, to have the prince reject her as Andersen himself had been. Since he could find no way to describe the appearance or the behavior of the mermaids so as to make them seem inferior to human beings, Andersen posited that mermaids have no immortal souls. He cannot say what this means, however, since the mermaids seem to lack nothing possessed by human beings except legs. The sea-witch tells the mermaid she can have a soul if a mortal will love her, which reduces "soul" to a romantic and sexual prize; worse, the mermaid has vastly more of something like a soul than does the prince. Then, since Andersen partly wants to revenge himself against the prince for rejecting the mermaid, he has the mermaid's sisters tell her she can become a mermaid again if she will kill the prince, which makes the mermaid's love into even more of an unnatural passion than it is before this. Finally, since of course the mermaid will not kill the prince, Andersen must invent a trapdoor to escape from these impossible tangles, and so he invents the daughters of the air, who "have no immortal soul either, but they can gain one by their good deeds." But the trapdoor refuses to open, since Andersen cannot imagine why daughters of the air, any more than mermaids, should have to work for immortal souls, while human beings have them as part of their birthright. Indeed, the whole question of an immortal soul is much trickier in a story like this than Andersen realizes, and it illustrates the great good sense of earlier oral and written tellers of fairy tales in leaving out all explicit religion. To make socially inferior into sexually inferior, and to make sexually inferior into naturally inferior, is bad enough, but to make naturally inferior into religiously inferior is sheer desperation. The original longings which created the story are, I think, the

reason for its continued popularity; all the snobberies and reverse
snobberies that follow seem just to be ignored, at least by people I
know who claim the story as one of their favorites—and they invariably first read it early in adolescence.

"Thumbelina" has the same kind of difficulty, though the surface
of the story is much more clear and calm. Thumbelina, born tiny,
on the pistil of a tulip, is captured by a toad who takes her away so
she can be married to the toad's ugly son. Andersen must have
known many stories in which such a kidnapping was threatened or
achieved by giants, ogres, and dwarves. But the toads here, though
indeed ugly, are not the least wicked or brutal, so that when Andersen says "She did not want to live with the horrid toad, neither did
she want the toad's ugly son for a husband," he is once again confusing difference and inferiority. The toad isn't nasty at all, just a
toad. James Thurber has a fable about a crow and a Baltimore oriole
which employs this same situation, but Thurber's aims are far
different from Andersen's. Thurber's crow may be a fool for falling
in love with a Baltimore oriole, but the pretty oriole is no prize
either. Andersen, though, can't avoid sanctioning Thumbelina's
distaste for toads by implying that toads should stay in their place
and know better than to want Thumbelina. Indeed, the same thing
happens a second time when a field mouse rescues Thumbelina from
the oncoming winter and very pleasantly thinks she would make a
good mate for her friend the mole, who is prosperous and has a
shiny dark coat. Thumbelina understandably does not care for this
idea, especially since she doesn't want to live underground and pre-
fers sunshine and song. But Andersen persists in blaming the field
mouse and the mole for being a field mouse and a mole, ground and
underground animals: "For their neighbor, the tiresome mole in the
black velvet coat, had proposed to her"; "But she was not at all
happy, for she did not care one bit for the tiresome mole." It is as
though Andersen never asked what the implications were of his
projecting his own feelings of being rejected onto the animal world.
Stranger still is a little story called "Sweethearts," which makes a
class matter between a top and a ball, so both the top who wants and
the ball who rejects are figures of mere silliness. Andersen was always improvising, outfitting objects and animals with his own

feelings, and so seldom stopped to respect the nature of his characters.

Fortunately, some of Andersen's stories are more impersonal and therefore much better than "The Little Mermaid" or "Thumbelina." "The Snow Queen" is riddled with faults, but it shows what Andersen could do well, which was something that older tellers and writers of fairy tales had not tried to do. By the time he wrote "The Snow Queen," a long, loose narrative in seven stories, he had done a lot of traveling, and everyone he met in Germany, France, England, and Italy knew he was a Dane, a man from a little-known northern country. In this tale he seems to be asking what it means to be from such a country, considered not as a place where Andersen had suffered, and not as a society, but as a climate. He opens with some little devils that go everywhere with their looking glass, "reducing the reflection of anything good and beautiful to almost nothing, while what was no good or was ugly stood out well and grew even worse." The devils take their mirror too high in the heavens, and it breaks, but that only means that its pieces, when they fall to earth, can become lodged in the eyes and hearts of people: "A few people even got a splinter of it into their hearts, and that was terrible indeed, for then their hearts became exactly like a lump of ice." Andersen knew all about ice, and when, one summer day, a bit of the glass strikes a boy named Kay in the heart, and another lodges in his eye, Andersen knows this lump of iciness can have little effect in the summertime. Come winter, though, Kay starts trying to act more grown-up; he ridicules the childish delights of his friend Gerda, and then he begins to offer clever parodies of his grandmother and to insist that a snowflake under a magnifying glass is better than one that just falls to the ground, and much better than a rose's petals.

One day Kay goes out into the square with his sled, and soon a big sleigh comes along and the driver ties up Kay's sled and carries it out of the village: "All of a sudden they flew to one side, the big sleigh stopped, and the person who was drawing it stood up. The fur coat and cap were made entirely of snow. It was a woman, tall and slender, and glittering white. It was the Snow Queen." She kisses Kay, and:

Kay looked at her. She was so beautiful. He could not imagine a brighter or more lovely face. She didn't seem to be all ice now, as she did when she sat outside the window and beckoned to him. In his eyes she was perfect. He was not at all frightened; he told her he could do mental arithmetic even with fractions; that he knew the areas of all the countries, and the answer to "What is their population?" And she went on smiling. Then he began to suspect that he did not know so much after all. Bewildered he gazed into space. She flew away with him, flew high up onto the black cloud, while the storm howled and roared—it sounded very much like old folk tunes. They flew over woods and lakes, over sea and land; below them the cold icy wind went whistling, wolves howled, black screaming crows flew low over the glistening snow, but over it all shone the moon, large and clear, and on that Kay gazed during the long, long winter's night. By day he slept at the feet of the Snow Queen.

We have seen nothing like this before; it is grand, atmospheric writing about nature, seeking effects the teller of "The Juniper Tree" would not have needed or understood. Andersen here is finding something new for a fairy tale to do. This abduction is thrilling as well as frightening, because Andersen has pondered what it means to be a snow *queen* as well as a *snow* queen. Unlike the devils, the Snow Queen is a natural force, and therefore powerful, and to be queen of such a force is to be beautiful and perfect, so that all Kay's homage to her, his fractions and facts, is not enough. By introducing the little devils, by having them make Kay susceptible with the glass caught in his heart and eye, Andersen frees the Snow Queen of any suggestion that she is demonic or malicious; she is really only claiming her own.

Just as the author of *Beowulf*, of an earlier time but a similar latitude, knew that what lay outside the meadhalls was named Grendel, and that what lived in the meres was Grendel's mother, so Andersen knows that even in a city snow and cold can grip and dominate, finding the victims of the imps and claiming for them a particularly northern fate. But the Snow Queen must take Kay out of Denmark, because spring and summer return there, and up to Lapland, her home. Gerda, the child who didn't want to be grown up, sets out to find him. She visits an old wizard woman who is kind to her but wants to keep Gerda for herself, which makes her like the Snow Queen except her dominion is a flower garden, not a sleigh, and that makes all the difference. Gerda keeps asking the flowers where Kay is, and they all give lovely irrelevant answers, lovely because each tells a fairy tale, irrelevant because they know nothing of Kay, and Gerda can barely understand them. That all things are bright and beautiful does not connect them, or make them know each other— the world is too large and various for that, especially in the warmer months.

But as autumn comes, Gerda sets out again, and meets a crow who tells her about a princess who has announced she will marry any young man who can come and talk to her as though he were at home. Most young men became so nervous at trying that they failed, but one lad finally appeared and said to the palace guards, "It must be boring standing on the stairs; I'm going inside." That is exactly how Kay sounded after the glass pierced his heart and eye, so Gerda goes to the palace, is sneaked in by the crow's sweetheart, only to discover the prince is not Kay. Very nice he is, as is the princess, and they listen to Gerda's tale and offer to outfit her trip north. "How good they are, human beings and animals," Gerda thinks as she tries to overcome her disappointment, and to remember that everyone she has met on her journey has been as helpful as he or she could be. So it is with the rough robber band that captures Gerda, where a woman wants to kill her but her perky daughter gets her mother drunk so Gerda can escape; so too with the Lapp woman and the Finn woman and the reindeer who guide and take her to the Snow Queen's palace. The story is long because it must be, in order to show the world, when it is not dominated by the Snow Queen, is not paradise but the world, multiple, varied, usually helpful to a distressed girl if it doesn't have to go far out of its way to do so. Gerda, seen by herself, is an awfully passive, pallid heroine, but Andersen, though he praises her highly, only offers sweetness and innocence as her virtues, and he does not pretend they light up the sky.

In the Snow Queen's palace all is cold, ordered, and dazzling; Kay drags about pieces of ice, makes shapes and words, because the

Snow Queen has told him "you shall be your own master, and I will give you the whole world, and a new pair of skates" if you can spell the word "eternity." But he cannot, and it is winter now, so the Snow Queen is off in more southern regions; Kay "looked at the pieces of ice and thought and thought for all he was worth." This is satire, of course, derived from Andersen's dislike of the math and spelling taught in schools, but here it is decently muted, and the point Andersen makes is not entirely irrelevant. At least as good, surely, to have the Snow Queen set Kay the task of spelling "eternity" as it is to have Winnie-the-Pooh hunt for a backson because Christopher Robin doesn't quite know how to spell "back soon."

Then, at the climax:

> She walked into the big empty hall, caught sight of Kay, and knew him at once, and flew towards him and flung her arms around his neck, held him tight and shouted: "Kay! darling little Kay! At last I've found you!"
>
> But there he sat quite still, and stiff and cold. Then Gerda shed hot tears, which fell on his breasts, and penetrated right into his heart. They thawed the lump of ice, and dissolved the splinter of glass that was lodged in it. He looked at her, and she sang:
>
> > As roses bloom in the valley sweet,
> > So the Christ child there ye shall truly meet.
>
> Kay burst into tears. He cried and cried so hard that his tears washed the tiny chip of glass out of his eyes. Now he knew her and exclaimed for joy.

The Savior makes a much better appearance here than the immortal soul does in "The Little Mermaid." Salvation is in the world, not in eternity, and we can know this by knowing the roses in the valley, which fade and are not perfect. Roses have no place in the Snow Queen's palace, no more than do hot tears and hymns, and it is Gerda's "heroism" that her persistence has allowed her to do so much with the little she has, and it is the glory of the world that it has, this way and that way, shown her the way.

The symbols and actions all work in "The Snow Queen" because Andersen has asked what it means to be captured by the queen of the snow, and what power can rescue what she has captured. Gerda is no Beowulf or Siegfried, and the Snow Queen cannot be killed, and it takes all the power of the spring and summer, all the determination of Gerda, plus a prince, a princess, a crow, reindeer, and two women who live up north just to release the lad with the glass in his eye and heart. Someone who lived much south of Denmark might not need to know all this, and someone who lived much north of Denmark might not be able to. But, knowing what he knows, and, for once, trusting what he knows, Andersen can release his story from the personal bondage that ties up so much of his other work. To be sure, there are the nips and barks of the satire, the idealization of the child for her innocence only, the lengthy clumsiness of the stories of Gerda's journey, and we can see that it is always unfortuate that Andersen was a *writer* in ways earlier tellers of tales did not have to be, and in ways that Tchaikovsky and the great choreographers and dancers did not have to be either. But Karen Blixen once said she had been able to live her later years more bravely because she had read Andersen all her life, and one understands that, too, with "The Snow Queen" in mind.

It is often said of Andersen, and of many later successful storytellers for children, that they never grew up themselves and so could better speak to the young. There is perhaps truth in this, but most of the conclusions one might want to draw from this idea seem false. In Andersen's case it is demonstrable that what retarded his maturing as a person handicapped him as an author, and all his defects, by comparison with the earlier authors of fairy tales, seem the result of an inability to be calm, confident, transparently anonymous, a partaker in a tradition older than he, and wiser. Andersen's century and our own are the latter days, to be sure, but in the next chapter we will see that some of the traditional sources of strength remained for authors of children's literature if they knew how to employ them. True, the two most famous writers for children in the last century were Andersen and Lewis Carroll, both of whom were clearly retarded in their growth, and in Lewis Carroll's case that retardation is something like a major source of his power. But this is not, I think it can be shown, what made or makes him popular, and I sense nothing like childishness in Beatrix Potter, L. Frank Baum, Jean de Brunhoff, or Dr. Seuss, no serious adult shortcoming. Each of us remains a child in certain respects for most or all of our lives, and the great writers of children's books seem no more paralyzed by their childhoods than Wordsworth or Dickens or Emily Brontë or D. H. Lawrence.

What can be said in this regard is that many, though far from all, writers suffer in their early years in ways that have the effect of setting them apart, or of making them feel set apart. Whatever the mainstream is, they feel they are not swimming in it, and, quite often, when they become writers, they do not write in the literary mainstream, and many then write books designed for children or that become popular with children. But their successes are too varied to be set under one rubric, and in many cases the authors did not know children, did not like children, did not have anything that could possibly be construed as the point of view of a child. Their feeling of being set apart did not, in most cases, make them secret or active allies of children. Of all the odd or queer people who have written books we call children's books, only Lewis Carroll seems to have had the genius to express his oddness in a way that seems impervious to changes of fashion and the erosions of time. He allied himself with children, at least at times, but he has never been as popular among children as among adults; his strength, though very great, is very narrow because his was such a devastatingly restricted view of life, and many children can't understand him or be anything more than frustrated by his power.

But the category "children's literature" is too vague, too loose, to allow much generalizing, and the great children's books are too different one from another to suggest more than occasional comparisons between two or three. Kipling and Grahame share a rich sense of wonder, but Potter and Lewis Carroll offer very little of this. Potter and Grahame are visually rich authors, but Baum and Lewis Carroll, who are not, make great words for others to illustrate. Baum and Kipling yield attractive images of children, but Potter and Grahame barely have children in their works at all. None of the writers considered from here on seems to have learned much from, or been heavily dependent on, fairy tales as a source of strength, except in an altered and modernly adapted form. So we had best leave generalizations aside, and take each author in turn. First, though, a look at what survived from the former days that helped make some children's literature strong.

(4)   Animals

We are at the end of "Fairy Tales," and with Lewis Carroll in the next chapter we begin the "and After." The present subject, "animals," is a crude label to signify the strongest link between fairy tales and modern written children's literature. The animals in question are creatures who talk or in other ways act like human beings. They are present in most children's literature, ancient and modern, and they are the major source of the power of the best children's literature, a source that other kinds of literature had abandoned and forgotten well before the nineteenth century. It is a power that helps explain why certain people wrote books for children, or good books for children, while others did not or could not. It is certainly a more important consideration than any question of liking or understanding children, or particular individual children, and so is worth separate description and analysis.

In older literature we can find some realistically described animals, though few are any more important than the cow in "Jack and the Beanstalk" or the horse for which Richard III would have given a kingdom. Animals talked or acted like human beings in some ways, and most were to be found in fairy tales or beast fables. Fairy tale animals are usually enchanted and live in a world of human beings; beast fable animals usually participate in no magic and live in a world where human beings play a minor role. The distinction is not crucial, because the similarities between these two kinds of animals are, for our purposes, more important than their differences; but we should begin by looking at each separately to see the possibilities inherent in the talking animal.

Any animal seems able to serve as the enchanted beast of fairy tales: the bird in "The Juniper Tree," the fox in "The Golden Bird," the frog prince, the ram, snake, cat, deer, and blue bird in Countess d'Aulnoy, Beast himself. These animals do not wish to be animals, and, while enchanted, they are the kindest, the most patient, the most gentlemanly or ladylike, the most civilized creatures in the stories. They are willing to put up with faithless, inconsiderate, and rude human behavior in order to regain human form, often so they can marry the very people who are hardest on them. Their exquisite behavior might lead us to think they are used for satiric purposes, like Swift's Houyhnhnms, to show how animals can be closer to what human beings ought to be than people are. In fact they serve an opposite purpose. The enchanted animal, when unenchanted, is royal and behaves beautifully not because it is an animal, but because the spell under which it has fallen cannot enchant the beauty of its spirit or the sweetness of its manners. The spell is limited because the power of evil is limited to altering appearances. We can all be magnetized by beauty, or repelled by ugliness, and we usually want human beings for our dearest companions and mates and so find ourselves condescending even to the most impressive of animals. So fairy tale heroes and heroines can be deceived when they see an enchanted animal, and only the animal's patience and kindness can wear away the deception, establish trust, and thereby begin to break the spell. The metaphor thus created becomes so familiar that only the most interfering storytellers seek to spell it out: beauty in the flesh beguiles, beauty in the spirit endures, both are magical and can enchant; when the spirit is beautiful the enchantment can be called love.

In beast fables animals talk like people, but in most other respects they are more realistically described than animals in fairy tales. Human beings are usually absent because the animals are, or represent, human beings. Beast fables are at least as old as fairy tales; the most famous early collection is Aesop's, which gives us the tortoise and the hare, the fox and the grapes, and the habit of ending with one-line morals. Descending from Aesop are some stories told in medieval bestiaries and some by La Fontaine and Thurber. Other beast fables seem more directly to derive from folktales of barnyard and forest that were inspired by shrewd amusement at the actions of animals and by the animal behavior of many people. They are capable of yielding conscious high art; what we know as city and country mouse in Aesop becomes stern inquiries by Virgil, Horace, and Juvenal into the pleasures and limits of retirement into the country; a traditional story of a rooster, a hen, and a fox becomes the lavish comedy of Chaucer's "The Nun's Priest's Tale." Compared to fairy tales, beast fables tend to be worldly, slightly cynical in observation and in their conclusion that human beings are closer to chickens and pigs than they are to angels, or closer than they would like to admit.

One can find beast fables as well as fairy tales in modern written children's literature, and "The Three Little Pigs," "The Little Red Hen," and "The Gingerbread Man" are still staples of books given the very young. But the real legacy of both the beast fable and the fairy tale is not a matter of their lineal descendants, but something that derives from what the two genres have in common. Let us pause to think about how we speak of "conventions" in literature. Latter-day people, when looking back at earlier literature, will speak of its various conventions: the masks, the chorus, or the dramatic unities in ancient drama; the dream vision or the alliterative line in medieval literature; the "conventions" of Renaissance love poetry often lumped under the name "Petrarchan"; the "conventional happy ending" of fairy tales. All this bespeaks an obtuseness about the nature of older literature. Of course certain "conventions" *were* employed in older literature, such as various verse forms, or carrying out the bodies of the dead in Elizabethan tragedies, but these tend to be simple or technical matters, and a great deal of what we know as conventions in older literature is not like this. Their usage is seldom set or rigid, and they aren't technical matters since they derive not so much from an idea of literature as from an implicit idea about the whole of creation, an idea that was dying in the very centuries when childhood, the education of children, and children's literature itself began to take modern shape. C. S. Lewis's interesting book, *The Discarded Image*, attempts to describe and chart creation when it was seen as an image.

For our purposes, however, it is enough to point to uses of language, first in which the world outside human beings is described in human terms: the rosy-*fingered* dawn, a star *danced* when I was born, great *frowning* hills of Westmoreland, the heavens *declare* the glory of God, the morn in russet mantle *clad;* second, in which human beings and human actions are described in terms derived from the non-human world: "It is the east, and Juliet is the sun," "My love is like a red, red, rose," people described as foxy, wolfish, chicken-hearted, lion-hearted, "O tiger's heart wrapped in a woman's hide." Thus human activity is like every other activity in creation, and creation itself wears a human face and speaks in a human voice. What might at first look like a great batch of conventions—a lover's eyes are like the sun, a hen in a story means a fox is not far away, animals that suddenly turn out to be enchanted—was all part of an understanding of human life and creation that was fundamental to older cultures, and animals were not, therefore, employed as conventions, devices, or symbols. In *Animal Farm* George Orwell adopts the beast fable as though he were putting on a piece of armor, while Chaucer writes a beast fable as he wrote romances, fabliaux, and dream visions, depending simply on the kind of poem he wishes to make. When a songwriter writes the line, "Willow, weep for me," he is speaking to an audience who cannot imagine a willow actually weeping for a lover—willows have their ways, and we have ours, so we can weep when they die, but we do not imagine any tree will cry because a young man has lost his young woman. We are so used to *not* imagining, or believing, this way that when Hamlet speaks of "this goodly frame, the earth . . . this most excellent canopy the air, look you, this brave o'erhanging firmament, this majestical roof fretted with golden fire," we find it hard to imagine he is being anything but poetic and fanciful. If he is *not* being this, how are we to take such language?

We need not try to name when the former days ended and the latter days began, because we already have all the dating we need in the fact that children's literature was invented along with the latter days. Children's literature shows signs of a persistence in speaking and writing in "old ways" that most older literature relinquished as long ago as the seventeenth century. We find these most notably in the talking animal and the animal endowed with what we think of as human power. Children's literature has, by and large, resembled other modern literature in making its sun hot and silent, its rain fall without rain gods, its willows not weep over human disaster; nor are its human beings described in terms we normally use to describe sun, moon, earth, and oceans. Fairies, elves, leprechauns, and the like play only an infrequent part in modern children's literature. But its animals talk, wear clothes, live in houses, and, even when otherwise described in realistic terms, think and feel like human beings. Many of these animals are created or rendered with the same ease and lack of self-consciousness that used to animate the descriptions and stories of almost all literature. We do not speak of Beatrix Potter "adopting a convention" in *The Tale of Peter Rabbit* because the conventions at work there permeate it so completely and unselfconsciously that it seems almost impertinent to think of it as we might think of George Orwell "adopting the beast fable convention" in *Animal Farm*. Thus, in dealing with modern children's literature —though perhaps with no other current mode or genre—we feel the effects of the magic long before we inquire after its formula.

Perhaps most surprising about the use of animals in modern children's literature is this fluid ease, this rich sense of possibility, that was able to outlive the scientific and industrial revolutions, the rise of secular education, and the discrediting of magic. We know from our discussion of fairy tales that one impulse in the secular education of children was to decry the fairy tales and to substitute literature and learning that was rational and empirical. We know, too, that much of this effort partially failed. Fairy tales continued to be collected, read, heard, translated, and enjoyed long after they lost their initial bearings as oral literature of the hut and castle. In England, at least, childhood came to be thought of, often in the most grossly sentimental ways, as a special time, as the one period of life in which it was acceptable to believe in the magical, the imagined world, the speaking animal. The child was imagined to be able to enjoy an instinctive sympathy with and understanding of animals and an alliance with animals against adult human beings. Andrew Marvell had, in the middle of the seventeenth century, been able to ask about a young girl he called T. C., "Who can foretell for what high cause/ This darling of the gods was born," and then to describe her naming the flowers, taming them, and herself becoming like the rose. This was perhaps too lofty a sense of possibility for anyone in the nineteenth century; Wordsworth might insist that Lucy was claimed by Nature for its own, but even this was more than the major authors of children's books could claim. But many children in children's literature could "magically" ally themselves with animals —the Bastable children with the Psammead, Dorothy Gale with Toto and Billina, Mowgli with the jungle animals, Nils with the wild geese, Jackie Paper with Puff the Magic Dragon, the heroes and heroines of countless dog and horse books that tell their wonder tales in apparently realistic terms. All the old metaphors which showed human beings at home in a nonhuman universe were lost by this time except those which related children to animals, and there the old vitality seemed to have rich potential life, and the range of the metaphors was still large, from the splendid realism of Selma Lagerlöf's talking wild geese to the equally splendid nonsense of Edward Lear's owl serenading the pussy-cat as he looked at the stars. Everywhere that Mary went, the lamb was sure to go.

It is time to look at some examples more closely, and the first is so deliciously trivial it secures the point almost all by itself. To ask about the robin in Beatrix Potter's *Peter Rabbit* is like asking Sherlock Holmes's famous question about the dog in the night time. The robin is there, though, if not in the text and if only in four of the twenty-five illustrations. Reading the book quickly, as one does, one might casually notice the robin as decorative background for Peter's adventures in Mr. McGregor's garden, as though Potter enjoyed drawing robins and wanted to put one in. A robin is atop a pitchfork, singing during Peter's one happy moment, when he is eating carrots. A robin is there on the following page, turned away from Peter as Peter is beginning to feel rather sick. A robin stares at one of Peter's shoes when Peter first tries to escape from Mr. McGregor. A robin stares at a wet, forlorn Peter just out of Mr. McGregor's watering can. We may be looking at one, two, three, or four robins. Since it does not speak, we cannot call it a talking animal, but since this is a book where animals do talk, and where a rabbit conveys a wide range of attitudes we associate with human beings, it is fair to ask what the robin(s)' attitude toward Peter is, what choral commentary it might offer had Potter given it a voice.

We can ask, but cannot be sure what answer we get. We cannot say there is no connection between the robin and Peter's joy and sorrow, and we cannot say, if there were such a connection, what it is. It sings *while* Peter munches carrots, but not necessarily *because* Peter is happy. When Peter feels rather sick, the robin faces elsewhere, but even to say it "turns away" implies an attitude, an indifference or a disgust, that may be irrelevant. If it stares at Peter's shoe, that does not mean it is more interested in Peter's shoe than in him. If we are sentimental to think the robin is sympathetic to the wet and bedraggled Peter, we may be callous to deny the possibility. We might then look at the other animals in Mr. McGregor's garden, and they give us a number of answers, but no certain conclusion. The sparrows implore Peter to escape from the gooseberry net, and this tells us birds can be responsive to rabbits. The sparrows may even be cheering Peter on when, near the end, he finally escapes from the garden. The mouse doesn't answer Peter's plea for information about the gate, but only, so we are told, because it has a pea in its mouth. The white cat stares at goldfish and never sees Peter. Which tells us too little, by telling us too much. The robin emerges as a riddle, inviting us to imagine its feelings, but repudiating that invitation at the same time.

Should the robin be deleted from the story, few would or should notice. The triviality of the example helps, though, to underscore how much Beatrix Potter can do even with the smallest and least important of her characters, and she can do this because she is constantly urging us to look at animals, and then to ask if they are people, if they are like people, if they are unlike people, if they are as responsive or as indifferent as people are to others, if they are just animals. Short as *Peter Rabbit* is, it would not be easy to list all the effects its words and pictures achieve concerning the animalness of people, the peopleness of animals. Potter rebukes us for noticing so little about the human qualities of animals, yet also chides us for easy and sentimental assumptions we make about her animals on the basis of our knowledge of human beings ("Isn't he cute?" being only an extreme form of this). Potter is a somber, witty riddler, teasing us in and out of thought, and she does so with the ease and economy of means we associate more readily with Chaucer or Spenser than with Potter's contemporaries Hardy and Yeats.

The slightness of this example keeps it from being more than a single and discrete instance of the simplest terms of a metaphoric formula: A is B, the robin "feels," "turns away," "sympathizes" because we interpret its actions as though it were human. The effect is riddling precisely because it cannot be cumulative, and what we might learn from one picture helps us little with the others. So we need to look at some examples where characterization and extended narration are involved, where we can inquire about total effect as well as about moments. I want to use two books, Randall Jarrell's *The Animal Family* and Selma Lagerlöf's *The Wonderful Adventures of Nils*. Placed on a scale that runs from the realistic to the magical, both lean strongly toward the realistic; each uses its magical or unreal elements sparingly and decisively and to yield different, even opposing, effects.

The Animal Family begins with a full realistic description of a hunter living in a cabin on a meadow next to an ocean, very much aware that he is alone. One day he hears a voice singing in the water, and, after returning to hear the voice day after day, finally identifies the singer as a mermaid. He learns her song, sings it, she sings back, and what seems like the beginning of a courtship ensues:

> The hunter had lived so long with animals that he himself was patient as an animal. He waited a long time, and then went home; he was not disappointed that she had gone, only certain that she would be back. He kept remembering how the laugh and the last notes of the song had sounded. When he was so nearly asleep that he could hardly tell whether he was remembering them or hearing them, he was still certain that she would be back—after he was fast asleep, neither thinking nor dreaming, he still smiled.

If this were a strictly realistic story, "she" would be a woman and the tale a romance, but it isn't, quite, because "she" lives in the sea. She sings, she responds to his attempt to sing her song, she goes away, and he is "only certain that she would be back." If a robin sings in my yard day after day, I can justifiably expect it to return on subsequent days, but that is not quite the hunter's situation. He is certain "she" will come back to him, and because of him, which is why this feels so much like a romance. Jarrell alerts us, thus, to two possibilities: "she" is human, somehow, and will become the hunter's mate; "she" is "animal" nonetheless and will become his guide, his pet, something not a mate. The word "mermaid" covers both possibilities without stressing one to the exclusion of the other.

The mermaid and the hunter learn to talk by her learning his language, but the major distinction Jarrell keeps making between them cuts across the two possibilities mentioned above, still without denying either: he is male, she is female; he is human, she is not. These distinctions, though, are then superseded by another: she is sea, and he is land. After she learns the word "mistake," which is for her not just a new word but a new idea, she says the sea people think she is "mistaken" to talk to land people:

> But that night she had her answer. Her first words were: "The land is new." The hunter gave her a puzzled look. She said swiftly, "*They* say all good comes from the sea. But the land is—" here she said one of her own words, and then asked impatiently: "You have legs, I have not legs. The moon is white, the sky is black. What is that?"
> "Different?"
> "Different! Different! The land is *different!*"

It is the land she wants, and gradually she comes ashore, finds out about fire, and cooked food, and fresh water, and the occasional boredom of the hunter.

In these pages Jarrell faces his biggest hurdles, and we can be aware of them even reading the book for the first time. The first concerns the part of the mermaid that is a fish and her ability to adapt to land. Jarrell solves part of the problem by making her breathe through her human mouth to gain oxygen, so while in the water she must occasionally surface, like a whale or a dolphin. He tries to solve the more difficult question of her perambulation by just ignoring it until late in the book, after she has been on land for years, and even then he explains nothing. A book so much concerned with physical detail and animal behavior is marred, thus, because its most interesting figure is a mermaid moving about on land. The second problem is perhaps more serious, and concerns the relation of *The Animal Family* to Andersen's "The Little Mermaid." It seems for long stretches as though Jarrell's book is best seen as a critique of Andersen's values. In "The Little Mermaid," as we have seen, life in the sea is inferior to life on land, as much so as life on earth is inferior to life in heaven; only human beings have immortal souls, and the best and brightest of mermaids is willing to suffer agonies in order to gain the love of a mortal prince and thereby to gain an immortal soul as well. Perhaps Jarrell's story can read perfectly well for a reader who has never read Andersen, but unquestionably it is in the awkward position of being tilted so it can be set against Andersen's tale. Jarrell's land is not superior to the sea, only different, and Jarrell delights in working back and forth between showing us the mermaid as animal—thus, given over to gathering food, sleeping, and unreflectiveness—and the mermaid as human—thus, able to talk, be interested in new things, eager to adapt to conditions for which she was not physically designed. Everything around her keeps strictly realistic bearings, but her presence, her questions and puzzlements about the ways of people and the land force Jarrell and the hunter into fresh examinations of the land, and of the difference that being human does and does not make. Jarrell insists we cannot grant Andersen's assumptions about the superiority of the human unless we can demonstrate it. But the hurdle of this book's relation to "The Little Mermaid" remains, for me, not so much jumped as walked around; little as I am fond of Andersen's tale, little do I enjoy what seems *The Animal Family's* parasitic relation to it.

What Jarrell wants, we soon see, is a romance, but one whose bearings are very different from Andersen's. I am going to break off the following quotation in mid-sentence for the purpose of asking what our expectations are about the way the sentence will end:

> She loved the look of the fire, but she hated anything cooked over it—she ate nothing but raw fish she herself had swum after and caught. (When one was particularly appetizing she couldn't resist offering the hunter a bite. "It's so good when you don't burn it in the fire," she would say.) She helped the hunter with the cooking as——

It is a comparison that is set up by that "as." If our expectations are derived from at least parts of our own world, or from Andersen's, the sentence might read "as a bride who had never learned to cook." Jarrell's text actually continues as follows:

> She helped the hunter with the cooking as a husband helps his wife: when he had gone out to hunt and had left something to stew, she would take the pot off the fire. But she never knew when to take it off; sometimes the meat was hard, and sometimes it was cooked to pieces, and she never got it right except by accident.

This is perhaps realistic, but not what we would expect nonetheless. Jarrell's realism wants, first, to alert us to the problems of mermaids and to the possibility that cooking is not the "natural" event we usually take it to be; and he wants, second, to reverse or negate our sense of the "natural" roles for the hunter and the mermaid. She is not the hunter's "husband," to be sure, and she is not his mate or his bride, but an outsider trying to be helpful.

We are now on the thirty-seventh page of a book of one hundred and eighty pages; where is it going to go? Not into an Andersen romance, not back into the sea, and not, unless it alters its engrossed tone, into a satire against mankind. The best we can say is that Jarrell thus far has employed his one nonrealistic element, the mermaid, to ask about and point our attention toward the land, so it should be that that Jarrell is interested in. And so it is. What follows is a myth of the family that is clearly designed to replace Andersen's myth of the romantic lovers. The hunter shoots a bear one day in order to escape from it, and he then captures her cub, brings it home, and feeds it, so the bear is soon part of the family. The hunter steals a lynx cub, claiming its mother will not miss it for long, and soon it too is part of the family. The lynx finds a boy in a boat that has washed up on the beach, and the boy is brought home and soon no one remembers a time before he came. The bear, being well fed, remains peaceful and sleeps most of the time. The lynx enjoys its loving family and yet remains independent in a feline way. The boy grows more slowly than the other two and knows instinctively not to put his hands in the fire. Jarrell makes it as close to realism as he can, and gains this kind of effect:

> That night they put deerskins and sealskins on the bed and let the cub sleep on the bearskin, in the corner. Sometimes he would wake and cry for a while, and then huddle in the corner with his face pushed into the bearskin, and go back to sleep. And in two days he was sitting on the floor by the table when they ate, eating with them; in a week it was as if he had lived with them always.

The hunter and the mermaid thus become parents to the bear cub; the young thing instinctively acknowledges its need of protection and food, and they, apparently just as instinctively, offer it to him. None of the three sees anything remarkable in what has happened, but Jarrell himself does, and expects us to.

Then comes the lynx:

> From the first the lynx loved being with the bear; he had
> started out with one big furry thing, his mother, and the
> bear was bigger and furrier. When he stretched himself
> against that great brown mound, so awkward and oblivious,
> the lynx looked very quick and smooth and small. Away
> from the bear, he looked quick and smooth and big. How
> deftly he sat at the table, delicately eating and drinking
> from his dish and bowl, purringly taking a bit of fish from
> the mermaid's fingers!

These aren't "magic" animals, not even talking animals, but the aim
of Jarrell's realistic rendering of them is not so much realism as myth,
and, as we begin to see this, we can also see why Jarrell wanted to
begin with the mermaid, for all the awkwardness he gets into with
her. The mermaid wants to live with the hunter, not as his mate, but
because she is curious about life on land; he sleeps underneath the
skins and she on top. The mermaid, however, being herself "magical," sets us up to expect the magical, so Jarrell then offers, as something magical but tantalizingly possible, his mythical version of the
real. Having started with a mermaid, rather than a woman, our questions about the romantic and sexual possibilities between the mermaid and the hunter are transformed into assurances about their
grand worth as parents, since the cubs and the boy want warmth,
food, and protection, and, receiving it, they grow into themselves,
fully and peacefully. Start with the mermaid, and use her as the one
magical ingredient in a myth of the real and the natural.

Hovering over the entire story is a question: why couldn't life be
like this? Why do we live in isolation and division when harmony
seems possible? When we first ask it, the answer is obvious: because
this is a story with a mermaid, and mermaids don't exist. As the story
unfolds, however, that answer comes to seem shallow and inadequate, and another, though never offered explicitly by Jarrell, seems
more to the point: because we don't separate family life from sexual
and procreative life. The hunter and the mermaid are of different
species, so they don't mate, and, since they are not the natural
parents of the bear, the lynx, and the boy, there is never any fuss
about father-roles or mother-roles, any more than there is about
husband-roles and wife-roles, and male-roles and female-roles. They

nurture instinctively, not because they love to—though they do—
but because they must. Jarrell cannot, to be sure, solve our sexual
and procreative problems by avoiding them, but he can show us the
animal family we could make were we able to solve, or ignore, those
problems.

How wonderful, or so it all seems to the alien, the mermaid, who
tells the hunter near the end of the book, as they are lying on the
beach one day:

> "And then I knew how you feel when it rains and there's
> nothing for you to do. I knew, but none of them knew.
> They don't know how to be bored or miserable. One day is
> one wave, and the next day the next, for the sea people—
> and whether they're glad or whether they're sorry, the sea
> washes it away. When my sister died, the next day I'd for-
> gotten and was happy. But if you died, if he died, my heart
> would break."

The point, she insists, is not that she is female and he is male, not
that she is "animal" and that he and the boy are "human," for
these are subsidiary points. The crucial difference is still that she
is sea and they are land, and she has come to live with them:

> "But on land it's different. The storm's real here, and the red
> leaves, and the branches when they're bare all winter. It
> all changes and never stops changing, and I'm here with
> nowhere to swim to, no way ever to leave it or forget it. No,
> the land's better! The land's better!"

The lynx is moving away down the beach, and presumably at some
point it will not come back. The bear, at the end, is sound asleep,
because bears sleep. The boy, at the end, is talking to his parents,
because boys talk and ask questions because they are curious. The
family doesn't change the nature of any of its members, and it
must be strong enough to protect against the pain of those who feel
pain for longer than a moment or two. The family is the land's
great creation, made possible by the magical mermaid, and the longing that lies behind the resultant myth wants it to be true that such
a family does not need a mermaid in order to be made real.

The crucial use of the talking mermaid for Randall Jarrell is to
help make a myth, and in this making we are not strongly aware of

story beyond the opening sequences. Our task as we read is to see what we know to be prefitted parts being fitted into their prefitted places. In such a book, nothing is a mere thing, a mere dialogue, a mere animal or person, and such books always run the risk of seeming too pat and too preachy, and perhaps concerning that little more need be said here than that Jarrell runs these risks better than most such books. In such a book, also, we don't, I think, become actively aware of an "A is B, animal is like person" metaphor, at least not past the opening scenes, because we are being asked to say, in effect, A (animal) and B (person) belong to class C (family), and the real metaphor is between C and the "real world." In a very different kind of work such as we are about to turn to, we are much more actively aware of an author making choices as to means of characterizing animals and as to where the story is going, choices which keep the A is B metaphor more alive for us in a page-by-page way. When the sense of the author's inventing seems more improvised, perhaps, we are more forced to see how the metaphor is being handled, since we are not being drawn toward seeing one big picture, as in Jarrell's myth, but into the constant activity of seeing, as in Selma Lagerlöf's *The Wonderful Adventures of Nils.*

Nils opens, like *The Animal Family,* with quiet realism. Nils is an adolescent Swedish lad who, since he has refused to attend church with his parents, is told by them to read the Sunday morning service at home. He promises, but it is a lovely early spring day, and he has no intention of more than halfheartedly keeping his promise. He starts to read the service, falls asleep, and wakes to discover that some thief has apparently left open the lid of his mother's chest:

> While he sat there and waited for the thief to make his appearance, he began to wonder what the dark shadow was which fell across the edge of the chest. He looked and looked—and did not want to believe his eyes. But the thing, which at first seemed shadowy, became more and more clear to him; and soon he saw that it was something real. It was no less a thing than an elf who sat there—astride the edge of the chest!

Already the story has taken a turn, Lagerlöf has made a choice. It might well have been a human thief that ransacked Nils's mother's chest, as could happen in Robert Louis Stevenson or Stephen Meader. But instead, "it was no less a thing than an elf."

Elves are less precisely literary figures than mermaids. They appear in various folk literatures, though, so far as I know, in this century only Tolkien has ever taken elves seriously. Knowing this, we might quickly check the date of *Nils*, which is 1907, to see what we might expect to be Lagerlöf's attitude toward elves. Since elves belong to an older world than ours, most latter-day authors tend to be a little cute or self-conscious about them. The more a writer believes in elves the easier that writer will find it to bring them into a realistically described world, while the writer who uses elves as an admitted contrivance is more likely to transport the story to an alternative world of the magical, where elves can safely exist. Lagerlöf settles the matter very quickly: "To be sure, the boy had heard stories about elves, but he had never dreamed they were such tiny creatures." In other words, Nils had heard about elves as he might have heard about Stockholm, as a matter of lore, other people's knowledge. But the lore is not to be doubted. From what he had been told Nils had wrongly imagined the size of elves, just as, from what he had been told, he might have wrongly imagined the height of the tall buildings in Stockholm. But he does not doubt the existence of either. "It was no less a thing than an elf" means that, tiny though they are, elves are important.

But Nils is not awed, or respectful, or even curious about the elf. He catches it in a butterfly net, and the elf pleads with Nils for its freedom, offering "an old coin, a silver spoon, and a gold penny" in return. Small and captive though it is, Nils is rather frightened of the elf and quickly agrees to the bargain: "He felt he had entered into an agreement with something weird and uncanny; something which did not belong to his world, and he was only too glad to get rid of the horrid thing." Again, Lagerlöf has made a choice, turning her story one way so it will not go another. E. Nesbit's Londoner Bastables see the Psammead, of whom they have never even heard, and they brightly start asking it questions. Nils is a darkly and narrowly raised country boy, uncertain of his world and its limits. With a "weird and uncanny" elf, "the horrid thing," Nils is almost certainly not going to find any wet magic, or a trip on a magic carpet, or a road to Oz.

Nils quickly regrets his bargain when he thinks he might well have asked for more than the elf offered, and he tries to recapture the elf.

Suddenly he is hit on the head, sent reeling from wall to wall until he falls senseless on the floor. Again, we might read this as a cue to transport the lad away to an elfin world, rather as the cyclone does Dorothy Gale. But again Lagerlöf chooses to keep her Swedish country world intact: "When he awoke, he was alone in the cottage," and still with the Sunday service to read too. As he makes his way back to his book, however, Nils discovers he has been transformed into the size of an elf. Imagine the possibilities once again, remembering we are on page 17 of a book of over five hundred pages. Lagerlöf could still transport Nils out of Sweden, but everything she has done thus far shows she accepts elves and their magic powers as part of Sweden. Yet, accepting of elves or no, the more Swedenlike she keeps her world, the less elflike it must be. To have Nils now become part of a community of elves, running around the house of his parents, perhaps, might work for a little joking, like the invisible Faustus and Mephistophilis at the papal court in Marlowe's play, or for a little doing good, as in *The Tailor of Gloucester*. Such stories must be short, though, since their narrative possibilities dwindle quickly. If Nils isn't going to go visit elves, what is Lagerlöf's point in changing his size?

The answer comes quickly: to make him smaller than animals. The elf has disappeared, Nils is alone, and he goes into the barnyard only to learn he has long been despised as a bully there:

> Instantly, both the geese and the chickens turned and stared at the boy; and then they set up a fearful cackling. "Cock-el-i-coo," crowed the rooster, "good enough for him! Cock-el-i-coo, he has pulled my comb!" "Ka, ka, kada, serves him right!" cried the hens; and with that they set up a continuous cackle.

This is a wonderful passage for showing the suppleness of the metaphor of the talking animal when used by a good author. Lagerlöf on the one hand goes out of her way to insist she is a close observer of real roosters and knows the sound of their crowing is not the standard "cock-a-doodle-doo." On the other hand, "good enough for him" and "he has pulled my comb" are the words of a standard talking animal. The effect of this is to make us ask what real roosters, "cock-el-i-coo" roosters, say to each other, or to us, could we hear them rightly. A child is apt to wonder about such questions, but so too is anyone who has spent slow, careful time looking at and listening to roosters. The answers are potentially frightening, and Lagerlöf's turning of her story as she has implies that if we were the size of elves we could hear what roosters say; and we would also be powerless to alter whatever judgment they might levy against us.

By this point we can be fairly sure this is not an elf story. The elf has been useful to clarify Nils's character, and to make him small, but it looks now as though his adventures are to be as a tiny Nils, in Sweden. Finding it unbearable to be told he might now be punished for past wickedness, Nils hurls a rock at the birds, who charge at him. A house cat appears, the barnyard birds disperse, and Nils is momentarily saved:

> Immediately the boy ran up to the cat. "You dear pussy!" said he, "You must know all the corners and hiding places about here? You'll be a good little kitty and tell me where I can find the elf."
>
> The cat did not reply at once. He seated himself, curled his tail into a graceful ring around his paws—and stared at the boy. It was a large black cat with one white spot on his chest.

Like *The Animal Family*, this keeps combining the talking animal with careful descriptions of the real, and for the sake of such careful descriptions. But the effect is very different, and nothing in Jarrell's book could be as ominous as this. Nils assumes the cat can talk since the barnyard birds can talk, but he forgets he can assume this because he himself is very small, much too small to be patronizingly jolly to a cat. This creature is no monster, but it is a real cat, not a "dear pussy":

> "I know well enough where the elf lives," he said in a soft voice, "but that doesn't say I'm going to tell *you* about it."
>
> "Dear pussy, you must tell me where the elf lives!" said the boy. "Can't you see how he has bewitched me?"
>
> The cat opened his eyes a little, so that the green wickedness began to shine forth. He spun round and purred with satisfaction before he replied. "Shall I perhaps help you because you have so often grabbed me by the tail?" he said at last.

Then the boy was furious and forgot entirely how little and helpless he was now. "Oh, I can pull your tail again, I can," said he, and ran toward the cat.

Compare this with another difficult moment for a child magically reduced in size, Alice's "Conversation with a Caterpillar." Lewis Carroll describes his caterpillar as three inches high, and he will eventually become a butterfly, but essentially his conversation with Alice is between a schoolmaster and a pupil. By comparison, Lagerlöf's cat is frightening not because it acts like a figure of human authority, but because it acts like a real cat, its green wickedness shining forth from its eyes, able to talk, but only to remind Nils what any abused cat might say to any bullying child.

Then Lagerlöf reaps her first important reward for having adhered so closely to realism in her tale of elves and talking animals: "Then the cat made one spring and landed right on the boy; knocked him down and stood over him—his forepaws on his chest, and his jaws wide apart—over his throat." This is unimaginable in Wonderland, or in a fully realistic story, or in *The Animal Family*. Anyone who has looked inside a cat's mouth, or seen a cat play with a captive mouse or bird, or seen a child grab a cat and call it "dear pussy," knows the horror of this moment. How much, Lagerlöf asks us to see, does mere size and strength determine the order of creation; how casual we are, too, in using our strength; how awful for Nils, whose punishment is juster than nightmare: " 'There!' he said. 'That will do now. I'll let you go this time, for my mistress' sake. I only wanted you to know which one of us has the power now.' " The cat that can remember the unkindness of one person can remember the kindness of another, and his dismissal of Nils shines forth, like his own green wickedness, as a gesture of sinister contempt.

Alice, when she is made small, is frustrated and irritated; Gulliver, in the country of the giant Brobdingnags, is disgusted; Nils here is plain scared, because Lagerlöf has made his world so coherent with the one he left when he first saw the elf. In going the direction she has gone thus far, Lagerlöf seems now in some danger of making her story into a lecture to Nils for his past sins, such as one finds in Carlo Collodi's *Pinocchio*. One of the laws of Kipling's jungle is that punishment must not be followed by recrimination, and clearly Lagerlöf must not break that law. We are not going on with the elf, the barnyard animals, or the cat, but we are going on with Nils's wonderful adventures, and Lagerlöf has gone as far as she can go in teaching her hero humility. Fortunately Lagerlöf has pondered her materials slowly and patiently, so she doesn't go Collodi's way. What she has pondered, we know, is Sweden, and especially, it soon becomes clear, the life of its wild animals. Nils goes back to the yard and watches a flock of geese fly over, calling to the tame geese on the ground to join them. One eager young gander agrees to leave. Nils climbs up on his back, and soon both have joined the flock in the air; for the first time, Nils's reduced size is a benefit for him. First, Nils learns the wild geese don't expect the gander to be able to keep up and have invited it along in order to watch it fail, and fall. Second, Nils is told the wild geese shun human beings because all people, large and small, are cruel to other animals. So we have abandoned the simpler sorts of didacticism. The wild geese are in their way as bullying as Nils, but they are grand, too, and not in the least in need of being punished. Likewise, if Nils has behaved badly, he has been no worse than most people tend to be. We are in open air, free to ponder such bracing grimness, and by comparison with these wild geese, Randall Jarrell's animals seem tame, human-oriented.

Some time later Nils is able to help one of the wild geese, and in return the leader of the flock, Akka, goes back to Nils's house and secures the elf's promise to return Nils to human size again:

> But the boy was thinking of the carefree days and the banter; and of adventure and freedom and travel, high above the earth, that he should miss, and he actually bawled with grief. "I don't want to be human," said he. "I want to go with you to Lapland."

"I don't want to be human" might be Gulliver denouncing a race of odious vermin, or Peter Pan wishing no one would ever grow up. But anyone might want to pursue adventure and freedom and travel, when it is not with Kenneth Grahame's Mr. Toad but with this stern, wild old goose. We may seem here to be edging toward satire, judgment against human ways, but Lagerlöf is still pondering:

> It was a strange thing about that boy—as long as he had lived he had never cared for anyone. He had not cared for his father or mother; nor for his schoolteacher; nor for his

school mates; nor for the boys in the neighbourhood. All that they had wished to have him do—whether it had been work or play—he had only thought tiresome. Therefore there was no one whom he missed or longed for.

This passage is perhaps the greatest triumph of Lagerlöf's way with people and animals. "He had never cared for anyone" is offered simply as a fact. It does not make Nils a freak, though it helps explain his past cruelty to animals. The very quietness with which the discovery is made serves to authenticate it, as though anyone might make such a discovery, as though we should not be surprised or aghast should we discover it about ourselves even without riding on the back of a wild goose. In their very grimness, such sentences offer bracing assurance.

Each time Lagerlöf has chosen how to place Nils within her shifting context of speaking animals, she has insisted, we can now see, on making a point about strength and power. There is the wrong kind of harsh strength, as we see when Nils's parents leave for church, when we learn about Nils's past behavior with animals, when the wild geese mock and tempt the tame ones. All these seem ugly and nasty. There is also a right kind of harsh strength, as we see in the cat and the geese handling Nils, as we see especially in Lagerlöf's handling of Nils. All these seem beautiful. Nils thinks of "adventure and freedom and travel" when he thinks of the geese, but it has been hard adventuring, not so much liberating as invigorating. The discipline of the birds is genuine, worthy, anything but tiresome, although very tiring. Slow and pondering though she is, Lagerlöf has actually moved rather quickly toward this cleansing moment when Nils discovers he does not want to be human again, and it is hard to see how she could have done this without the talking animals and the magical changes in Nils's size.

Each choice a storyteller makes works to deny other possible choices. Having kept her story in Sweden, she cannot move it much farther away than Lapland. Having stressed the fierce discipline of the geese, Lagerlöf cannot make them warm, nice, or very pleasant companions. Having chosen to use talking animals to reveal the nature of real animals, she has deprived herself of any large or enveloping plot, because the real life of wild animals can yield only episodes, and the long story of survival. As a result, after the moment I have just described, *The Wonderful Adventures of Nils* becomes more plainly episodic than it has been thus far, since Nils's essential choices have been reduced to two: stay with the geese or leave them. The driving narrative impulse which is sustained as long as Lagerlöf is shifting her contexts and our way of seeing Nils has been spent and, after this, can be recaptured only within episodes, and cannot be generated through the book as a whole. The book has become "adventures."

We have now looked at two latter-day writers working with animals, especially animals who speak, and their relation to people. I have not tried to enumerate or classify the techniques, or even to mention all those used in these two books. Rather, I have been concerned with stressing the variety of possible effects and the great and exciting ease with which they have been employed by writers who are not self-consciously adopting conventions, or employing techniques, but who are exploring materials capable of yielding great expansiveness and great precision. In both books the talking or magical animal is the key, but the door the key opens is different in each case. It is probably true that it takes a rather special talent to see the possibilities of these animal metaphors, and it is certainly true that many more have presumed they possess this talent than have been able to demonstrate they do. The terrible cuteness and triteness of most children's books sometimes seems little more than the result of ignorance or incomprehension or carelessness about the materials being used, most of which concern animals in one way or another. In the introductory chapter I spoke about the snobbery that animates many of A. A. Milne's stories about Winnie-the-Pooh and Christopher Robin, but, compared with most writers of children's books, he achieved an almost unqualified success because he understood his materials, he wanted the effect he achieved. Most never get this far because their observation and understanding of the potentially magic relations between animals and people, especially between animals and children, is dim, thoughtless, or merely clever. The point needs no belaboring here since our concern is with the classic successes, but it should never be thought that a writer who employs a metaphor therefore will employ it successfully.

This is only another way of reminding us that children's literature is not a genre even though most children's books use talking or humanized animals. There is no necessary reason why *The Animal Family, The Wonderful Adventures of Nils,* or even *The Tale of Peter Rabbit* has to be thought of as a book for children, though we can understand historically why this has happened. Nor should we assume that writers of children's books, or employers of talking animals, have much in common. Some writers derived their animals from close observation, as was the case with Selma Lagerlöf and Beatrix Potter; others from folk or fairy tales or beast fables they felt close to, or from other books written for children, or from a wholly "adult" desire to make a myth, as with Randall Jarrell. Potter, Grahame, and Kipling were almost exact contemporaries, and all were English people of approximately the same class. Externally nothing could have been more fully contrived to make them partakers of the same tradition, yet Peter Rabbit, Rat, and Shere Khan reveal that in literary matters the three writers seem to have shared almost nothing at all.

Yet the very fact that talking animals exist in children's literature reveals the persistence of a tradition that mostly died or disappeared in other writing and must count for something in the way of shared assumptions. Animals, talking animals, animals that are children or specially allied with children, creatures that can recreate, flatter, and repudiate the human wish that we are not alone—that is the backbone of children's literature as we know it. I would not care to speak for all writers of children's books, but of many it can be said that they shared the myth of adult life as a prison house, as announced in Wordsworth's classic passage in his "Intimations of Immortality" ode:

> Shades of the prison-house begin to close
>   Upon the growing Boy,
> But he beholds the light, and whence it flows,
>   He sees it in its joy;
> The Youth, who daily farther from the east
>   Must travel, still is Nature's Priest,
>   And by the vision splendid
>   Is on his way attended;
> At length the Man perceives it die away,
> And fade into the light of common day.

Wordsworth did not, at least in this poem, believe that the light and joy which attended the child at birth need be totally lost as we grow older, but in other poems he did believe this, and many writers of children's books seem to have shared this belief. They accepted childhood as a time of instinctive oneness with the surrounding world and used talking animals to signify the potential connection between the human and the surrounding.

Accompanying this belief is, quite often, the correlative one that understands adults as people who can see only "the light of common day," and in many stories we find a relation between a child and an animal that adults cannot understand, or have, or wish to have, because custom lies on them with a weight, heavy as frost, and deep almost as life. In fairy tales there is no trace of this, because distinctions there between older and younger people are never mythic or romantic, but we find it in *Nils*, in Felix Salten's *Perri*, in Frances Hodgson Burnett's *The Secret Garden*, in E. Nesbit's Bastable books, in *Peter Pan* and the *Jungle Books* and *Charlotte's Web*, and it is on the fringes, playing an implicit role, in almost all children's books. Since Blake and Wordsworth were among the first to offer the terms of the myth of the prison house, we should not be surprised that in many children's books the impulse propelling the myth is romantic, though Selma Lagerlöf shows this is not always so. Many writers of children's books do not enjoy adult life, and the myth offers great consolation and power for those who do not. It yields for many thoughts that do not, alas, lie too deep for tears, but for many others it yields gaiety, joy, and cheerful realism, and for them the availability of the tradition of the talking or humanized animal provides the terms for expressing what the myth has given.

Yet even as we move toward a generalization, we must be wary and remember that the tradition of the talking animal in children's literature is too varied, geographically too widely dispersed, for a single romantic myth to encompass it or even always to accompany it. Kate Seredy in Hungary, Salten in Austria, Lagerlöf in Sweden, Johanna Spyri in Switzerland, de Brunhoff in France, all the writers considered in the ensuing chapters in England and America reveal this variety more than they encourage very much in the way of generalization. Just naming this short list of writers shows how hard a task it will be to write a true history of children's literature.

(5)   Lewis Carroll

There is nothing odder in the annals of children's literature than the
position occupied by the *Alice* books. They are the irreplaceable
classics that everyone is supposed to know, and yet few people, so
far as I can tell, sit down of their own volition to read them, or are
unhappy when an episode or a book is over. Jan B. Gordon in *Aspects
of Alice* has a shrewd observation on this score: "The adult who,
because of traditional respect for its legendary greatness or the desire to inculcate its morality, elected to read *Alice's Adventures in
Wonderland* to a child before bedtime, may well prompt a sudden
flight into dreamland." When this happens, *Alice* resembles the book
Alice herself was bored with when she first spotted the White Rabbit
and fell down his hole. Yet there is barely a passage in the book that
does not ring a bell for an educated reader, and at the level of word
and phrase Lewis Carroll is the most memorable author of children's
books who ever lived, and one of the most memorable of any kind:
" 'Twas brillig, and the slithy toves"; "curiouser and curiouser";
"It was the *best* butter"; "The time has come, the walrus said, to
talk of many things"; "Reeling and Writhing and Fainting in Coils";
"*There's* glory for you"; "jam tomorrow and jam yesterday—but
never jam today." Everyone has favorites, the list goes on and on.

There is nothing contradictory in the fact that these classics, filled with memorable phrases and incidents, are not read or reread with much genuine enthusiasm. The same might be said of Shakespeare and certainly could be said of the King James Bible. What we remember most clearly is what we should remember, bits and pieces, and we do not have to reread either book all the way through to go back and pick these up. This means, however, something that those who write about Lewis Carroll seldom wish to admit: the generalizations one wants to make about him tend not to hold. Alice, for instance, does not "grow up," or grow in stature, in either book. The events in neither book are consistently narrated as if taking place in a dream. Time, space, and chess are not consistently handled in *Through the Looking-Glass*. What Alice meets is not always fantastic, topsy-turvy, frightening, or nonsense. The two books are different from each other, but some episodes in each could safely be moved into the other book. Alice is not always priggish, or concerned with rules and manners, or a symbol or a type of anything or anyone. "Dodgson," asked the Canon Duckworth as he chaperoned the Liddell children and Dodgson up the Thames, "is this an extempore romance of yours?" "Yes," Dodgson replied, "I'm inventing as we go along." Which is precisely what we would have surmised had we not been told. As a consequence of this "inventing as we go along" the books don't make very satisfactory or interesting wholes, but they do contain a great many memorable individual phrases and episodes. In an essay on the *Alice* books, written some years after they were published, Lewis Carroll insisted on this very point:

> *Alice* and *Looking-Glass* are made up almost wholly of bits and scraps, single ideas which came of themselves. In writing it out, I added many fresh ideas, which seemed to grow of themselves on the original stock; and many were added when, years afterwards, I wrote it all over again for publication; but (this may interest some readers of *Alice* to know) every such idea and nearly every word of the dialogue *came of itself*. Sometimes an idea comes at night, when I have had to get up and strike a light to note it down —sometimes when out on a lonely winter walk, when I

have had to stop, and with half-frozen fingers jot down a few words which should keep the new-born idea from perishing—but whenever or however it comes, *it comes of itself.*

The point was apparently so important for Lewis Carroll that he had to say it four times in one paragraph and italicize it twice as well.

It should not be surprising, then, that many of those who have written about Lewis Carroll and the *Alice* books are not literary people. They tend to fall into two groups. The first accepts and even delights in the fragmentary nature of the books, because, like Humpty-Dumpty, their pleasure comes from picking up brilliant bits and scraps and writing as though the others did not exist. Martin Gardner and Peter Heath have editions of the books, for instance, that offer a running marginal commentary on the semantic, philosophical, mathematical, and historical problems and allusions that dot Carroll's pages. A recent book dedicates itself to solving Lewis Carroll's riddles, beginning with the Mad Hatter's "Why is a raven like a writing desk?," for which Lewis Carroll himself had no answer. Since these inquiries can almost be carried on as though Lewis Carroll were not an author, it is understandable that many such commentators are physicists, logicians, and mathematicians. The second group are psychologists, and they seek to explain Lewis Carroll's bits and scraps by recreating Charles Dodgson, the shy donnish lover of little girls. The words "Freudian" and Jungian" crop up here, used rather loosely, especially by those who think the psychologists are wrong, vulgar, impertinent, or all three. Since the Humpty-Dumpty commentators tend to be English, and the psychologists tend not to be, questions of national habit enter in as frequently as questions of aim or method.

Later I would like to see how Lewis Carroll's ways of working with his fragments elude even good Humpty-Dumpty critics, but first we can look briefly at a psychologist. Here is a passage from Florence Becker Lennon's interesting and suggestive *Life of Lewis Carroll*; the subject is "Jabberwocky": "The book has one grim defeat in the trappings of victory. Humpty-Dumpty demonstrates *Looking-Glass* methods by analyzing 'Jabberwocky.' The youth slays the Jabberwock—is the author trying to tell himself, by writing the poem backwards, that this is a disastrous victory? What drove Charles back into himself and his childish memories? Was it not his acceptance of ordination without resolving his doubts? For him, taking orders was, implicitly, giving in to his father. No one, reading the elder Dodgson's letter, would say he exercised no tyranny over his son." First we need to make some quick emendations. "Jabberwocky" is not "written backwards," but in mirror script, a fact which by itself says nothing about the quality of the victory in the poem. Nor is there anything distinctively *Looking-Glass* about Humpty-Dumpty's methods. Finally, Dodgson's ordination in 1861 could not by itself have "driven" him back into "himself and his childish memories" since there is the same kind of playfulness, the same kind of childishness, in Dodgson's bits and scraps written before 1861 as there is in the later work.

But what of Lennon's most important point, that, in slaying the Jabberwock, Dodgson is showing us a castration story, the boy presenting the father with a triumph over a monster that is really the boy's desire to be a man? Lennon points out that the boy in the poem does not, as a result of his triumph, become heir to a kingdom, like Beowulf, and is not given a princess in reward, like many young lads in fairy tales. The fact, furthermore, that the last stanza repeats the first gives us a static world in which nothing is significantly changed by the triumph over the Jabberwock, so that the victory, if not exactly a defeat, effects nothing beyond making the father happy. So far as it goes or can go, Lennon's point suggests something that Dodgson may well have felt and that may well have driven Lewis Carroll into poetry to express. *Through the Looking-Glass* is filled with battles, between Tweedledum and Tweedledee, between the Lion and the Unicorn, between the Red and the White Knight—and they all resemble the battle against the Jabberwock in being somewhat obscure and pointless, as if governed by a fate the combatants cannot control. Dodgson said or wrote nothing explicitly about his feeling concerning his ordination, but he did dither some years before accepting orders, and he proceeded no further in the church than to become a deacon, which was enough to encase him in vows of celibacy but not enough to give him anything more in the way of authority in the church. And Dodgson's father, by 1861 himself Archdeacon of Ripon, wanted his son to join the church and was capable of exerting strong-willed control beneath a generally unruffled and gentle exterior. On the face of it, then, an interpretation of "Jabberwocky" that sees it as expressing a dubious victory gained by Dodgson to please his father is not at all out of the question.

Lennon's reading, nonetheless, seems to me the obverse of Humpty-Dumpty's, each being evasive but in opposite ways. Humpty-Dumpty explains the poem by explaining some of its words, as though the meaning were nothing more than the sum of the definitions of its individual words. Some of Humpty-Dumpty's readings are silly—"brillig" does not "mean" "four o'clock in the afternoon" —while others can hardly be improved upon, like "lithe and slimy" as the definition of "slithy." What he leaves out is what Florence Becker Lennon leaves out, too: Lewis Carroll, the author of a poem that may be only a fragment in *Through the Looking-Glass* but is by itself a full and suggestive whole, with meanings that exist apart from whatever motives propelled it into being:

> 'Twas brillig, and the slithy toves
>   Did gyre and gimble in the wabe;
> All mimsy were the borogroves,
>   And the mome raths outgrabe.
>
> "Beware the Jabberwock, my son!
>   The jaws that bite, the claws that catch!
> Beware the Jubjub bird, and shun
>   The frumious Bandersnatch!"

Like all Lewis Carroll's poems, "Jabberwocky" is assured, free of doubt or tangle or explicit mystery. Here, too, we have no impulse to say, as Alice does after her recital of "Father William," "That's not right." "Jabberwocky" is clearly right.

Except for certain words, furthermore, we know perfectly well what it means. The rhythm and grammar are coherent; it is a ballad, a scene is set, a warning is given. As in all ballads, the sense of danger and ominous future is set off against the assured meter. As the poem unfolds, if anything allows the boy to kill the Jabberwock, it is words: the Jabberwock can whiffle through the tulgey wood, but the boy can in his turn galumph, and he has a vorpal blade besides, to shut off the Jabberwock's burbling. If this is heroism, like David against Goliath or Beowulf against Grendel, it is obscure heroism, since the sword may be magic and the Jabberwock, for all his jaws and flames, seems easy to kill. If it is a ritual killing, then "brillig" is a time of year or a time of life, but the terms are otherwise unclear. The poem exudes mystery, not about its action, only about its words, its sounds, its apparently great distance from us, and Humpty-Dumpty does not help when he explains the words because the mystery lies in the fact that the words are self-sufficient, without need of being explained, so that "galumph," "beamish," and "chortle" could enter into the common language without having first been defined. To ask, then, what kind of nonsense this is is only to say what kind of sense it is: ballad sense, sound sense, the ability of words to suggest their own meanings. The action itself is conclusive, but our sense of it must remain inconclusive, though no less satisfying for that. The effects are rigged, "poetic," beyond the touch of analysis, and its delights are solemn. Which is to say it resembles a good deal of Tennyson, Swinburne, and Hopkins, and that the poet who learned its lessons best was the young Eliot writing about wearing trousers rolled as a consequence of aging.

None of this denies Lennon's "reading" of the poem, though it might help to make that reading seem less relevant or decisive. The real trouble with the psychologists is that even if they are entirely right they usually leave the major work of description and analysis and synthesis undone, and the most a reading of the life of Charles Dodgson can give us is some clues as to how best to conduct our proceedings. The task with the *Alice* books, as with most children's literature, is to stick to the surface of what is presented to us and to read that surface hard. A writer whose "bits and scraps" "came of themselves" is willing to acknowledge mystery in what he did, but the mystery is in the writing, in the special unyielding quality of the *Alice* books. "Words mean more than we mean to express when we use them; so a whole book ought to mean a good deal more than the writer meant." Lewis Carroll said that, not, presumably, in order to give his readers full license to read his books any way they wished, but in acknowledgment that what we find and what he meant might well be very different.

I hope I have not suggested that the life of Charles Dodgson isn't fascinating or is irrelevant to our study of Lewis Carroll, but I don't think Florence Becker Lennon, Phyllis Greenacre, Géza Róheim, or Martin Grotjahn has ever succeeded in being precise about the relevance of Dodgson's life for the reader of the *Alice* books. One reason for this is that Dodgson seems really to have been the person he presented himself as being, which is a fact many psychologists find difficult to live with. He was born in 1832 and died in 1898, and he spent forty-seven of his not quite sixty-six years in Christ Church, Oxford, as fellow, don, lecturer, writer, and cleric. He was an interesting, suggestive, but minor scholar of works on mathematics and logic. He was a fanatic keeper of order who indexed and filed his voluminous and not very interesting correspondence; he loved puzzles and games, many of which he devised late at night, suffering from insomnia; he loved the theatre and knew that such a love was not, as some others thought, incompatible with his clerical position. He wrote a great deal, all bits and scraps, some of which he put together into books, some of which went into his diary and letters, some of which he fired off to fuel donnish disputes. He was an avid and excellent photographer, a great many of whose best pictures, or so he thought, had to be destroyed because they were of girls in the nude.

His passion for girls is the most famous fact about him and probably the most important fact as well, and it is certainly the one people find hardest to accept at face value. What he wanted from his relations with girls he almost certainly got: their attention and companionship, their willingness to pose for his camera, their responsiveness to his kisses and to his black box of puzzles and games, which he used to introduce himself to girls he met on trains or in parks. Gradually he accustomed himself to the fact that girls become, about the age of fourteen, young women, and except near the end of his life he wanted no more to do with young women than with boys or with adults of either sex. His diary reveals no sign of sexual torment in him, and his letters to girls and to their mothers show nothing hidden or forbidden in what he sought. When one girl turned fourteen and "came out," he dropped her and found another; Alice Liddell, being his first girl after his own sisters, he gave up more grudgingly, and he only gradually became cheerfully resigned to finding new girls every few years. Sometimes he was rebuffed or warned off by an anxious parent, but he came to expect that too. In religious matters he was inclined to be reticent and slightly priggish; with girls he was open, direct, playful, frequently sentimental and mawkish.

It is hard, as William Empson has said in what is still the best essay ever written about him, not to cock one's eye at Dodgson's way of living, and we must wonder why someone wanted what he wanted. He was so active and diligent in pursuing his pleasures with girls, however, that it seems unwise to begin by seeing him as someone fearfully repressed, constantly "driven back into his childish thoughts." He never grew up and was surely blocked or retarded in important ways, but he lived with himself remarkably well after he came to understand the essential configurations of his life, desires, and possibilities. I don't mean to say he was happy, and one quality that emerges very strongly in his writing is a cruel desire for revenge that the surface of his life would seem to deny. He found life difficult and found himself unfit to live as many or most others seemed to live. His equipoise was sporadic, bits and pieces like everything else, so that his attitude toward living was essentially defensive. Everything was unstable, and if he strikes one note repeatedly it is that rules, orders, courtesies, and generalizations all break down under the pressure of selfishness, cruelty, idiocy, pedantry, shortsightedness, passion, and even, occasionally, decency. Dodgson adored Alice, but Lewis Carroll was merciless toward her, exposing her to everything he had himself suffered: teachers who made him reel and writhe, governesses who resembled the Red Queen and dowagers who resembled the Duchess, robust boys who acted like Tweedledum and Tweedledee, Humpty-Dumptys who stayed too long on their walls, footmen who wanted to know if he was to be allowed in at all. Yet, if Alice's defenses against these onslaughts were generally inadequate, Dodgson's own seem gradually to have become successful, perhaps because he was so very good at showing in his writing all that he feared and disliked.

The one thing that Dodgson was not is paranoiac. He imagined no conspiracy, no sense that anything in the world connected coherently enough for that. So we are forced back on to the bits and scraps, and we must try to see what kind of coherence and connection they offer when taken a bit at a time. "Jabberwocky," we have seen, is a poem of beautiful obscurity and untriumphant finality whose nonsense, should we choose to call it that, is neither funny nor threatening. Now here is a conversation from "A Mad Tea-Party," whose ways, means, and effect are almost entirely the opposite:

> The Hatter opened his eyes very wide on hearing this; but all he *said* was "Why is a raven like a writing desk?"
>
> "Come, we shall have some fun now!" thought Alice. "I'm glad they've begun asking riddles—I believe I can guess that," she added aloud.
>
> "Do you mean that you think you can find out the answer to it?" said the March Hare.
>
> "Exactly so," said Alice.
>
> "Then you should say what you mean," the March Hare went on.
>
> "I do," Alice hastily replied; "at least—at least I mean what I say—that's the same thing, you know."
>
> "Not the same thing a bit!" said the Hatter. "You might just as well say that 'I see what I eat' is the same thing as 'I eat what I see'!"
>
> "You might just as well say," added the March Hare, "that 'I like what I get' is the same thing as 'I get what I like'!"
>
> "You might just as well say," added the dormouse, who seemed to be talking in his sleep, "that 'I breathe when I sleep' is the same thing as 'I sleep when I breathe'!"

As the scene unfolds, it is quite clear why it is irrelevant if an answer to "Why is a raven like a writing desk?" is never found. The phrase is a riddle, and when Alice hears what sounds like a riddle, she feels she can relax because she knows how to play. When she says "I believe I can guess that" she does not mean she knows the answer but that she can guess, which is most of what one does with riddles. But, since "I believe I can guess that" does not mean, or say, that Alice can "find the answer to it," the March Hare trips her up when she says "Exactly so." Alice's certainty is social, the result of knowing that the connection between a raven and a writing desk is a riddling one, and the March Hare is determined to upset her certainty.

"Why is a raven like a writing desk?" is as obscure a set of words as
" 'Twas brillig and the slithy toves," but in each case the form—a
riddle or a ballad—allows us to relax rather than to feel uncomfortable about the obscurity. Such relaxing is possible only as long as
everyone goes along, which the March Hare, and then the Mad
Hatter, won't do, and that makes them rude, difficult, fussy, sharp,
naïve, or some combination of these qualities. Immediately the nonsense of the tea-party becomes difficult and unpleasant, but it was
the quality of Lewis Carroll's imagination that, once something difficult or unpleasant was opened up, he pursued it. The conversation
gives us six statements, in effect, two from Alice, two from the
Hatter, and two from the March Hare:

> *Alice:* "I say what I mean" and "I mean what I say"
> *Hatter:* "I see what I eat" and "I eat what I see"
> *Hare:* "I like what I get" and "I get what I like."

The Hare and the Hatter claim Alice's mistake is to equate her two
statements, but we know her mistake is to misread the situation and
to relax when a riddle is asked. The Hatter and the Hare then equate
Alice's pair with theirs, implying that if what they assert is silly or
wrong then Alice's must be silly and wrong too. In fact, however,
Alice's statements *can* be equated, though in ordinary usage "I say
what I mean" is either naïve or pedantic while "I mean what I say"
is threatening. But if one statement is true then so is the other, and
the real complications lie elsewhere, in the difficulty of people saying what they mean, as Alice is demonstrating right here. The Hatter's statements cannot be equated, and each taken by itself is rather
daft, "I see what I eat" making life a matter of blindfolds or dark
rooms, and "I eat what I see" belonging to a gastronomic tyrant of
grand proportions. The Hare's statements not only cannot be
equated, but are close to being an obverse pair, since "I like what I
get" is the cheerful assertion of a wondrous observer or an obedient
slave, while "I get what I like" is the assertion of a tyrant or a god
whose subjects, at most, "like what they get."

What is perhaps most interesting about this passage is the way,
once a social situation has been frustrated or diverted by the desire
to intimidate and obscure, character can be suggested and elucidated.
The obvious clue to this comes from the Dormouse offering his pair:

"I breathe when I sleep" and "I sleep when I breathe," which is, as the Hatter says, true indeed for the Dormouse. Alice, after all, *is* pedantic and naïve, and just a little bit threatening in her way of being so. The Hatter *is* daft and is as much of a gastronomic tyrant as he can be, spending most of his time eating what he sees and seeing what he eats. The Hare *is* both something of a tyrant—just before this we have had his exchange with Alice that goes "Have some wine," "I don't see any," "There isn't any"—and the generally willing slave of this loony situation who can only mutter to himself he wishes it were time for dinner, so he can, for once, like what he gets and get what he likes. That is, whatever it was that began this scene for Lewis Carroll, once into it he found ways to be expressive about his characters that are a good deal more suggestive than our general awareness that this is a "stupid tea-party" might allow for. We will see a brilliant and profound instance of this later, when we come to "Wool and Water," where the hardest thing to do is to take the White Queen seriously. There is nothing brilliant or profound about the Hatter and the Hare, but what gives them their nasty and mad interest is Lewis Carroll's way of making language adhere to character to make his situations rich.

For it isn't ever the characters as such that count, but the bit or the scrap, the episode, which is why learning to read one scene helps us very little in reading the next one. A good deal of what makes the books unnerving, especially *Wonderland,* is that they offer no sense of continuity, or of a past or future tense. Alice herself makes only one effort to use an earlier experience to get her through the agonies of a new one. It comes in the croquet game, when the Duchess, in a strikingly more cheerful mood than she was during "Pig and Pepper," tries to make love to Alice:

> Alice did not much like keeping so close to her; first, because the Duchess was *very* ugly; and secondly, because she was exactly the right height to rest her chin on Alice's shoulder, and it was an uncomfortably sharp chin. However, she did not like to be rude, so she bore it as well as she could.
>
> "The game's going on rather better now" she said, by way of keeping up the conversation a little.

> " 'Tis so," said the Duchess: "and the moral of that is—
> 'Oh, 'tis love, 'tis love, that makes the world go round!' "
> "Somebody said," Alice whispered, "that it's done by
> everybody minding their own business!"

This is Alice's wittiest moment, because it was the Duchess herself
who had said earlier how much better the world would get on if
everyone minded their own business. Precious little good it does
Alice, though, to remember this:

> "Ah well! It means much the same thing," said the
> Duchess, digging her sharp little chin into Alice's shoulder.

The terrible triumph of adult passion, as Lewis Carroll knew it, is
right there. Love does make the world go round when everyone
minds his own business, and the Duchess' loving of Alice is a hunting love, and the Duchess' business is finding victims, taking care, as
one of her later morals has it, that the more there is of mine the less
there is of yours. Anyone innocent of sexuality, though not necessarily free of it, is thus forced to see adults playing their great game of
hunter and hunted, minding their own business, calling it love, obliterating the past. The playful terror of the Duchess here has very
little to do with the brutal mania of the Duchess in "Pig and Pepper."

This is why it seems right to say that Lewis Carroll, for all that he
adored Alice Liddell, for all that he idealizes his own Alice, treats his
heroine mercilessly. She is idealized because she is free of the passions that rage in many of the other characters, but this does not keep
her from rebuke and ridicule, and all she can do is to escape from
each situation. She is never able to connect with anyone, never gives,
never takes, so that she seems odd, alone, as much unyielding as
brave. There is no clearer instance of the strange results of letting
scenes "come of themselves" than in the one moment when Lewis
Carroll gives Alice power over a situation. In her first meeting with
the Duchess, Alice walks into a scene of casual savagery, the cook
hurling pots and pans, the baby howling and sneezing, the Duchess
speaking with the erratic violence of an aged filthy steam engine:

> "It's a Cheshire Cat," said the Duchess, "and that's why.
> Pig!"
> She said the last word with such sudden violence that

Alice quite jumped; but she saw in another moment that it was addressed to the baby, and not to her, so she took courage, and went on again—

"I didn't know that Cheshire Cats always grinned; in fact I didn't know cats *could* grin."

"They all can," said the Duchess, "and most of 'em do."

"I don't know of any that do," Alice said very politely, feeling quite pleased to have gotten into a conversation.

"You don't know much," said the Duchess; "and that's a fact."

Alice did not at all like the tone of this remark, and thought it would be well to introduce some other subject of conversation. While she was trying to fix on one, the cook took the cauldron of soup off the fire, and at once set to work throwing everything within her reach at the Duchess and the baby—the fire-irons came first; then followed a shower of saucepans, plates, and dishes. The Duchess took no notice of them even when they hit her; and the baby was howling so much already that it was quite impossible to say whether the blows hurt it or not.

"Oh, *please* mind what you're doing!" cried Alice, jumping up and down in an agony of terror. "Oh there goes his *precious* nose!" as an unusually large saucepan flew close by it, and very nearly carried it off.

Alice's locutions always tend to be a little cozy, as with "did not at all like," "thought it would be well," "it was quite impossible to say," but nowhere else are they made to seem so pathetically inadequate as when they meet this stark violence. Furthermore, her efforts to keep up—"*please* mind what you're doing," when the cook *is* minding what she is doing, and with a vengeance; "there goes his *precious* nose," when, as Alice soon discovers, the nose is anything but precious—make Alice herself seem obtrusive and irrelevant.

Soon, however, the rampant disorder breaks down the customary locutions, and Alice can begin to occupy some of the empty space:

> "If everybody minded their own business," the Duchess said in a hoarse growl, "the world would go round a good deal faster than it does."

"Which would *not* be an advantage," said Alice, who felt very glad of an opportunity of showing off her knowledge. "Just think what work it would make with the day and night! You see the earth takes twenty-four hours to turn round on its axis—"

"Talking of axes," said the Duchess, "chop off her head!"

Alice's not taking offense at the Duchess' offensive remark, her transformation into a pedant, ballooning her pittance of knowledge out into the room, make her seem actually to belong to this appalling scene now, an equal partner in the cacophony. Poor Alice, one might say, but think what it would be like to listen to her.

So the Duchess launches into her lullaby, "Speak roughly to your little boy," and then turns the "nursing" of the baby over to Alice, who, entering right into the spirit of things, soon discovers that the "proper way of nursing" is to "twist it up into a sort of knot, and then keep tight hold of its right ear and left foot, so as to prevent its undoing itself." For the first time, Alice has some power to wield, and a way to wield it, and she becomes like the Duchess very quickly. The baby, having been twisted into such a shape, grunts, so Alice reproves it: "That's not the proper way of expressing yourself." Such a scene must have "come of itself," because it is hard to think of how else it could have happened. But what was Alice Liddell, or others in her position, to make of this Alice, speaking severely to the little boy and beating him when he sneezes?

Nor is the worst over:

No, there were no tears. "If you're going to turn into a pig, my dear," said Alice seriously, "I'll have nothing more to do with you. Mind now." The poor little thing sobbed again (or grunted, it was impossible to say which), and they went on for some while in silence.

Alice was just beginning to think to herself, "Now, what am I to do with this creature when I get it home?" when it grunted again, so violently that she looked down into its face in some alarm. This time there could be *no* mistake about it; it was neither more nor less than a pig, and she felt that it would be quite absurd for her to carry it any further.

So she set the little creature down, and felt quite relieved to see it trot away quietly into the wood. "If it had grown up," she said to herself, "it would have been a dreadfully ugly child; but it makes rather a handsome pig, I think." And she began thinking over other children she knew, who might do very well as pigs, and was just saying to herself, "if only one knew the right way to change them . . ."

The language, both Alice's and Lewis Carroll's, carries on with its cozy aplomb—"I'll have nothing to do with you," "the poor little thing," "there could be *no* mistake about it," "it would be quite absurd"—as Alice is transformed into a kind of Circe, turning all those she controls into swine. In this scene the only pretense at order is the ostensibly polite language; everything else is given over to violent fantasy. When this fantasy is what is released, one understands more easily why playing with words and puzzles and fussing with the accouterments of order were so important to Lewis Carroll. Take them away and Alice, and Lewis Carroll, become like the cook, or the Duchess, or anyone else who does not mind the cost to others when seeking relief from the intolerable fact of all of us having been born. There is nothing I know in nineteenth-century literature quite as nakedly revealing; Dickens, who could write magnificently when pushing out the edges of his fantasies, would not have dared expose a little girl as ruthlessly and fully as Lewis Carroll does here.

Charles Dodgson himself had certain things on which he could rely, such as his station in life, his position at Oxford and in the church, his trust in God. But he denied himself all these in his transformation into Lewis Carroll, who had, also, no tradition or inherited form or direction. Lewis Carroll had only his native wits, his loneliness, his intense alertness, his passion for girls. Reading "Pig and Pepper," "A Mad Tea-Party," and the second scene with Alice and the Duchess in "The Mock Turtle's Story," I sense not so much a desire to expose or excoriate Alice as released anger and hatred—of domineering duchesses, squalling babies, insolent servants, and cavalierly rude people in general. Other things equal, Lewis Carroll in *Wonderland* always works to protect Alice, to make even her folly and pettishness seem more decent than anything she confronts. But other things are not always equal, and when a scene, coming and taking shape of itself, began to appeal strongly to Lewis Carroll's desire for revenge, then even Alice could be left in the wake of the waves.

There is much less of this in *Through the Looking-Glass*, which is altogether a softer and sadder book than *Wonderland*. Some of its episodes, we know, were written in at least some form before *Wonderland* was published—"Jabberwocky," the scene with the live flowers, and Tweedledum and Tweedledee are at least likely candidates—but there were nine years between the July 4 boat ride to Godstow in 1862, after which *Wonderland* began to take form as a book, and the publication of *Through the Looking-Glass* in 1871. If, in those nine years, the shapes of Dodgson's life became clearer to him, some of those shapes were signs of defeat, signs that, for all the great popularity of *Alice in Wonderland*, little was ever going to change for its author. The sharp, jabbing, nasty quality of much of *Wonderland* is almost gone, to be replaced by obscure battles and by three figures, two of which are versions of Lewis Carroll, who are fully grown, defeated, and pathetic: the Gnat, the White Queen, and the White Knight. Lewis Carroll had lost all touch with Alice Liddell, and he wanted, he said openly, to try to recapture whatever remained of the golden afternoon of their relation.

Alice Liddell, however, had passed on into adolescence, and Dodgson had not quite settled into a life devoted to her successors:

> I have not seen thy sunny face,
> Nor heard thy silver laughter:
> No thought of me shall find a place
> In thy young life's hereafter—
> Enough that now thou wilt not fail
> To listen to my fairy-tale.

Alice was seventeen, and not yet married, so perhaps she would at least read his book, even if she no longer sat by him in his rooms, punted with him on the Thames:

> Come, hearken then, ere voice of dread,
> With bitter tidings laden,
> Shall summon to unwelcome bed
> A melancholy maiden!

Older children now, they fret to find their bedtime near, which for Alice would be the marriage bed, for Dodgson the grave, for Lewis Carroll silence, and it is not surprising to find Lewis Carroll equating all three. Nor is it surprising that he should have begun to find something ineradicable in the human condition, as is most clearly heard in the cry of the baby deer in the dark wood: " 'I'm a Fawn!' it cried out in a voice of delight. 'And dear me! you're a human child!' A sudden look of alarm came into its beautiful brown eyes, and in another moment it had darted away at full speed."

A sense of loss, and then of something ineradicable, not so much frightening as saddening and deadening, leading to a withdrawal into obscurity, all dominate *Looking-Glass,* and nowhere more clearly and wonderfully than in "Wool and Water," the scene with the White Queen. It has been possible to patronize or even to ignore the White Queen ever since Lewis Carroll described her, not in the book but much later, as "gentle, stupid, fat, and pale; helpless as an infant . . . just suggesting imbecility but never quite passing into it." What has hurt commentary on this scene even more than Lewis Carroll's own remark, though, has been the intervention of the Humpty-Dumpty critics, who have tried, in the face of all evidence, to see the White Queen's talk about "living backwards" as part of some philosophical game of Dodgson's. Even before we get to "Wool and Water," we should know that the chess game, the mirror effects, the running hard just to stay in the same place, are all games Lewis Carroll plays only when he wishes to, and says he is, and so does not play when he has other bits and scraps in mind.

Here is Roger Holmes, though, in "The Philosopher's *Alice in Wonderland,"* saying that "The Looking-Glass country was a place in which time moved backwards." There is some playing with this possibility concerning the Looking-Glass cakes in "The Lion and the Unicorn," but Holmes's major exhibit must be the White Queen. But, as the opening of "Wool and Water" makes amply clear, in "the Looking-Glass country," time does *not* run backwards, and, apparently, not even the White Queen thinks it does:

> "I don't know what's the matter with it!" the Queen said, in a melancholy voice. "It's out of temper, I think. I've

pinned it here, and I've pinned it there, but there's no pleasing it!"

"It *can't* go straight, you know, if you pin it all on one side," Alice said, as she gently put it right for her; "and, dear me, what a state your hair is in!"

"The brush has got entangled in it!" the Queen said with a sigh. "And I lost the comb yesterday."

If one loses one comb yesterday, and entangles one's brush in one's hair as well, then by today one's hair may well be in a state. Everything here is in perfect temporal order, or at least normal temporal order. But the White Queen needs a rule to explain why things are in such a mess: "jam to-morrow and jam yesterday—but never jam to-day."

"It *must* come sometimes to 'jam to-day'," Alice objected.

"No, it can't," said the Queen. "It's jam every *other* day; to-day isn't any *other* day, you know."

"I don't understand you," said Alice. "It's dreadfully confusing."

"That's the effect of living backwards," the Queen said kindly: "it always makes one a little giddy at first—"

The White Queen knows today is the crucial day, and she also knows there is never any jam. Whatever the reasons for "no jam," her explanation has nothing to do with living backward or forward, since today "isn't any *other* day" regardless of whether it is preceded or followed by tomorrow. What the White Queen and Alice agree upon is that there ought to be rules for things. What the White Queen also knows is what Alice has persistently refused to learn in spite of all the evidence: things never go right, rules don't hold, explanations confuse as much as they explain, and there is never any jam.

The idea of living backward, as we approach it, thus, is not an idea offered by Lewis Carroll. It is the White Queen's effort to explain the mess that is her life:

"What sort of things do *you* remember best?" Alice ventured to ask.

"Oh, things that happened the week after next," the Queen replied in a careless tone. "For instance, now," she went on, sticking a large piece of plaster on her finger as she spoke, "there's the King's Messenger. He's in prison now, being punished; and the trial doesn't even begin until next Wednesday; and of course the crime comes last of all."

In *Wonderland* the Knave of Hearts is on trial for having already stolen the tarts, but it is also true that the Queen of Hearts does a good deal of sentencing before there has been either a crime or a trial. That is not a matter of time but of royal caprice, and here the White Queen seems to want to devise rules that will reverse crime and punishment. Still, if we just once imagine that the King's Messenger is in fact currently in jail, being punished for a crime not yet committed, then it will be tyranny we will be led toward. Certainly what Alice finds hard is not a matter of time running this way or that, but of justice:

"Suppose he never commits the crime?" asked Alice.

"That would be all the better, wouldn't it?" the Queen said, as she bound the plaster round her finger with a bit of ribbon.

Alice felt there was no denying *that*. "Of course it would be all the better," she said, "but it wouldn't be all the better his being punished."

If it would be better for the Messenger never to commit the crime, the reason must be simply so that fewer crimes will be committed. Since the White Queen is imagining that it might be possible for the Messenger to break what seems an irreversible chain of events (punishment-trial-crime), then, if it can be broken by his choice, why not break it earlier, with the King's choice to punish him?

"You're wrong *there*, at any rate," said the Queen. "Were *you* ever punished?"

"Only for faults," said Alice.

"And you were all the better for it, I know!" the Queen said triumphantly.

"Yes, but then I *had* done the things I was punished for," said Alice: "That makes all the difference."

"But if you *hadn't* done them," the Queen said, "that would have been better still; better, and better, and better!" Her voice went higher with each "better," till it got quite to a squeak at last.

Roger Holmes cannot imagine that anything is happening here other than a philosophical puzzle, and even he must admit that as a puzzle it seems to make little sense: "It just does not make sense. Punishment exists in a Bergsonian time-with-direction. As everyone knows who has seen movies run backwards, most human actions so lose their significance when reversed as to appear hilarious. One of the standard amusements in the nickelodeon days was to run backwards a film of a man eating steak. Bergson had much to say about memory: he must have been amused at the Queen's remark that she remembered best things that happened the week after next." This is badly deflective from the passage in question, but in ways characteristic of those who are more interested in problems or puzzles than in Lewis Carroll.

To say the White Queen does not make sense is to fail to consider the kind of sense she might be making. Elsewhere in either of the *Alice* books, an explanation is usually the act of a tyrant trying to make Alice into a victim. In this scene, we may want to assume, as Roger Holmes does, that the White Queen is trying to justify the intolerable, as if she were master of the world and as if the rules were her own invention. She is in fact inventing the rules, rather as the White Knight invents anklets for warding off sharks, because she is not at all the tyrant in her world, but the victim. The first rule is that there will be punishments; that goes along with "never jam today." If she were interested in puzzles, then time might be the subject, and Holmes would be right to say she makes no sense. But suppose the facts of life are the subject. The White Queen, Alice, and all the rest of us have been told, as if it were a fact of life, that punishments make one better. Having endured the punishment, having been "improved," the White Queen assumes she still can choose whether or not to commit the crime. The point at issue is not the way time runs, but how to respond to punishments for crimes one has not, or not yet, committed. Alice, like Roger Holmes, thinks it would be better if the White Queen, and the King's Messenger, would only be punished for crimes they have committed. The White Queen might like that arrangement better too, but she doesn't live in a world where that happens. The beauty of the White Queen is that, living in a tyranny as she does, where punishments often or even always precede crimes, she still imagines moral autonomy for individuals. In a world beyond politics, revolutions, or justice, people must still run their own lives, and therefore it would be better not to commit the faults one is going to be accused of anyway. Not because God is watching, because Lewis Carroll knows no God. Not because it makes one feel better, since the White Queen is clearly unhappy. But, as we say, just because. Of course, as Alice says, "there must be a mistake somewhere," but the White Queen knows she can do nothing about that.

Defeated and helpless the White Queen is, but imbecilic or stupid she is not. If her explanation for the world is that time runs backward, she is quite right to believe it, because she will prick her finger, after all, and there is much to gain by screaming first:

> "I haven't pricked it *yet*," the Queen said, "but I soon shall—oh, oh, oh!"
> "When do you expect to do it?" Alice asked, feeling very much inclined to laugh.
> "When I fasten my shawl again," the poor Queen groaned out: "the brooch will come undone directly. Oh, oh!" As she said the words the brooch flew open, and the Queen clutched wildly at it, and tried to clasp it again.

So she cuts herself, and when Alice asks why she doesn't scream now, she answers cheerfully that she has done the screaming already. One deadens the pain of punishment by not committing crimes, one kills pain by anticipating it, one keeps from crying, as she goes on to tell Alice, by considering things.

Roger Holmes's comment on this grand moment glimpses some of this, but almost by accident, since what he is considering is not the White Queen, but whether or not she could exist: "One *might* live in a world in which the screams and the pain came before the pin prick. Here is reversible time, the time Mechanists insist on, strange only because misunderstood. Within this temporal frame one must eliminate purposeful significances, such as catching at a brooch *in order* to pin it. But such a world is possible: certain philosophers from Democritus through Spinoza to the present have recommended it." Holmes's knowledge is all drawing-board knowledge, what might be possible in theory, so he cannot imagine that Lewis Carroll is using reversible time and causation in order to reveal the White Queen's way of living in her intolerable world, in which of course there is injustice and of course time runs forward only. Holmes makes his own units, his own frames of reference, and cuts out much smaller bits and scraps than Lewis Carroll's and examines them in isolation from each other, so that the White Queen on justice is considered as a totally separate subject from the White Queen on brooches and screams, and the question of why the White Queen should want to apply the plaster before pricking her finger is never raised.

This conversation with the White Queen is so dazzling in its implications, it seems to me, that it is not surprising that Holmes is far from the only one who does not want to imagine them to exist. To think of a world in which the punishments come first is frightening, and most of us have too strong a sense of fairness not to protest bodily when confronted with such a world. It is easier just to think of the White Queen as daft, and she herself wishes she could remember the rule for being glad. When we think about a world in which there is jam, but never jam today, we usually are more comfortable doing so with a totally different part of our minds from the part we use to devise rules for explaining and accepting the painful and hateful. One could not develop such a beautiful, if despairing and deadening, view of life as the White Queen's either easily or willingly, and it is one of Lewis Carroll's most brilliant insights to sense that, after the scene is over, we might want to know how old she is. It is the only time in either book that it could matter. "Now I'll give *you* something to believe," the White Queen says, "I'm just one hundred and one, five months and a day." Alice says she cannot believe that, but I can. Time does run one way only, after all, and one would have to go back at least a century to find the White Queen starting out on her lonely life. She knows what she has learned and what she has endured. We that are young can see that this is Lewis Carroll's saddest, wisest, best moment.

The White Queen is a sheep, but we know that even before she begins to bleat like one. What we could not have known, though, is that she keeps a shop on St. Aldgate's directly across from Christ Church and Tom Quad, where Dodgson lived. But how else, if one stops to think about it, could Lewis Carroll have found out what she knows if she hadn't chanced to live nearby. If such a woman actually was there, and if she did occasionally puzzle her customers by selling eggs, five pence farthing for one, two pence for two, Dodgson must have seen he had met someone as eccentric as he knew others took him to be, and so he paused to ponder, and she thereby became the only adult from whom he ever tried to learn. "The helplessness of the intellect," writes Empson about the White Queen's claim that one can keep from crying only by considering things, "which claims to rule so much, is granted under the counterclaim that since it makes you impersonal, you can forget pain with it." This certainly says a great deal about Lewis Carroll, but the White Queen herself is really better, sillier, and much older than this. Her way of understanding has to terrify a young person; less than half her age, I find it hard to imagine I might one day come to her pathetic lucid understanding, and so I continue to apply plasters only after I have cut myself. Like Lewis Carroll, however, I am moved by the White Queen and need to honor her. She is one of those very old people, such as one might run across in a shop, who can tell us much about what might be in store for all of us, and what we should know in any event, since never was a defeated message so assuring.

But, like everything else in the *Alice* books, "Wool and Water" is only a bit or a scrap, so that just as the horrors of "Pig and Pepper" pass, so too does the sweet and defeated beauty of the White Queen. "Wool and Water" gives way to Humpty-Dumpty and, once put in its place, becomes no more animate or useful, especially for children like Alice and Lewis Carroll, than a piece in a jigsaw puzzle or a square on a chessboard. There is nothing structural in any large sense about Lewis Carroll's imagination, nothing that accretes, gives from one moment to help the next. Within the episodes, as I have tried to show, there is a good deal more that is coherent and resonant than most people, and especially the Humpty-Dumpty critics, have cared to realize. These episodes are the crucial units; often they are not as long as a chapter, or a page or two, but, knowing what we know of Lewis Carroll's methods of composition, it should not be surprising that within these units much is going together, building up and breaking down, that only frequent careful rereading can show.

As long as we bear this in mind, there surely is no harm done if we say that Lewis Carroll's fragmentary view of life is a child's view; one suspects that children are more often forced to accept life as bits and scraps than are adults. This hardly means that the *Alice* books are, or ever really were, popular among children; the evidence is that some children like Carroll very much, as do some adults. His great appeal is to those people, who can be any age at all, who happen to find life as stern, sad, and intractable as he found it; who feel that what we need most in order to live are good defenses; who know that what schools teach is Ambition, Distraction, Uglification, and Derision; who know, concerning words, that the question is not whether one can make words mean different things, but who is to be master; who know that at the end of the mouse's tail, or tale, we all stand condemned to death. Such people find in Lewis Carroll not only the great quotable things anyone can find, but strength, courage, and consolation, because his great talent was for putting awful truths in ways that did not crush. If Alice learns little from what happens to her, she keeps up her end of the bargain and remains undefeated. "No longer a baby," W. H. Auden writes as a true admirer of Alice, "she has learned self-control, acquired a sense of her identity, and can think logically without ceasing to be imaginative." Auden then adds that "what she is . . . is what, after many years of countless follies and errors, one would like in the end to become."

I don't myself feel that way, and can find much more enduring models in Grahame's Water Rat and Kipling's Kim. Those who see life as Auden says he does, however, as a succession of follies and errors, will find nothing that can take the place of Lewis Carroll and Alice. As might well be imagined, Lewis Carroll himself said it best. "There's nothing," says the White King, "like eating hay when you're faint." Alice finds that prescription almost as puzzling as I find her author, and so the White King explains: "I didn't say there was nothing *better* . . . I said there was nothing *like* it."

(6)   Beatrix Potter

The books, all save one, are small, about four by six inches, so small an adult finds it difficult to hold one without the hand's seeming clumsy. There are twenty-four books, and again if we exclude the one large book, *The Fairy Caravan*, their total number of words is less than that of one of the *Alice* books. The pictures are simple, and their artist found people impertinent who said she was an important English watercolorist. Yet they may have been looked at as much as any pictures ever made; these books are much the most popular ever made for small children. People read them, not just over and over, but over and over and over, until each picture, each rise and fall in the prose, becomes a mark on a chart by which one can steer one's consciousness, and at a level one would have said only music can reach. People often say they love, or loved, this or that children's book, when in fact they don't, or didn't, but no one seems ever to be lying when they say they love these books. Their maker, Beatrix Potter, had a life that is hard to understand, but it is as clear as the water of mountain streams compared with the mystery of her achievement.

It has to do with smallness, one knows that, with the way Potter uses smallness to force concentration from her reader. The page is important, even the large amount of white blank space on many pages is important, because that too forces us to concentrate. But somehow these matters are difficult to speak of directly, so let me begin by quoting some sentences from a few of her major books, sentences that are clearly typical and distinctive enough even out of context. Then, as we go back and look at her life and her early work, we can keep in mind and ear the hard, bright, solemnly playful prose:

> Peter was most dreadfully frightened; he rushed all over the garden, for he had forgotten the way back to the gate.
> He lost one of his shoes among the cabbages, and the other shoe amongst the potatoes. [*Peter Rabbit*]

> As there was always no money, Ginger and Pickles were obliged to eat their own goods.
> Pickles ate biscuits and Ginger ate a dried haddock.
> They ate them by candle-light after the shop was closed. [*Ginger & Pickles*]

> Moppet and Mittens have grown up into very good rat-catchers.
> They go out rat-catching in the village, and they find plenty of employment. They charge so much a dozen, and earn their living very comfortably.
> [*The Roly-Poly Pudding*]

It is so apparently unremarkable, this writing, yet everyone who knows Potter knows that yes, that's it, the unmistakable Potter sound. It will take, however, many more words than are in one of her books to say how that prose came to be hers, as recognizable as Jane Austen or Dickens, and in its way every bit as good. In the process of discovering how she came to write as she did, we should also be able to learn about the kind of artist she is, and why smallness is so important to both the writing and the pictures.

Beatrix Potter's life was a long journey home. During her last thirty years she was Mrs. William Heelis, of Castle Cottage, Near Sawrey, in the north-country county now known as Cumbria. During those years she worked hard and became known among the people of the Lake District as a successful sheep farmer. She loved the Lakes, and prospered, and gradually acquired farms totaling thousands of acres, most of which she left to the National Trust at her death so that they could always be farmed. She published a number of books during this period, but all from material that had been lying in her portfolio from earlier years; her last published book, *Little Pig Robinson*, is a long discursive tale written more than thirty years earlier and not good enough to publish until she was beyond caring about such things. When an admirer addressed her in a letter as "Dear Miss Potter," she replied, "When a person has been married nearly thirty years it is not ingratiating to get an envelope addressed to 'Miss'." She was Beatrix Potter no longer, and she was happy for the first time in her life, at home, hard at work, in the country of her ancestors.

She died in 1943, at the age of seventy-seven. Her first book, *Peter Rabbit*, was written in 1901, and between then and her marriage in 1913, she wrote and illustrated all the books of hers that still matter. We see her first thirty-five years, before *Peter Rabbit*, as a long getting-ready, but she saw all the years before her marriage, including the years of her great books, as a long time of waiting, for marriage, farming, independence, and literary and artistic silence. As far as she was concerned the caterpillar didn't become a butterfly until she had more to do with her life than draw, paint, and write. Much as our perspective must be different from hers, it helps to keep remembering what hers was. It shows, among other things, that hers was not the art of a strangely or sadly stunted person so much as it was the first public appearance of a life that was growing, finding itself, with almost terrifying slowness.

We can say of her contemporaries Kipling and Grahame that a great deal went wrong as they were growing up. Grahame was effectively an orphan at five, and at sixteen he was exiled, for life as it were, when he was told he could not go to Oxford and was sent instead to City of London offices. Kipling was also effectively an orphan at six, and he too was told as an adolescent he could not go to the university and instead had to grub out a living putting together provincial newspapers in India. Grahame and Kipling, though, at least could do something, and they could become the writers they were because they had to do what they did not want to do. Beatrix Potter could go to no school, take no job, suffer no exile. When she was forty-seven and told her parents she was going to be married, they responded as to an ungrateful and disobedient child. Helen and Rupert Potter were from the north, and their ancestors were intelligent, hard-working, and successful merchants and manufacturers; they took themselves away from all that, moved to London, did almost nothing, and looked down on those who worked for a living. This does not seem to have made them happy, and it almost killed Beatrix before she had a chance to live. Their son, being a son, was sent to school, and he was allowed, after he tried being an amateur painter, to buy a farm and even to live on it. Understanding his parents well, he waited ten years after his wedding to tell them he was married to a farmer's daughter.

England, its industrial revolution almost over, its arteries hardening into a Bank and an Empire, its future lying mostly with those parts of its society it was most afraid of, paralyzed people like the Potters. The one activity Rupert Potter allowed himself was photography, and almost all his surviving pictures show people in rigid poses, just as almost every picture taken of him shows his own rigidity. So too with his wife, whose days were highlighted by a drive in her carriage every afternoon at two. So too, for most of the years she lived at home, with their daughter. They were people with money, and therefore time, to relax, be expansive, and gain the broad tolerance that can come from travel or the pursuit of all that makes one curious; yet they were people not just serious, not even just solemn, but so stiff and inactive as to leave a caricaturist with very little to do.

Beatrix Potter's journal, written between the ages of sixteen and thirty-one, could serve as a major exhibit in any demonstration of the ravages of the lives of the idle bourgeois late Victorian rich. Although it has no secrets to tell and never had to be hidden from anyone, Potter wrote it in a code she invented, not a particularly difficult or elaborate one, but a full written language nonetheless. The handwriting ranges from tiny to minuscule; there are sheets of six-inch by eight-inch paper that have 1,500 words on them. It is also very long, running well over 200,000 words, and it reads like the work of one who had either been so paralyzed she had nothing to say about herself, or who was so secretive she could not trust her private thoughts even to a journal that was written in code and that no one knew existed until a decade after her death.

The Journal of Beatrix Potter is unnerving reading, but it is seldom dull, and it is often compelling for one who knows, as she of course did not, how her life was to turn out. February 8, 1884, Potter is seventeen, being, after her fashion, personal:

> Afterwards papa went to Christie's and saw a modern picture of a mythological subject as large as the pier glass, sold for 30 shillings! A modern portrait of Macready(?) an actor, as Hamlet, began at fifteen shillings. It's an extraordinary business the price of pictures. Alma-Tadema wanted £1000 for that little water colour at the Exhibition. Papa got one sepia drawing of Landseer for £5 at Christies, but could not secure another, the Jews being woken up.

November 26, same year, this time on the national scene:

> Radicals furious because old Gladstone is trying to make terms with the Tories. There is no doubt what has driven him to his senses, it is the Egyptian difficulty. He is going to get the Franchise Bill through as best he can, retire to the House of Lords, and leave the Tories to make the best of twenty millions deficit.

Domestic matters are reported with distance and astringency, while national matters are reported as though they were domestic, so the tone alters very little when it moves from one arena to the other.

The range of tone is fairly wide, though the extremes are rare. She can, on the one hand, allow her detached tone to reveal genuine callousness: "Mr. Millais very much shocked at the shooting incident. Then the explosion (the latest news is that the fellows may have blown themselves to pieces, but it is too good to be true)." On the other hand, something may happen that forces her to drop a veil or two. Here she is writing after the death of the Rev. Mr. Gaskell, husband of the novelist, and beloved by Beatrix from her earliest years:

> Shall I really never see him again? but he is gone with almost every other, home is gone for me, the little girl does not bound about now, and live in fairyland, and occasionally wonders in a curious, carefree manner, as of something

not concerning her nature, what life means, and whether
she shall ever feel sorrow. It is all gone, and he is resting
quietly with our fathers. I have begun the dark journey of
life. Will it go on as darkly as it has begun? Oh that I might
go through life as blamelessly as he!

The fact that we see very little of Potter being callous, and almost
as little of her being precocious and anxious about herself, would
seem to imply that in her journal she was guarded, intense, detached,
and knowing. Nor does the essential tone change in the next dozen
years, except that passages like the last disappear after 1887, and
for the most part it is a steady run of reporting, comment, and
opinion, written as though the author did not change much.

Beatrix Potter's voice when she speaks about public matters is
someone else's—her father's, her father's friends, her father's newspaper. It knows neither doubt nor shame, but it does know Gladstone, the true sentiments of the working class, the way to run an
army or an empire, and the disgusting evil of riots. The leaders of a
demonstration protesting a rise in unemployment "ought to be hung
at once like dogs"; the Irish plague her as constantly as they did
Gladstone: "What have the Irish done that we should add 210 millions to the national debt for their benefit?" Born into a paralyzed
situation and allowed to do little, Potter presumably had little choice
but to become like a ventriloquist's dummy, but she became this
eagerly and completely, which she need not have done.

Yet it seems unnecessary and not relevant to pile up passages in
support of the proposition that she was an insufferable snob and
prig. For one thing, the fact of the journal is indicative of great
energies, used both in the actual writing and in exercising the self-
command required to keep it up. After reading it, one is more inclined to think the code was designed not to hide anything but to
give her something difficult to do. Since there is no reason to believe
that any Potters ever laughed or enjoyed doing something together,
we can see the journal as her fun, or relief. That she seldom wrote
about anything personal probably means she had little personal to
say; her feelings and desires were never consulted by others, so
she seems to have suppressed or ignored them herself, and she
does this so well, and so completely, that after a while one is not

aware as one reads of any deep restraint being imposed. She does not know what life means, does not feel sorrow, and she is aware of the lack, but does not find it worth carrying on about. If we feel the voice of the *Journal* is missing the sense of a person, or the sense of a personal shaping in the writing, then we must listen again to the voice of her more mature prose:

> Peter was most dreadfully frightened; he rushed all over the garden, for he had forgotten the way back to the gate. He lost one of his shoes among the cabbages, and the other shoe amongst the potatoes.

That is not the voice of the *Journal*, to be sure, but it is not personal either, and is not shaped according to the outlines of a person or personality. What the *Journal* lacks in this respect the books do not provide. The books offer a sense of words being chosen, of pressure being put on language by an intentness the *Journal* remains innocent of, but that is another matter altogether.

The one subject in the *Journal* where Potter always expresses her own taste and is never secondhand in her judgments is art, painting and drawing, her own and that of others:

> Dislike is a mild word for my feeling toward Burne Jones.

> I notice one thing not quite right in the *News from the Sea*; children who habitually go barefoot always have the toe joint larger and, I am afraid, are generally flat-footed.

> The former showed that Raphael had never looked at a horse.

> A great master's worst pictures have generally something in them which is wanting in the best work of his inferiors.

The tone may be the same as the one she uses to describe the servants in a resort hotel, but the observation and the opinions are, clearly, strictly her own, because she herself drew and painted and had struggled hard to develop and understand her own talent. There are moments in the *Journal's* early years when she will allow herself a paragraph about herself and her art, of which this is perhaps the most interesting:

It is all the same, drawing, painting, modelling, the irresistible desire to copy any beautiful object which strikes the eye. Why cannot one be content to look at it? I cannot rest, I must draw, however poor the result, and when I have had a bad time come over me it is a stronger desire than ever, and settles on the queerest things, worse than queer sometimes. Last time, in the middle of September, I caught myself in the backyard making a careful and admiring copy of the swill bucket, and the laugh it gave me brought me round.

One wishes there were more such passages, but still, this one tells us a good deal.

If Potter was lucky in anything, it was that the kind of art she wanted to do—copying, as she calls it—was work a young woman in her position could be encouraged to do. That her passion to copy was genuine is clear enough from "Why cannot one be content to look at it?" She drew out of boredom, she drew to escape bad times, but she also loved it. She stared, not as in a trance but with cleansing alertness, intensity, and impersonality, because the concentration could bring her out of herself and give her purposefulness. Her work was not bold or adventurous, because it was meticulous copying, but the results were seldom drawings that give us any sense of the second-hand. Her most frequent medium was pen and ink, with watercolor saved for more formal efforts. For a long time the work was what we would call studies, of animals, insects, flowers, and, in her most dedicated and sustained "copying," fungi. Her uncle, Sir Henry Roscoe, became interested in her drawings of fungi and in her ideas about them, and the later years of the journal are much taken up with their joint efforts to interest officials of the Royal Botanical Gardens and the Linnean Society. The results were typical. Potter was not only a woman, but she had never been to art school and had never formally studied botany, so the people she and Roscoe met almost had to be bullied to pay any attention, and Potter herself was painfully shy. The one written result of her work was a paper, "On the Germination of the Spores of Agaricaceae," which was read to the Linnean Society, but not by its author, because women could not be present at its meetings. More important were the more than two hundred painting of fungi which no one would publish, coldly beautiful works many of which, fortunately, were reproduced in 1967 in W. P. K. Findlay's *Wayside and Woodland Fungi.*

This was the serious work of her twenties and early thirties, but good as it is, and much as one wants to protest against the shabby treatment it received, one can hardly lament, as things turned out, that she did not go on with it. If such work could bring her out of herself, if she could keep from crying by considering fungi, the paintings lack the bright, haughty assertiveness of the *Journal.* The work had enabled her to focus and clarify her small-scale meticulousness, but it lacks life. On the other hand, her landscapes of the period are warm, but are inclined to prettiness, and the larger the landscape the less good the result. The earliest drawings of animals are, like those of insects and flowers, only careful work, but gradually she began to put these animals within a closed space—a garden, a doorway, a mousehole—and when she did, something began to happen. The enclosed space became the external equivalent of her own staring field of vision. Within it the care is still manifest, within it the less interesting parts of her landscapes could be pared away, but, most important, within it the faces of the animals begin to come to life, to be expressive, alert, amused or amusing, as though this rabbit, cat, or mouse were about to do something. Like Potter herself.

Given the confined nature of her life, given her tendency to write in tiny letters, given her desire to copy little things other people usually ignored, it is not surprising that enclosed spaces gave her the crucial assurance that within them she could be brash and full of pronouncements and could, as it were, safely drop Gladstone and the Irish question as she did so. The point is perfectly clear to anyone who goes through the indispensable *The Art of Beatrix Potter.* In the sections called "Houses, Village Scenes and Landscapes," "Gardens, Plant Studies, and Still Life," and even "Interiors," Potter is an artist who, even in her full maturity, is never more than admirable. But in "Animal Studies," in a woodmouse sent as a Christmas card when she was twenty, in a deer and fawn seen at the Zoological Gardens and done when she was twenty-five, one sees what was about to happen. Most noticeable are the limbs, drawn at rest but filled with potential energy, and the facial expressions just marked enough so we can imagine the same faces having other expressions than these.

There is no space at all in the drawing of the woodmouse, and the background for the doe and fawn is indifferently articulated. But in two other 1891 drawings, "The Rabbits' Potting Shed" and "The Mice in Their Storeroom," one sees the real thing, and so wonderfully done it is surprising that Potter did not recognize all she had discovered. The limbs that had been potentially capable of motion are now moving, the faces reveal thought and feeling, and from there is it only a small leap to showing animals doing human activities. The enclosed spaces seem to have had no effect on the animals, but they have helped Potter herself immensely, to imagine a scene, to suggest a drama, to lower the sky so all these are possible. The mice in their storeroom are doing nothing remarkable. One, facing us from a distance, is staring intently, while the other, nearer and with its back to us, is turning its head slightly to the left so we can see one eye focused, it seems, on the same spot the other mouse is looking at. If anything is happening for them to see, four bags, full of whatever it is mice store, hide it from us. It could be danger, or a companion coming through a mouse hole, but with such intent looks on the faces of the mice, it could not be a flyspeck or a mote in the sunlight. Something is going on. Get down low, cut out the farther space, note the haunches, ears, and eyes of mice, and everything comes to life. The drawing is funny, though the mice themselves are extremely serious. The meticulous care of the drawing keeps the scene looking realistic, free from caricature, so that the mice have become more like human beings as they have become more intensely mouse-like. What is happening? The artist, master of the scene because herself free within the enclosed space, is thereby free to imagine, and when she does so she will begin to tell a story.

In 1893 Potter did a series of sketches for "Brer Rabbit and Brer Fox" and a sequence of six paintings for the rhyme "Three little mice sat down to spin," some of which, in revised and inferior form, were incorporated into *The Tailor of Gloucester* almost ten years later. Here the art is full-blown, because the story told in the rhyme enables each mouse to look somewhat different in each picture as the cat comes, tries to get in, and is thwarted. No longer studies of mice, but a mouse world. That the mice are spinning coats for gentlemen does not so much make them human as give them a great variety of things to be doing. The enclosing of the space allows us to imagine the domestic lives of mice as being like those of people, but what interests and amuses us most is the mouselike quality of these intense activities. Potter is still copying, but copying to put her own animals in her own world. She has discovered her métier, though her silence about all this in her *Journal* must suggest either that she did not think so, or was not sure of what she had done, or did not find it sufficiently different from what she had done in her head while staring at animals to be worth noting as a discovery.

There is nothing in the *Journal*, either, about a letter she wrote on September 4, 1893, to Noel Moore, the child of a former governess, the famous letter that begins:

> I don't know what to write to you, so I shall tell you a story about four little rabbits whose names were Flopsy, Mopsy, Cottontail, and Peter. They lived with their mother in a sand bank under the root of a big fir tree.

The story is only half as long as the *Peter Rabbit* published eight years later, and the drawings are crude indeed compared to the Brer Rabbit, Brer Fox, and three little mice she had done the same year. But it is a real story, and it ends, quite properly, with Flopsy, Mopsy, and Cottontail having bread, milk, and blackberries for supper. The young woman of eighteen who had wondered if she would ever feel the great adult feeling of sorrow, who had been depressed and ill quite often during the years when she was cabined, cribbed, and confined in her parents' house, was not free now by any reckoning, and by her own she would not be for another twenty years. But she had truly begun, at the age of twenty-seven, to find herself.

In the eight years between the letter to Noel Moore and the publication of *Peter Rabbit*, between "The Mice in Their Storeroom" and the wonderful witty robin who may or may not be paying attention to Peter, Potter did not develop much as an artist, and the entries in the *Journal* maintain the same tone they had in 1884. But the animal world was getting larger; there are letters in these years which mark the first appearance of Jeremy Fisher, Tom Thumb and Hunca Munca, Tabitha Twitchit, and Little Pig Robinson. What keeps the work in these letters from being as good as it could have been, and as it was soon to be, is that it is too obviously meant to amuse a child. There is no evidence anywhere to suggest that Potter liked children or knew how to speak or behave when around them. "I don't know what to write to you," begins the letter to Noel Moore. What she shared with children was the fact that she was treated as one until well into middle age, which made her as desperate as the most desperate child to find an area, a small enclosed space, of her own. As long as her animal worlds were part of letters to children, though, she tossed off her drawings and stories, treated them as something essentially trivial.

The *Journal* makes no mention of Canon H. D. Rawnsley, which is surprising given the ground rules for inclusion that she had apparently established for herself. Rawnsley was a friend of the Potters, vicar of Wray and then of Crosthwaite in the Lake District, a voracious enthusiast and battler for causes, best known today as one of the co-founders of the National Trust. In her admirable *The Tale of Beatrix Potter*, Margaret Lane writes: "To Beatrix he was even more appealing, for in the warmth of his physical and mental vigour, which was prodigious, her shyness melted, and she made the stimulating discovery that it was possible for grown-up people to have enthusiasms." Rawnsley saw a lot of Potter's work, liked it, encouraged her in her paintings of fungi, and established himself as someone she could trust. When she began thinking in 1901 that she might make a book of the story she had written for Noel Moore —who had, luckily, kept the letter—she turned to Rawnsley as a citizen of the worldly world for help and advice. He kept her from being discouraged when the first six publishers to which she sent *Peter Rabbit* returned it, and then he urged her to take some money of her own and have it privately printed. Given her shyness, and the tribulations she had endured just to meet people at the Zoological Gardens, his help may have been crucial. Just by showing her little book to friends she sold two hundred copies almost immediately and was very proud she had made a profit of £12. Early in 1902 Frederick Warne & Co., one of those who originally had rejected the book, offered to publish it if she would redo the illustrations as watercolors. She agreed and did the new pictures quickly. She also cut out some late pages that eventually found their way into *Ben-*

jamin Bunny, and one of the most profitable publishing ventures in the history of children's literature was begun.

Later Potter came to say she detested *Peter Rabbit,* and I can see why, though I continue to find it one of her best books. Warne still insists on speaking of the entire series as "The Peter Rabbit Books," as though all twenty-three were only a series of adventures about Peter. Too many people have only scant knowledge of everything else she wrote. By comparison with many of her later books *Peter Rabbit* seems terribly uncomplicated, and by virtue of its great popularity it was responsible for much of the sentimentalization of her conceptions by her readers and successors. One can imagine Potter wanting to scream when told for the hundredth or thousandth time, "Peter's cute," since even accurate praise becomes tiresome, and this is not accurate. Nonetheless, there is ample reason for its great popularity, and it much more accurately reflects Beatrix Potter's genius than *The Wizard of Oz* reflects L. Frank Baum's; on the fiftieth or hundredth reading one still finds much to enjoy.

The original letter to Noel Moore was tossed off; the published *Peter Rabbit* was carefully made, because it now had to meet Potter's own high standards even if it was to be thought of, still, as a book for the very young. The offhandedness of the letter is most marked in the pen-and-ink drawings, in which the animals are lacking in expressiveness, but in the text too we can see significant differences between letter and book, even when the actual words are virtually identical in both versions. The number of words per page and per illustration is markedly reduced in the book, so that pauses come at the end of almost every sentence, and we are forced to move more slowly and to look much harder than in the earlier version. For instance:

> First he ate some lettuce, and some broad beans, then some radishes, and then, feeling rather sick, he went to look for some parsley; but round the end of a cucumber frame whom should he meet but Mr. McGregor!

The differences between this, from the letter, and the printed text are insignificant. In the letter all this comes on one page, accompanied by two pictures, a bland one of Peter staring blandly at some lettuce, and the confrontation with Mr. McGregor much as it is in the book. When the text is broken up, as it is in the book, into material for three pages and three illustrations, subtle and important changes take place. The robin appears, caroling away atop the pitchfork while Peter gorges himself on carrots, then "turning away" on the next page as Peter goes to look for some parsley. The gorging and the illness become intense separate events, and the prose seems much less designed to run along hurriedly to get to the meeting with Mr. McGregor. The watercolors show the garden as a lush place, great for rabbits, and this effectively and properly makes equivocal the earlier judgment of Peter: "But Peter, who was very naughty, ran straight into Mr. McGregor's garden." Peter may be naughty for doing as he was told not to, but anyone, especially a rabbit, might want to be here.

It is very much a rabbit who is doing these things, but, especially in the early going when Peter is dressed and walking on two legs, it is also very much a child, something much more faintly suggested in the original letter. It is a boyish Peter who wears a blue jacket, as opposed to the pink ones of his sisters, and a boyish Peter who knows the moment his mother tells him not to go to the garden that he must go there. What this means is that the story takes a real turn when Peter loses his clothes and goes about on all four legs. In the letter to Noel Moore the escape from the gooseberry net, which is on page 34 of the book, leads directly to the escape from the garden, which is on page 51 of the book; in that version, thus, the story is simply about being naughty and escaping, in which the punishment for naughtiness is not having bread, milk, and blackberries for supper. In the book Peter goes from the gooseberry net to the watering can in the tool shed; then he forlornly gets lost in the garden, sees the field mouse and the cat, then climbs the wheelbarrow, from which he can see the gate, far away across the garden. What this means is that as Peter "reverts" from clothes to no clothes, from boyish rabbit to rabbity rabbit, we move into a story where the trip to the garden becomes its own reward and punishment, and the sense of what Peter must endure becomes stronger, and the sense of Peter's mother as a dominating moral agent diminishes. Thus, when Peter collapses after returning home, the sense of exhaustion is paramount, and Potter's picture does everything she can to stress the exhaustion;

Peter's mother is looking at him not as though he had been naughty, but as though she were perplexed and he were beyond the touch of any admonition. Peter's sisters get their berries, as why should they not, since they had gathered them, while Peter, put to bed with camomile tea, feels the consequences not just of his naughtiness but of his adventurousness and daring. Of course one would rather be Peter than his sisters, but that is no reason why they should not get their blackberries, just as Peter's silly courage is no reason why the world should suddenly be as he wants it to be. Mrs. Rabbit was right to warn her children about the garden, but of course we are glad Peter went, not because defiance is a virtue but because of all that Potter made him go through, wonderful but mostly miserable, while he was there.

The original letter only glimpsed this and offered Potter an outline when she returned to the story to take it seriously, which meant slowing the pace of the text, lengthening and thickening the story, working harder at the pictures so they were more interesting in themselves and commented on the text as well as illustrating it. With Jean de Brunhoff's elephants one feels a sense of the marvelous, so that one stares, relaxes, and asks for more. With Potter's animals one's role as a reader and watcher is much more active, and one feels a questioning, absorbed sense of the wonderful: Should rabbits wear jackets? Is Mr. McGregor a fool, or a bad gardener? Is Peter more a "true rabbit" when he eats green vegetables than his sisters are when they eat currant buns and blackberries? De Brunhoff's world is full, as large as a large page or pair of pages, so that to question it would be like questioning God; Potter's world is sharp, small, and it keeps changing on us ever so slightly, page-by-page, picture-by-picture, page-by-picture. As a result we leap, ask questions, feel content with our author because her demeanor is very knowing as well as very active: "He lost one of his shoes among the cabbages, and the other shoe amongst the potatoes." On the opposing page there is a picture of cabbages and a robin, and the precision of Potter's tone makes us want to know where the potatoes are, because we are as much inside Potter's knowingness as Peter is inside the garden. De Brunhoff invites us to look, and wonder, and be glad; Potter invites us to stare, and ask questions, and delight in never having answers enough.

Slight as it is, *Peter Rabbit* shows as much as anything Potter ever did what intentness could yield; a tossed-off cautionary tale is transformed into a story of sad adventure that has no moral but does have a complicated moral tone. It must have shown Potter herself all this too, because this time she followed up her success, exploited her discoveries. It must have mattered to her that the success was public and financial as well as artistic, and it brought her out slightly into the world, to talk things over with the Warnes, to put her profits in the bank. All this was too much like being in trade to suit her parents, but, if only for that very reason, it was what she needed. *The Tailor of Gloucester, Squirrel Nutkin, Benjamin Bunny,* and *Two Bad Mice* all followed within two years, and she became secretly engaged to Norman Warne in 1905. Warne, sadly, had always been in modest health, and, only a few months after the engagement, died. Heavy as that blow must have been to Potter, this time she was not to be totally denied, and that same year she bought, entirely on her own, Hill Top Farm, Near Sawrey, in the Lake District. She had been unable even to tell her parents of her engagement, and she was still tied to them, so that she could get to her new place only to paint rooms and to plant bulbs. She had a large enclosed space of her own now, though, and a whole slew of books followed, from *The Pie and the Patty-Pan* of 1905 to the climactic *Mr. Tod* eight years later. In 1910 she bought a second farm in Near Sawrey, and the agent for the sale was a Hawkshead solicitor, William Heelis. Some time later, after a critical illness and a struggle with her parents, Potter and Heelis were married, in October 1913. "I hold an old-fashioned notion that a happy marriage is the crown of a woman's life," she had written a distant cousin many years earlier, and now her life had been crowned. The great years of her books were put behind her, apparently as easily and eagerly as she put behind the long years of waiting in London.

So much of what went into her books was a combination of old drawings and stories with new work and revisions that it is difficult to divide her books into periods. As we have noted, Potter was drawing almost as well as she ever did as early as 1893, and the writing as such does not get much better than *Peter Rabbit*, though it does get much fuller and much more daring. In the art of making a book where words and pictures play back and forth, with and against each other, *Peter Rabbit* shows her at close to her best. Nonetheless, the books that come after she bought Hill Top Farm are, on the whole, longer, richer, slightly darker, and better than those that come before, even though the pressure to keep new things in front of the public forced her to publish quite inferior books, often in the same year that she was also publishing one of her masterpieces. Individual tastes vary, and in the case of Potter many readers feel compelled to remain loyal to the books that made the deepest impression on them when they were very young. *Squirrel Nutkin*, for instance, which to me is one of the lesser Potters, offered C. S. Lewis an idea of autumn that gave him a joy deep enough to last a lifetime. There is no quarreling about things like that. My own list has four books to go along with *Peter Rabbit* as being her very best: *The Roly-Poly Pudding* (1908), *Jemima Puddle-Duck* (1908), *Ginger & Pickles* (1909), and *Mr. Tod* (1912). In a group just below these I would place four more: *Two Bad Mice* (1904), *The Pie and the Patty-Pan* (1905), *Mrs. Tittlemouse* (1910), and *Timmy Tiptoes* (1911). Rather than try to defend my choices, or to discuss them all in order, I would like to comment on those qualities in the Sawrey books that make them different from *Peter Rabbit* and that reveal her art at its densest and best.

The best of the Sawrey books are quite a bit longer than any of the early ones, and this means not only more pages, but more words per page, and some pages where there is no facing watercolor and only a line drawing for illustration. None of these facts represents an advantage in itself, and the relatively fewer illustrations per sentence and word seem a positive drawback. Even though Potter got to be very incisive with her line drawings, especially in building turns in extended sequences, the classic Potter book for many people remains the short text facing a watercolor. But there are many compensating gains. The world is fuller not just because the stories are longer, but because we have different kinds of animals having to live somehow, often in close quarters with each other, and we are asked to face the satisfying and nasty facts of life for those who live in barnyard and woodland, farmhouse and village. Satisfying and nasty—the terms consort very well with the young author of the *Journal*, but now her talents for relating the nasty and the satisfying found a subject she could stare at, ponder, play with. On a farm one kills one's pigs and ducks, and one tries to kill rats and mice and allies oneself with otherwise independent cats to do so. In a village slight nods of the head and small shifts in tone of voice reveal, to the practiced eye and ear, friendships and hatreds of many years standing. In the woods Peter Rabbit and Benjamin Bunny must learn to live, if they can, with foxes and badgers. In all these matters Potter found abundant material for her own careful, intent, complicating, and dispassionate genius. A question about manners can become, with nothing more than a turn of the page, a question about living and dying, and the variety of tones that can thus be evoked, still within small enclosed spaces, is greater, more amusing, and more somber than anything we find in the early books.

Potter always called her animals "rubbish," rabbits and mice and ducks and the like; they were not "serious" animals like sheep, dogs, and horses. When one visits Hill Top one is struck by how hard it must have been for her to keep "serious" animals out of her books, since sheep and dogs are everywhere, the basic work of the farm. Until she was married, though, and no longer an author, this work had to be left in the hands of others, which implies that she felt that she should not draw, or write about, the really serious matters. There was plenty to do with the "rubbish" animals, however, since even rats must live somehow, must they not, and how a rat is to live is not a trivial matter. That is to say, both Samuel Whiskers in *The Roly-Poly Pudding* and Peter Rabbit have adventures, but Peter's remain a naughty prank, while the struggle between cat and rat in a farmhouse is eternal and to that extent beyond moral questioning. This allows Potter a certain extravagance, whereby she can imagine whole families of cats and rats, each with their domestic problems, each therefore resembling human beings, and still never lose her sense that these animals are doing what comes instinctively to them. We find these instinctive activities in all the stories, of course—rabbits hunger for lettuce, squirrels hunt for nuts, mice are afraid of cats. But when, in *The Roly-Poly Pudding*, Potter gives us a family of cats and a family of rats, and makes them both long-time residents of a household, the instinctive desire of the cats to catch the rats implies an extended action, one which can also be played against the internal or domestic relations within each family. A story can then move in a number of directions without Potter's ever losing track of the fact that these are animals, doing what animals do. A mother worries for a lost child, a creature is annoyed when its privacy is invaded, a mate must trust another mate even when the other is essentially untrustworthy, and these are "human" events performed by cats and rats in ways that seem entirely "natural," so that when Potter leaps from one strand of her tale to another it simultaneously feels like an artistic feat of some magnitude and a simple underlining of an essential fact of animal, and human, life.

Near the opening of *The Roly-Poly Pudding,* a housewife talks with her guest, and the fact that both are cats keeps coming in and going out of our view of them:

> Mrs. Tabitha came downstairs mewing dreadfully— "Come in, Cousin Ribby, come in, and sit ye down! I'm in sad trouble, Cousin Ribby," said Tabitha, shedding tears. "I've lost my dear son Thomas; I'm afraid the rats have got him." She wiped her eyes with her apron.
>
> "He's a bad kitten, Cousin Tabitha; he made a cat's cradle of my best bonnet last time I came to tea. Where have you looked for him?"
>
> "All over the house! The rats are too many for me. What a thing it is to have an unruly family!" said Mrs. Tabitha Twitchit.

The picture facing the text here shows Cousin Ribby entering the door, altogether too well-dressed and too liable to demand the full attention of her hostess for Mrs. Tabitha to be able to handle in her already chaotic household. The bad pun about the cat's cradle really works against Ribby and shows that she objects to Tom Kitten's perfectly natural fooling around with her bonnet, or perhaps to Tom's more "human" but equally natural desire to annoy such a fussy visitor. When Mrs. Tabitha and Ribby set out to look for kittens they are mothers, and when they worry about rats they are cats, so that a line like "The rats are too many for me" combines harried housewife and frustrated hunter.

"He's a bad kitten," says Ribby about young Tom, but the case is not proven here. He had run away because his mother wanted to shut him and his sisters up in a cupboard while she baked, and "Tom Kitten did not want to be shut up in a cupboard." Tabitha wants to shut him up because he is young and cannot, presumably, look after himself, but her worry on that score, given the presence of the rats that are too many, seems not altogether fussy. Tom, on the other hand, knows nothing of rats and can only interpret being shut up as the restrictive act of a fussy mother, which hardly makes him a "bad" kitten, though of course any fussy adult might think it does. Tom is young and curious, so he climbs the chimney and gets lost, simply because the world is larger than his reckoning. More dangerous as well; there are mutton bones lying in a flat place in the chimney and the mutton bones are a typical perfect Potter stroke, simultaneously startling, piquant, and sinister. If a sheep has been killed, it was neither cat nor rat that did the slaughtering, and this has the effect of making Tabitha less a mistress of the house, of reminding us that those who do slaughter sheep are dangerous creatures, especially to sheep, and of hinting that Tom is in a world *much* larger than he realizes.

Whoever killed the sheep, however, was probably not responsible for the bones ending up in the chimney:

> "Who has been gnawing bones up here in the chimney? I wish I had never come! And what a funny smell? It is something like mouse; only dreadfully strong. It makes me sneeze," said Tom Kitten.

Tom is a kitten, and thus an innocent, and thus doesn't know what even we know: rats are near. But what do we know, after all? Do rats and mice smell alike? Does the smell of rats make a cat sneeze? There is a similar moment in *Peter Rabbit,* when Peter stares tearfully at the field mouse, and then solemnly watches the white cat staring at goldfish, and is very much out of his depth, as Tom is here. In *Peter Rabbit* there is, from the beginning, an ethical framework, so that Peter is breaking his mother's rules as well as Mr. McGregor's trespassing laws, and as a result we know he must be gotten home safely so he will be forced to face his mother. There is no such original framework operating here, where the cats are all out of their depths in trying to handle the rats, who are stealing Tabitha's dough and rolling pin so she cannot bake, and who are such a threat that she must look for her children as the rats run wild. We assume Tom will be rescued, but his lostness is more perilous than Peter's since it directs the story much less securely; suddenly the mutton bones, which look as big as Tom Kitten's backbone in the picture, play strongly against our protective sense of young Tom, two-footed Tom, blue-jacketed Tom. There is violence in the world and some of it is right here. The background in this picture of Tom staring at the bones is precise in its sinister vagueness. We may know Tom will somehow be saved, but, really, we are as lost in this story as he is.

Then, at the climax, Tom stumbles into the rat hole where Samuel Whiskers is sitting oafishly against a wall:

> It was a very small fusty room, with boards, and rafters, and cobwebs, and lath and plaster.
>
> Opposite to him—as far away as he could sit—was an enormous rat.
>
> "What do you mean by tumbling into my bed all covered with smuts?" said the rat, chattering his teeth.

Samuel Whiskers' "bed" consists of nothing more than scraps of cloth and paper, but the indignation is real: Tom is trespassing, and rats who object to intruders all covered with smuts are not going to enjoy trespassing youngsters. A rat is a rat, to be sure, but Samuel Whiskers' outrage is perfectly understandable, which makes his chattering teeth a delicious expression of any kitten's, or any person's, fear of rats and anyone's instinctive dislike of intruders, especially when the intruders are the youngsters of one's natural and traditional enemy.

Potter is too intent, staring, busy, and amused to congratulate herself on the astonishing number of distinct but overlapping effects she can create simultaneously as her stories reach their climax. Samuel Whiskers calls his wife, Anna Maria, and we soon learn what a rat does with a captive intruding kitten. Tom is "rolled up in a bundle, and tied with string in very hard knots," and everything in that sentence works to shift the problem away from Tom and onto the question of what the rats are going to do with him. Such a shift is hard to manage in a story with a central character, such as Peter Rabbit, but it is easy where the subject is the endless battle between cats and rats in a farmhouse. Furthermore Potter enjoys the shift because it is a shift from child to adults, and one can do so much more with adults, such as make them into gourmets and pedants:

"Anna Maria, make me a kitten dumpling roly-poly pudding for my dinner."

"It requires dough and a pat of butter and a rolling-pin," said Anna Maria, considering Tom Kitten with her head on one side.

This is at the end of a page in which Samuel watches Anna Maria tie Tom up, and on the next is a line drawing of Tom, securely tied and ready to be made into a pudding, and we watch him as we hear Samuel say:

"No," said Samuel Whiskers, "make it properly, Anna Maria, with bread crumbs."

And on the next, under a drawing that shows a very well-fed Samuel Whiskers and a thin and perhaps overworked Anna Maria, she insists:

"Nonsense! Butter and dough," replied Anna Maria.

By stretching the dialogue onto three pages Potter effects the shift to the rats more easily than she could have done had all the dialogue fallen onto one page. By the time this little sequence is over we are focused on a marriage. First we presume all the power lies with the oafish and well-fed Samuel, and then we see that Anna Maria can at least prevail in selecting the choice of dressing for the pudding. After a consultation Samuel sneaks off down the staircase to steal some butter, and he then returns, after a second journey, with the rolling-pin: "He pushed it in front of him with his paws, like a brewer's man trundling a barrel."

To consider the problems rats may have in their domestic relations, or in their struggle to stay well fed, is not actually to want Tom made into a roly-poly pudding. This is not particularly a matter of our emotional investment in a hero, or of any moral sense that cats are superior to rats, which might have been the case in anyone else's rendering of this material. In a climactic moment such as this, one can hear almost every note Potter has sounded earlier. As Samuel Whiskers is pushing the rolling-pin like a brewer's man trundling a barrel we can remember, for instance, the mutton bones—maybe rats this resourceful did kill the sheep?—and back before that, "The rats are too much for me," and why should they not be when they can roam at will in the house just to have dough and butter rather than bread crumbs for their meal? So the house seems full, Tabitha and Ribby at their wits' end, Moppet and Mittens off wandering somewhere, Tom tied up, Samuel obeying his wife's choice of recipe, Anna Maria looking so thin she never could actually have eaten a roly-poly pudding, could she? Yet, with all this in play, there is still no reason to want Tom actually put into the oven—or, we may ask, what oven? where?

Tom is then well buttered and wrapped in dough made by his mother, Anna Maria insisting the knots will not be hard to digest. She is just about to say the soot that covers Tom is no problem either when the rats hear noises: a saw, a dog scratching and yelping. Earlier Tabitha had sent for John Joiner, the handyman, and the serious animal makes his appearance. But this moment of rescue does not much interest Potter. Rescues are properly so called when an emotional or moral investment has been made about whoever is being rescued, and while neither we nor Potter want Tom eaten, we are clear that being rescued or being eaten is not the point of this tale. No, we are concerned with cats and rats:

> "I fear that we shall be obliged to leave this pudding."
> "But I am persuaded that the knots would have proved indigestible, whatever you may urge to the contrary."
> "Come away at once and help me to tie up some mutton bones in a counterpane," said Anna Maria, "I have got half a smoked ham hidden in the chimney."

Respectable and an anxious provider even as a fugitive, Anna Maria is only "obliged" to leave Tom behind; pedant and gourmet even as a fugitive, Samuel cannot be construed as intending to comfort his wife in their distress. Potter's coolness deliciously pays off in high comedy found in that very unlikely place, the domestic concerns of rats on the run. Her years of painful and absorbed waiting, of staring at objects and gradually finding something worthy of her commentary, of finally finding her place within the confines of a space small enough and alive enough to make one rat into Samuel Whiskers and another into Anna Maria, are all amply rewarded here.

By 1908, in the middle of her first Sawrey period, Potter could command everything that had ever been potentially part of her talent. She might occasionally toss off a *Miss Moppet* or a *Fierce Bad Rabbit*

just to keep the presses rolling. She might, in apparent exasperation
with the continued success of *Peter Rabbit,* write an anti-Peter-
Rabbit-lover book, *Tom Kitten,* in which she set up the story to be
like *Peter Rabbit* and then deliberately refused to let the story fulfill
its own expectations. She could even introduce John Joiner, the
serious animal, into her tale of rubbish animals without seriously
marring her story, because John Joiner is just a handyman that any
housekeeper might be able to call on in an emergency; in the context
of householding cats and intruding rats, dogs and cats might easily
seem natural allies. She could even insist that the endings of her
books not resemble those of other stories for young people. John
Joiner rescues Tom Kitten on page 63, but *The Roly-Poly Pudding*
goes on until page 75. *Mr. Tod* reaches its climax on page 84 and then
slides downhill for ten more pages. Most extravagantly in this respect, *Ginger & Pickles* has fully twenty pages after it is apparently
over.

Since these extended endings are such a definite sign of the freedom of Potter's mature books, they are worth comment. In the
Sawrey books she is, as I have said, describing a world within which
we are asked to consider an episode, the morning Mrs. Tabitha
Twitchit started to bake, the day Tommy Brock stole the Flopsy
Bunnies, the outcome of the policy of extending unlimited credit in
the shop run by Ginger and Pickles. Always we are asked to consider
the episode in the context of the everyday life of a barnyard, a woodland, a village. "The rats are too much for me" is a statement about a
state of mind as well as about what Samuel Whiskers had done that
morning. "Nobody could call Mr. Tod 'nice'. The rabbits could not
bear him; they could smell him half a mile off." This is daily life,
rabbits and foxes living in a world of predator and victim. "The shop
was also patronized by mice—only the mice were rather afraid of
Ginger." Ginger is a shopkeeper, in need of the trade, but also is a
cat, and cats find it hard to see mice "going out at the door carrying
their little parcels." As we are introduced to a particular set of
characters in a particular episode, we are also learning the generic
facts of these animals' lives. The more Potter generalizes her story,
the less important any one character or event will be. Potter can
thus assure us, even at the most heightened moments in her tales,
that what is happening is to be expected, not extraordinary, even as
she narrates the most extraordinary events. Thus, after Tom Kitten

is rescued, Potter presses on, with the same air of knowing patience with which she does every other moment, telling us where Samuel Whiskers and Anna Maria went to live, how Mittens and Moppet became rat catchers when they grew up, how Tom even in his mature years was afraid of rats because of what had happened the day his mother began to bake.

In this as well as some other respects, *Ginger & Pickles* is Potter's most daring book, which is one reason why it has never been among her most popular books; it is very unnerving indeed, even after quite a few readings. It refuses, from first page to last, ever to say what is most important about what is happening, though each moment is carefully and clearly focused. Ginger, a tiger cat, and Pickles, a terrier, run a village shop. Among their customers are Peter Rabbit and the Flopsy Bunnies, Samuel Whiskers and Anna Maria, Jemima Puddle-Duck and Sally Henny-Penny and Mrs. Tiggy-Winkle. Briefly we are asked to consider how the "natural" desire of cats for mice, or of terriers for rabbits, can interfere with good business hospitality just as the perhaps "natural" prejudices of villagers—against the children of an enemy, maybe, or pushy fussy tourists—might interfere with good business hospitality. Then we shift. Ginger and Pickles extend unlimited credit, and the animals won't pay their bills, and soon a policeman appears with a rates bill the shop can't pay, so eventually Ginger and Pickles must close their shop. Clearly Ginger and Pickles are fools for running their shop on unsound principles, but they are pitiable because the other animals take such ruthless advantage of them, and because the bureaucracy is so stiff and persnickety it can come up with a rates bill of £3 19 11 3/4, or one farthing less than an even £4. But watch the twist that comes next:

> "This is the last straw," said Pickles, "let us close the shop."
>
> They put up the shutters, and left. But they have not removed from the neighbourhood. In fact some people wish they had gone further.

The tense shifts from past to present, life goes on, a business fails and so shutters must be put up.

This comes on page 50, and the book has twenty-five pages to go, and since page 16 we have been considering the downfall of the shop because it extends unlimited credit. But *Ginger & Pickles* is not just the name of a shop; these are the names of a dog and a cat, who must go on living. So then we learn they have taken to hunting rabbits, Ginger successfully, it seems, with traps, and Pickles unsuccessfully, it seems, as a gamekeeper with a gun. Then Potter turns her book once again, drops Ginger and Pickles entirely and returns to *Ginger & Pickles*, or to the store that once bore their name. How do the other animals manage without it and its extravagant generosity with credit? Potter spends the last twenty pages answering that question, looking at tradesmen's carts, at the brief and ill-advised efforts of dormice to run a business, and at a successful reopening by Sally Henny-Penny, who offers many bargains, but also demands cash payment. We are thus tempted to say this has been a story about a village all along, but Potter is more precise than that. It is a village story, but not thoughout, just finally, at the end, where the pages no longer follow a plot but the mind and energies of the teller. The teller is a villager, and a villager must invest her energy in everything surrounding her and with no one consideration allowed to dominate the others. The price of handkerchiefs, the variety of the merchandise, the instincts of animals, the prejudices of shopkeepers, the folly of mindless generosity, the fall of a business and the departure of its owners, the brief inquiry into where the failed business owners have gone to, the arrival of other businesses, the assurance that nothing is permanent, and that only the village and life itself may last beyond a season or one's own lifetime—all these are here, and each receives the same careful, amused scrutiny all things deserve. Villages cannot afford heroes or villains, and therefore they know no climaxes or irrevocable actions, and the villager who knows this best is Potter herself.

Still, though village and farmhouse life gave Potter much that enabled her to feel free, part of a larger world, able to create the likes of *The Roly-Poly Pudding* and *Ginger & Pickles*, she was nonetheless Beatrix Potter still, the Lake District landowner who was incarcerated for many months each year in her parents' house in South Kensington, where all seemed flat, stale, and unprofitable. Just once, so far as I can see, did she allow herself to do a book about herself, though it is not necessary that we see *Jemima Puddle-Duck* this way, or insist that Potter did. But it is singular among her later books for the kind of ambivalent focus it gains on its central character. Just having a central character is something Potter wisely put behind her after her earliest books about the naughtiness of Peter Rabbit, Benjamin Bunny, and Squirrel Nutkin, and she probably saw that in order to concentrate on one character she would have to make that character somewhat quirky, not quite natural, not part of farmhouse or barnyard life. Jemima's quirkiness, her not quite natural desire, is, seen from another point of view, perfectly natural: she wants to hatch her own eggs. Barnyard birds are, and aren't, birds; they lay their eggs but the eggs are taken away, to be eaten or hatched elsewhere. Jemima wants to do only what all birds of the air do, but for her to want this, since she is a barnyard duck, means she must be perverse. She must leave home.

It is hard to believe Potter did not see herself in all this. But at the age of forty-three, when she wrote this story, Potter was well beyond the childish consolation of simple protesting about her desire to be free, to make a nest, to do what seemed natural, except that in her it also seemed perverse. So she makes the story of Jemima's leaving home a type of the story of Little Red Riding Hood. Jemima is a silly virgin, closer in age as we see her to Potter than to Red Riding Hood; she has not learned to mistrust gentlemen with sandy whiskers, and so she lets herself be seduced with pathetic ease:

> "Madam, have you lost your way?" said he. He had a long bushy tail which he was sitting upon, as the stump was somewhat damp.
>
> Jemima thought him mighty civil and handsome. She explained that she had not lost her way, but that she was trying to find a convenient dry nesting-place.

Potter had never risked anything like this before, this beast fable sexuality and innocence of animals of different species:

> "But as to a nest—there is no difficulty: I have a sackful of feathers in my woodshed. No, my dear madam, you will be in nobody's way. You may sit there as long as you like," said the bushy long-tailed gentleman.

Thus Jemima, as she sits in the sandy-haired gentleman's woodshed, covered as it is with the feathers of previous victims, earns the full scorn of Potter's emphatic: "Jemima Puddle-Duck was a simpleton."

Yet before this Jemima has been very brave in her efforts to move out on her own, nowhere more so than in her attempts to use the wings she knows she was born with but which, even as a mature duck, she has seldom actually used. Potter says, "She flew beautifully when she got a good start," insisting that Jemima, and perhaps herself, could do quite well on her own just by using what nature gave her. But the picture that faces this sentence, which shows Jemima flying, blue bonnet tied around her neck, red shawl around her shoulders, does not show something flying beautifully. How well she does under the circumstances, not how gracefully, is Potter's picture of her. Yet even as she is earning Potter's scorn, Potter is finding ways to defend her; the picture opposite "Jemima Puddle-Duck was a simpleton" shows only a very natural and ducklike Jemima, nibbling in the garden. This kind of complexity of vision was pretty much beyond the early Potter, and Jemima is the only fully grown creature in all her books about whom we seem to be asked to care more than is wise or even sensible. We may know that in the real world Jemima would be eaten by the fox, and should be, but we want her saved anyway. It would take a miracle, a Prince Charming, to do the trick, and neither a duck nor Potter knows much about Prince Charming. She brings in the usually excluded work animal, the collie, but does not offer him, as she does John Joiner in *The Roly-Poly Pudding,* as an easily available member of an ongoing household. When he appears, Kep the dog is much closer to Rupert Potter than he is to Prince Charming. As he listens to Jemima's story the picture shows him standing over her, looking stern, while she confesses a story the pathos and danger of which she is unaware.

It is a tricky business, especially when we are aware of what it seems to reveal about Potter, her plight, her desires, and her attitudes toward all these. After Kep appears, as rescuer, father, prince, god from the machine, the story does not work very well, though it helps to bring the story back to the ordinary life of farm animals to have Kep's puppy cohort eat Jemima's eggs. Yet *Jemima Puddle-Duck* is, after *Peter Rabbit,* the most popular of Potter's books, and it seems reasonable to suggest that it is permeated with a personal need and power that readers can feel without inquiring into their source, and whereby it triumphs despite the tenuous control of tone in the later pages. I spoke earlier of the daring involved in making *Ginger*

& Pickles, but the daring here is really as great, because of all that is involved in making one's Little Red Riding Hood a mature female. The range of feelings thus brought in is not so much varied as schizophrenic, because Potter's admiration and scorn seem at war with each other. The power of this book seems less than fully controlled, which makes it all the more moving, for what it protects as well as for what it reveals.

So we have the farmhouse Potter, the village Potter, and the lonely determined foolish Potter that would fly from home and have a family if only she knew how. None of these are in evidence in her last great book, *Mr. Tod*, her story of the uplands, of the animal kingdom, of nature red in tooth and claw, of fierceness that wears a distinctly human face. The dates cannot be assigned with precision, but it would seem she wrote it after beginning the ordeal of her engagement with William Heelis and her separation from her parents. For most of its length *Mr. Tod* seems not so much to express that ordeal as to seek release from it, but then in the climactic battle we see something Potter could not have learned from staring at foxes and badgers, something she could often have observed by staring at people. Potter showed her own ability to be nasty as early as her *Journal*, but in *Mr. Tod* she seems to find such release in imagining the nastiness of others that she does not have to feel nasty herself, and her control is masterly throughout.

"I have made many books about well-behaved people," she begins, and "for a change I am going to make a story about two disagreeable people, called Tommy Brock and Mr. Tod." Since, of her previous seventeen books, no more than five could be said to be about "well-behaved people," we can only suspect how much she wanted a holiday from good manners and how much worse than usual were the characters she was about to consider. Note that she calls Tommy Brock and Mr. Tod people, something she had never done with a character before, but she turns from this to contemplate the disagreeable by contemplating the ordinary life of nature, the fox as known by rabbits:

> Nobody could call Mr. Tod "nice." The rabbits could not bear him; they could smell him half a mile off. He was of a wandering habit and he had foxey whiskers; they never knew where he would be next.

> One day he was living in a stick-house in the coppice, causing terror to the family of old Mr. Bouncer. Next day he moved into a pollard willow near the lake, frightening the wild ducks and the water rats.

The bright unpleasant assurance of the young woman of the *Journal* has found its home, so nothing unpleasant now seems alien to her. By having Mr. Tod be a "person" the rabbits "could not bear," Potter invites us to contemplate the equivalent of the town drunk or braggart. By having Mr. Tod seem almost to break laws of nature as well as of decency in his unpredictable moving about, she invites us to enjoy the feeling that we cannot bear certain people because they seem almost to break the laws of nature.

This mixing of the distinctively human with the decidedly animal and natural is done even better in the opening description of Tommy Brock:

> Tommy Brock was a short bristly fat waddling person with a grin; he grinned all over his face. He was not nice in his habits. He ate wasp nests and frogs and worms; and he waddled about by moonlight, digging things up.
>
> His clothes were very dirty; and as he slept in the daytime, he always went to bed in his boots. And the bed which he went to bed in, was generally Mr. Tod's.

A short bristly fat waddling person with a grin whose clothes are dirty because he goes to bed in his boots might be Sancho Panza, or Scratchy in Stephen Crane's "The Bride Comes to Yellow Sky." To add "he grinned all over his face" and "He ate wasp nests and frogs and worms" does more than make Tommy Brock into a badger; it has a splendidly nasty and sinister effect on the surrounding vague phrases over which they exercise control: "He was not nice in his habits," "he waddled about by moonlight, digging things up." Things —something worse, surely, than wasp nests and frogs and worms.

We may recognize in this, and in the following passage, a use of the fastidious tone that might remind us of some of the dainty phrases in the *Alice* books; "not nice" is very much unlike Potter's usual prose, and calls attention to itself as a clear sign that what we are about here is perhaps a little more disagreeable than usual for the clear-eyed Potter:

> Now Tommy Brock did occasionally eat rabbit-pie; but it was only very little young ones occasionally, when other food was really scarce. He was friendly with old Mr. Bouncer; they agreed in disliking the wicked otters and Mr. Tod; they often talked over that painful subject.

The repetition of "occasionally" implies a restraint on Tommy Brock's part; yes, he does catch and eat and cook, apparently, young rabbits, but really, only now and then when wasps' nests are scarce. A fine fellow really, Tommy Brock, which slides us into Mr. Bouncer's view of him. It would never occur to us to say Jemima Puddle-Duck and the gentleman with sandy whiskers, a duck and a fox, made up an animal kingdom, nor would we say it about the cats and rats of *The Roly-Poly Pudding,* though they do make a very full house. Here, though, simply by triangulating fox and rabbit with badger, Potter suggests something almost that large and something so sinister that fastidious language may be called for. Look at Tommy Brock by himself and nothing could seem worse. Look at Tommy Brock looking at Mr. Tod and discussing "that painful subject" with old Mr. Bouncer, and our view of Tommy Brock shifts. Surely no one will mind the loss of an *occasional* young rabbit; they do breed fast, don't they? How strange some animals are, and all must live together somehow, and one way to do this is to try to overlook the fact that Tommy Brock has dirty clothes and eats one's grandchildren. One cannot afford to be too nice about these subjects. Fox and duck, thus, make a villain and a victim, while fox, rabbit, and badger make a whole world.

It has often been said that in her later books Beatrix Potter was no longer writing for young children, who, it is surmised, cannot take such complications of tone as I have been trying to describe. One might reply that Potter is never best understood as a writer for young children, but that is probably beside the point. These later books, *Mr. Tod* especially, are harsher, more disagreeable by far than *Peter Rabbit* or *The Tailor of Gloucester.* Indeed, in *Mr. Tod* Potter takes two of her early heroes, Peter Rabbit and Benjamin Bunny, and makes them into something like young readers who are here forced into a world that is too much for them, as though she now wanted to reveal what she had held back from her "many books about well-behaved people." She was, after all, now in her mid-forties and well

versed in disagreeableness, her own and that of others. She might
well have wanted to have done with that sort of restraint which had
managed somehow to imprison her for so many years. Thus we are
not, for a long time in *Mr. Tod,* inside an enclosed space, nor are
we intently staring at anything. Potter is free, ranging up and down
the woodland hillside, shifting her point of view widely and easily.

The passage most often cited to show the change in Potter's out-
look comes almost halfway through *Mr. Tod,* when she is getting
ready to move back one last time inside an enclosed space. One
afternoon Mr. Bouncer is babysitting for his grandchildren. He lets
Tommy Brock into the rabbit hole and lets himself be put to sleep by
his own pipe smoke. When he wakes, Tommy and the Flopsy
Bunnies are gone, and so Peter and Benjamin must set out up the hill
to look for them. Knowing Tommy Brock, they know they will
probably find him in one of Mr. Tod's houses, as indeed they do, at
the top of Bull Banks. The bunnies are in the oven but still alive, and
Tommy Brock is nowhere to be seen:

> The sun had set; an owl began to hoot in the wood. There
> were many unpleasant things lying about, that had much
> better have been buried; rabbit bones and skulls, and
> chickens' legs and other horrors. It was a shocking place,
> and very dark.

It is one of Potter's most brilliant moments. The setting sun and the
owl give us atmospheric writing unknown elsewhere in Potter and
cue us into a world that will, this time, move toward the "things"
Potter had deliberately left vague hitherto. These things "had much
better have been buried," which seems to pull us up short of specifi-
cation, but then we are told: "rabbit bones and skulls, and chickens'
legs and other horrors." Potter is, unquestionably and understandably, shocked. Foxes and badgers here are like adults, and what they
do at night, after the sun sets and the owls begin to hoot, is best not
discussed, or even discovered if possible.

The *most* sophisticated reader might see this simply as a verbal
trick in which Potter giveth—look at these rabbit bones and skulls
—and then taketh away—but they had much better have been
buried, and it might seem even more of a trick since the taking away
precedes the giving. The *least* sophisticated reader might see this as
mere horror, and of course Potter's youngest readers are bound to

include some of the least sophisticated. But the phrase "that had much better have been buried" is too resonant and too delicate to be either mere trick or mere horror. Potter does not say Mr. Tod should have buried these bones and skulls, though they are presumably his leavings. After all, he did not invite Peter and Benjamin here, and if they choose not to keep their usually discreet distance, they must take the consequences, surely. Nor can the rabbits whose bones these are care much, since they are dead no matter what. Potter's cry is not for any rabbits as such, but for all those who remain among the living, especially rabbits. It is instinctive, unreasoning, though it will admit no theoretical justification, because no fastidiousness and no distance can keep us from finally acknowledging what foxes and badgers do to rabbits, or what people can and do do to all three. But like so many things we "must admit," we are happier admitting it from a distance, and this time Potter insists on taking all comfortable distance away from us.

We have come a long way from, and also not very far from, Peter Rabbit's father, who, we learn on the second page of Potter's first book, had an "accident" in Mr. McGregor's garden and was put into a pie. What happens to him is what might happen to his son, or what has happened to those distant cousins of his whose bones we are contemplating outside Mr. Tod's house. Mrs. Rabbit's word, "accident," is not just a euphemism, because it is also her way of saying that naughtiness in the face of clearly given warnings is not accidental, so that Peter's father is put in the role of a provider while Peter soon fits into the role of a willful child. That tone is just what one wants in *Peter Rabbit*, especially since it is not the only tone in the book, or its final tone. But here in *Mr. Tod* a word like "accident" would be all wrong. Peter and Benjamin may be like young readers out of their depths, but they are also mature rabbits and know that in nature there are few accidents.

"There were many unpleasant things lying about, that had much better have been buried." That is the worst Potter can say of nature red in tooth and claw; its violence is ruthless but mainly rudely untidy, since it is hard enough to face young rabbits dying without also being forced to face their remains. Potter's is a human cry, since even sentient and talking rabbits like Peter and Benjamin are simply too scared to be outraged. It is an unreasonable cry, too, pathetic and weak in its human nicety in the face of the central fact of nature:

all must live as they can, and all must die. It also expresses a limit, the farthest Potter will go in her contemplation of the disagreeable as seen in the lives of foxes, badgers, and rabbits. The story is only half over, but now we are to go back inside the enclosed space, and the horrors we will see there will bear a distinctively human face. To contemplate the disagreeable is, finally, to come back to people.

Tommy Brock is in the bedroom, lying in Mr. Tod's bed, and snoring, when Mr. Tod first comes in:

> For the next twenty minutes Mr. Tod kept creeping cautiously into the house, and retreating hurriedly out again. By degrees he ventured further in—right into the bedroom. When he was outside the house he scratched up the earth with fury. But when he was inside—he did not like the look of Tommy Brock's teeth.
>
> He was lying on his back with his mouth open, grinning from ear to ear. He snored peacefully and regularly; but one eye was not perfectly shut.
>
> Mr. Tod came in and out of the bedroom. Twice he brought in his walking-stick and once he brought in the coal-scuttle. But he thought better of it, and took them away.

This is much closer to human enmity than to anything we know of fox or badger, who are predatory animals here only in the sharpness of their teeth. It is difficult, in speaking of the shifting Potter, to say she has made a real shift here, but this *is* different. "When he was outside the house he scratched up the earth with fury." Scratching up the earth, of course, is the act of a canine animal; in its resemblance to throwing something or kicking a wall, it is the act of a frustrated child; in its fury it is the rage of anyone whose house has been broken into; in its fear it is the adult human calculation of having somehow been beaten, in response to which one must do that distinctly human thing: plan a revenge.

Mr. Tod rigs up a water pail scheme, all the time seeming more and more foolish and pathetic, a loser, because of course Tommy Brock is not asleep, and the rope, when pulled, will only get Mr. Tod's bed wet. But just before Mr. Tod discovers what we already know, Potter makes another shift, transforms Mr. Tod momentarily into a type of Beatrix Potter, returned to Hill Top Farm after a winter away and facing a large job of spring housecleaning:

> "I will get soft soap, and monkey soap, and all sorts of soap; and soda and scrubbing brushes; and persian powder; and carbolic to remove the smell. I must have a disinfecting. Perhaps I may have to burn sulphur."
>
> He hurried round the house to get a shovel from the kitchen—"First I will arrange the hole—then I will drag out that person in the blanket . . ."
>
> He opened the door . . .

There is nothing here resembling nature red in tooth and claw, though we are not more than a few feet from the rabbit bones and skulls. Mr. Tod is not hungry, nor is he going to feast on Tommy Brock. He is going to rid his house of a terrible smelly burden, and nowhere else does Potter come so close to casting a sympathetic glance at Mr. Tod. Mr. Tod is right, and righteous; it is time to be done with such nuisances.

The picture facing this passage, however, tells an entirely different story. It shows what happens just after Mr. Tod opens the door, and instead of a righteous angry spring housecleaner, Mr. Tod is a peeper in at the door, as though he were the intruder. Instead of being smelly and dead, Tommy Brock is standing next to Mr. Tod's kitchen table, a cup and a saucer in his hands, his jacket and waistcoat looking quite neat, just as though *he* were the righteous householder:

> Tommy Brock was sitting at Mr. Tod's kitchen table, pouring out tea from Mr. Tod's teapot into Mr. Tod's teacup. He was quite dry himself and grinning; and he threw the cup of scalding tea all over Mr. Tod.

Tommy Brock is awful, nasty and grinning, but he also is the victor, more clever in a fight where cleverness is all that counts. "Winner," of course, is a human word to describe a human victory, one made sweet for Tommy Brock because he has not attacked Mr. Tod, only offended him, and because he has been living in one or another of Mr. Tod's houses for so long it is quite natural for him to treat Mr. Tod's china as though it were his own.

It won't do to say that disagreeableness is only human. We have been acknowledging all along the real appropriateness of using a fox and a badger as the central figures in this horrible, sad, funny tale of the awful. But for true disagreeableness the place to turn is not to fox and to badger; in the rabbits' bones lying around outside Mr. Tod's house we see the worst they can do. Nor is it just human beings who we want to claim are caught in this climactic frame. The worst Potter knows is human beings who are righteous and who can offer ample reasons for doing as they do. This is the closest Potter ever came, perhaps ever dared to come, to pure beast fable.

After this moment Potter has Tommy Brock and Mr. Tod revert, and we back off from them. In the fight Tommy Brock's victory is overturned and Mr. Tod's house is left a shambles, and the two battle on and on: "There will never be any love lost between Tommy Brock and Mr. Tod." Peter and Benjamin take advantage of the battle to rescue the bunnies that would have been lost had either combatant won, and we all come back to the rabbit hole, where old Mr. Bouncer is allowed to reassume his dignity, and where, very soon, the whole long series of events will become just a story for the rabbits to tell the bunnies as they grow up. All's well that ends well. But—"They had not waited long enough to be able to tell the end of the battle between Tommy Brock and Mr. Tod." Endings are for stories, and if this one must end, it must be with the reminder that the great events are not easily rounded off, especially in a world where the only endings are to days, seasons, and individual lives. But in her other books with endings extended long after the climax we are invited to imagine the absorbing naturalness of ongoing life. Here we have that, but as well we have the reminder that the human desire for enmity and revenge outstrips anything in the nonhuman world, both in ferocity and in duration.

Mr. Tod is a brilliant book, the climax of a brilliant career. No one should mind if it, or *Ginger & Pickles* or *The Roly-Poly Pudding,* too, never replaces other and earlier Potters in the hearts of most people, though it would be a shame if any of these late masterpieces were kept, for whatever specious reason, from anyone who is capable of attending to their great beauties. *Mr. Tod* cannot warm the heart, Lord knows, but such warming lies outside the scope of Beatrix Potter's work. For that the chapters that follow, which concern

Grahame's Rat and Mole and Kipling's Kim, will give us a great deal. Potter's is a sterner beauty altogether. In almost every book she wrote she gave herself a task of such difficulty that even a small slip must seem like a glaring error, and when one writes that kind of book, where intelligence, intentness, and precision are crucial, one is not going to achieve, except very occasionally, warmth or compassion. In at least ten of these books Potter is nigh flawless in her difficult doing, and she emerges not just unscathed but triumphant, and cleansing.

A friend of mine once said, after comparing *Peter Rabbit* and *Mr. Tod*, that "disagreeableness as lovingly evoked as it is in *Mr. Tod* is the outer limit of unpleasant moral value, which makes the *Tod*-world nicely comfortable by comparison to, say, the world of Dr. Johnson's prayers and meditations." What I like best about that statement is that it properly suggests a limit to Beatrix Potter's achievement within a context entirely worthy of her. She was able to make smallness and enclosedness into literary and artistic virtues, as opposed to the moral virtue Kenneth Grahame made of these same qualities. The first, second, and third thing to do with Potter, unquestionably, is to say how wonderfully and memorably she animated and then filled her small worlds, and eventually one would want to go on to show how loose and baggy, how easy on themselves, she makes most other writers and artists seem. But the world of Dr. Johnson's prayers and meditations, for one, was both more horrible and more profound than anything she could express. Having discovered what smallness could do for her, she could never open out from it farther than she did at the end, in *Mr. Tod*. Though on the whole her achievement seems much more considerable than Lewis Carroll's, he has moments in *Through the Looking-Glass* where his capacity for tears seems able to rebuke Potter for being so determinedly knowing.

But hers, after all, was another voyage, and its destination was not *Peter Rabbit* or *Mr. Tod* or any of the way stations in between, but William Heelis, and the quiet, purposeful, and fulfilling life she could have with him, and the sheep, and the land. We must be thankful it took her so long to arrive at her goal, but we must be glad, too, that after so much waiting and patient learning to live within enclosed spaces she could be free at last to find the work, silence, love —and perhaps the sorrow too—she had most wanted.

(7) Kenneth Grahame

When I took a studio at No. 4 St. George's Square, Primrose Hill, the outgoing tenant said "Let me introduce you to Dr. Furnivall. He will ask you if you can scull. If you say 'No,' he will take you up the river to teach you. If you say 'Yes,' he will take you up the river to keep you in practice. He will take you anyhow." . . .

I could not help smiling as, after a little enquiry about my work, Dr. Furnivall asked, "Can you scull?" When I answered "Yes," his whole face beamed. "How jolly!" he exclaimed. "I hope you will often come up the river with us." . . . I met him shortly after nine o'clock on the appointed morning, as he was coming from his house. Two large string bags were slung over his shoulder—one hanging in front, the other behind. These, with a third bag in his right hand, were all full of good things to eat . . . Back at Richmond the club boats went on to Hammersmith, but the Doctor would take his party to the station by way of queer narrow back streets, in one of which there was a quaint little 'tuck-shop.' Into this he would suddenly disappear, and those of the party who did not know that the floor of

the shop was two steps below the level of the street, literally
dived after him.

In his biography of Kenneth Grahame, Peter Green quotes this
passage to illustrate the charm of F. J. Furnivall, founder of the
Early English Text Society and the New Shakespeare Society, whom
Grahame met shortly after he went to work for the Bank of England
in the mid-1870s. Readers of Grahame will identify Furnivall immediately; bluff, cheerful, full of purpose when coming and going
from excursions of great and active idleness, knowledgeable about
where to go and what to take along, Furnivall is the Water Rat of
The Wind in the Willows.

Furnivall must have been impressive, and Grahame's imagination
tenacious, since it was thirty years after Grahame's first friendship
with Furnivall that he published his little masterpiece, in 1908. The
picture of Furnivall is useful, too, in helping us describe what seems,
for our purposes at least, like a shift in Victorian consciousness.
Lewis Carroll, born in 1832, grew up as the Victorian cult of childhood was first taking shape; as we have seen, the adored child for
Lewis Carroll and his generation was a preadolescent girl, while the
awkward, unpleasant thing to be was an active boy. Grahame, born
a generation later in 1859, grew up as the cult was in full flower, and
the central figure was more and more apt to be a boy. F. J. Furnivall,
as Jessie Currie describes him in the passage above and as Grahame
first knew him, was a grown man, but at the same time he wasn't;
he is Rat, reflecting the excitement of being a fun-loving boy. Like
Rat, Furnivall enjoys the perquisites of being independent, but it is
his boyishness that charms our sense of him.

Grahame's first books, *Pagan Papers* (1893), *The Golden Age* (1895),
and *Dream Days* (1898), were published when this new version of
the ideal person had gained a firm grip on the English imagination,
a hold it would not lose until World War I, when the boy, slightly
older, gained his apotheosis as a young victim in Flanders. In Beatrix
Potter's work we see little direct evidence of this, but it is noteworthy
that all her young heroes are male, while her young females are
always a little too nice to be interesting. If we look elsewhere in the
period, we see signs of this cult of boyishness everywhere. Here is
how Angus Wilson describes it:

But perhaps the whole of the nineties represents the triumph of one prominent strand of romantic thought—the
cult of childhood. However different their purposes, however serious their aims, there is about Rhodes and Barnato,
Wilde and Beardsley, Shaw and Wells, Henley and Kipling,
a boyishness at once entrancing and at times maddening.
Max, the dandy born old, did well to show the Prince of
Wales standing like a schoolboy, face to the corner, before
the Queen's awful displeasure; the illustrator of *1066 and
All That* did right to show the naughty nineties as childish
old boys. It was, not too long after, that night after night
the upper and middle classes crowded out the theatre to
hear Peter Pan say, "I want always to be a little boy, and to
have fun."

The showiness or gaudiness of some of those Wilson mentions should
not deter us from seeing that the shy and quiet Grahame belongs on
this list and lived in this world. Henley published a great deal of
Grahame's early work, and a number of issues of the notorious
Yellow Book have Grahame stories and sketches alongside Beardsley
drawings and Beerbohm cartoons.

The Golden Age and *Dream Days* were immensely popular books
because they fitted so easily into this new phase of the cult of
childhood. These books are almost unknown today, except perhaps
for "The Reluctant Dragon," but we will understand Grahame much
better if we see why his early books were so popular, and how *The
Wind in the Willows* is a transmutation of his earlier materials into
ideal and enduring shape. It too is about boyishness, or, more properly, boyish manhood, about being free of adult restraint and responsibility and sex. Furnivall appears as Rat, messing about in boats
and taking along good food; the rural god Pan reappears, still
idolized; Oscar Wilde appears in Mr. Toad's adventures in jail. *The
Wind in the Willows* goes *Peter Pan* one better; Barrie and Peter Pan
acknowledge in the very act of saying what they want that it is
impossible, while Grahame's ideal world on the river seems more
palpable, more fully realized, more truly desirable, than *Peter Pan.*
As a result, *The Wind in the Willows* lives today, perhaps more
popular now than it has ever been, part of its time but blessedly not

limited to it. It is loved by lovers of children's books, and also by many who care little for, or even positively dislike, most children's literature. Its pleasure is the pleasure of enclosed space, of entering a charmed circle, of living in a timeless snugness. It takes so little to turn snugness into smugness that it is no wonder that many books that seem to resemble *The Wind in the Willows* are tiresome and even objectionable. If it did not exist it might rightly be claimed that a good book with its essential emotional bearings could not be written. To try to explain this, we must look at Grahame's life, and briefly at his early work, and then slowly and carefully at *The Wind in the Willows* itself. Grahame's was not a distinctly original genius, like Lewis Carroll's or Beatrix Potter's, and it takes some stretching to call *The Wind in the Willows* a great book. But its best pages are magical, fringed with joy, and therefore irreplaceable.

Kenneth Grahame was a Scot by birth; his mother died when he was very young, and his father soon decided he wanted nothing to do with his children and sent them off to live with their maternal grandmother, who lived at Cookham Dean, Berkshire, in the Thames valley. It is easy to surmise that Grahame came to idealize childhood because his own was anything but ideal. He went to St. Edward's School in Oxford and expected to go on to the university, but the uncle who was financially supporting him thought of a university education as a needless frill, so at eighteen Grahame went to work, first in the uncle's law firm, and then in the Bank of England, where he spent the rest of his working life. He was dutiful on the job, but never known for working hard, and he was lucky enough, and good enough, to become at thirty-nine the youngest Secretary in the history of the Bank. He lived in London most of the time between 1876 and 1906; his friends were mostly bohemians, artists, and gentleman scholars, all boyishly anxious to show they weren't entirely respectable, all willing to have along someone who was eminently respectable by day but eagerly escapist by night and by weekend.

Grahame married late, after gaining financial security as Secretary to the Bank and as author of *The Golden Age* and *Dream Days*. His wife was his age, also sexually shy, used to personal independence, and emotionally retarded; their correspondence was in a kind of cockney baby talk. The marriage seems to have been unhappy and might not have lasted except for its one offspring, Alistair, born in 1900. In 1906 the Grahames moved to the Thames valley of his childhood; in 1908 he published *The Wind in the Willows* and resigned from the bank. Grahame traveled, often by himself, and moved his family into different houses in Berkshire. He wrote almost nothing. In 1920 Alistair Grahame, a student at Oxford, committed suicide, and after that his father maintained himself as a kind of living corpse. He died in 1932, and was buried on top of his son, at St. Cross Church, Oxford.

The crucial fact in Grahame's life is that he did not become the Oxford don he wanted to be and seemed suited to be. Had he done so he could have retired early into a quiet single life, and, lacking Lewis Carroll's genius and urgencies, he might never have been heard from again. Thrust into the city, he found in the Bank of England an institution in which he could believe sufficiently to make him persevere successfully in his work, but for which he was sufficiently unsuited that he had to seek escape from it constantly. The more successful he became, the more he wanted to give a form to this constant need to escape, something beyond taking walking weekends in Berkshire and long holidays in Cornwall or Italy. When he knew he would soon be appointed Secretary, he became an author; when he realized his marriage was also something from which he needed to seek refuge, he began *The Wind in the Willows*. Never having the permanent haven Oxford might have provided, he had to invent it in his books.

The first readers of *The Golden Age* and *Dream Days* tended not to recognize them as literature of fantasy and escape, because they could also be taken as witty and satiric exposés that showed children and parents as they "really" are. They are short sketches and stories about a group of five children in the same family; they idealize the children, but not into an image satisfactory to their elders, because their ideal life is gained not by doing as they are told, but by escaping from "the Olympians," their elders. By a neat ironic twist, they were therefore not thought of as children's literature at all. Their readers were adults, and people like Richard LeGalliene and Swinburne reviewed them. Those who objected did so in the name of what one reviewer called "the sacred cause of childhood," while those who loved them claimed Grahame had told the truth about children at last. Children themselves were not encouraged to read the books.

The five children in these stories are Edward, Henry, Charlotte, Selina, and a nameless lad who doubles as narrator. They are a crew, which means they may quarrel among themselves but always unite in sympathy and action whenever any one is the target of Olympian attention or abuse. They exerted a strong influence, apparently, on E. Nesbit, Arthur Ransome, Edward Eager, Mary Norton, and others, all English, all more avowedly writers of "books for children" than was Grahame, all fond of imagining the need of children to build a bastion against parents, relatives, nannies, and teachers, all frank users of the magical, the exciting adventure, or the fantastic, as Grahame himself was not, because for him freedom was all one needed to be at the heart of all fantasy and escape. I confess to finding most of these books with a young community of secular saints rather shy-making, mostly because the authors tend to work too hard to give each character some distinctive or identifying trait, which leads to mechanical writing and often to mechanical re-lations among the children.

That Grahame was not really seeking a realistic version of child-hood in *The Golden Age* and *Dream Days* is most evident in his nar-rator, who experiences all the joys and dark gloom of the other chil-dren but who is frankly free to become an adult narrator whenever Grahame wishes. The result is a kind of double perspective: here is a child telling a story, building a fortress against adults; here also is an adult narrator authorizing and supporting that fortress in his nostalgia for its having never been, or its having been lost. The results tend to be unpleasant a good deal of the time. For instance, in a famous story, "Sawdust and Sin," the younger sister, Charlotte, is trying to make two dolls named Jerry and Rosa sit still so she can tell them stories, while the narrator watches from a convenient hiding place:

> At this point Jerry collapsed forward, suddenly and com-pletely, his bald pate between his knees. Charlotte was not very angry this time. The sudden development of tragedy in the story had evidently been too much for the poor fellow. She straightened him out, and wiped his nose, and, after trying him in various positions, to which he refused

to adapt himself, she propped him against the shoulder of the (apparently) unconscious Rosa. Then my eyes were opened, and the full measure of Jerry's infamy became apparent. This, then, was what he had been playing up for! The rascal had designs, had he? I resolved to keep him under close observation.

On the one hand the narrator can share with Charlotte the presumption that the dolls have ears, eyes, and intentions. On the other, he can laugh at Charlotte for not understanding what Jerry's "real" intentions are. It is a convenient perch.

Charlotte goes on with a quick recounting of *Alice in Wonderland*, but ends sooner than she means to:

> "I never can make my stories last out! Never mind, I'll tell you another one."
>
> Jerry didn't seem to care, now he had gained his end, whether the stories lasted out or not. He was nestling against Rosa's plump form with a look of satisfaction that was simply idiotic; and one arm had disappeared from view —was it around her waist? Rosa's natural blush seemed deeper than usual, her head inclined shyly—it must have been round her waist.

This is smug rather than snug. Charlotte is condescended to as the little girl who plays with dolls, so absorbed in telling her stories and "getting them to listen" she doesn't know what is "really" going on. She is hardly a worthy victim of any but the briefest sally, one would have thought, but Grahame and his narrator get much mileage out of her innocence. The narrator is of course male, and superior to the girl's naïveté, and by believing in Charlotte's fantasy that the dolls are real, by poking fun at Charlotte, Grahame can simultaneously indulge his sexual fantasy and deny it is fantastic.

Thus when, a moment later, Rosa falls "flat on her back in the deadest of faints," Grahame can giggle at the doll's orgiastic swoon and poke an elbow in a reader's ribs with double entendres: " 'It's all your fault, Jerry,' said Charlotte reproachfully, when the lady had been restored to consciousness: 'Rosa's as good as gold except when you make her wicked. I'd put you in the corner, only a stump hasn't got a corner—wonder why that is.' " Ostensibly, one presumes, this is Grahame's joke on "the sacred cause of childhood," or that part of it that elevated the purity and innocence of Alice and Rosa. But in his licentiousness Grahame only reveals *his* innocence. He and Charlotte mean different things by "good" and "wicked," but he accepts the equation of goodness and sexual purity just as much as Charlotte accepts the equation between goodness and correct manners. What makes Grahame's innocence all the more culpable is that it is all done with an ostensibly adult snicker that shows he would not have dreamed of giving a copy of "Sawdust and Sin" either to Charlotte or to her older brother. The story fits well, thus, into *The Yellow Book,* and one can feel justified in preferring either the frank decadence of Beardsley's drawings or the totally repressed sexuality of a contemporary book like Frances Hodgson Burnett's *The Secret Garden.*

But the stories are seldom as bad as "Sawdust and Sin," and Grahame can occasionally use his blend of child and adult narrator to real advantage. In "Dies Irae," for instance, the boy has begun his day of wrath by gloomy brooding. He wanders outdoors oblivious of his surroundings because he is busily fantasizing revenges against aunts and others like aunts:

> A well-aimed clod of garden soil, whizzing just past my ear, starred on a tree-trunk behind, spattering me with dirt. The present came back to me in a flash, and I nimbly took cover behind the trees, realising that the enemy was up and abroad, with ambuscades, alarms, and thrilling sallies. It was the gardener's boy, I knew well enough; a red proletarian, who hated me just because I was a gentleman. Hastily picking up a nice sticky clod in one hand, with the other I delicately projected my hat beyond the shelter of the tree-trunk. I had not fought with Red Indians all these years for nothing.

Here too a hierarchy is made, but the gardener's boy, unlike Charlotte, isn't really ridiculed, not even when he fails to distinguish a hat from a human head:

> As I had expected, another clod, of the first class for size and stickiness, took my poor hat in the centre. Then, Ajax-

like, shouting terribly, I issued from my shelter and discharged my ammunition. Woe then for the gardener's boy, who, unprepared, skipping in premature triumph, took the clod full in the stomach! He, the foolish one, witless on whose side the gods were fighting that day, discharged yet other missiles, wavering and wide of the mark; for his wind had been taken away with the first clod, and he shot wildly, as one already desperate and in flight.

The superiority of the gentleman to the gardener's boy is what it should be. He has read more stories, fought more Red Indians, learned about Ajax and the gods, and so knows an epic battle when he sees one and that the gods fight on different sides on different days. The style includes the gardener's boy rather than ridicules him, and so everything that shows the narrator is an adult as well as a boy shows only the boyishness of both.

In "Sawdust and Sin" the hierarchy makes a leer, while in "Dies Irae" it celebrates release, the fantastic becomes real, the gods become defenders in which anyone might wish to believe. With a writer like Lewis Carroll, leering can be a fascinating and poignant activity—as with Alice and the Duchess, or the Gnat—but with Grahame it is only a nasty trifling. He needed situations and materials in which he could be more open, where the pleasure of creating hierarchies was mostly the pleasure of being inside a charmed circle, as with the gentleman lad in "Dies Irae," and thus beyond care, however momentarily, and beyond snobbery or snickering. In these early books, or so it seems to me, only in "Dies Irae" and "The Roman Road," where a boy and a man discuss the places they'd like to go, does the open enjoyment of wanting bring pleasure free from any attendant restrictive absorption with victims, or from a nostalgia where there is no circle and the charm is all a blur.

In the decade after *The Golden Age* and *Dream Days* Grahame's life contrived to make him feel more alone and unhappy, more in need of flight and escape. After his marriage he drifted away from Furnivall and Henley and many of his bachelor friends with whom he had walked the Berkshire Ridgeway or messed about in boats on the Thames or on the Fowey in Cornwall. He also accepted a relation for which he was emotionally unfit and in which he was, apparently, sexually hopeless. After she had noted a lack of interest in him, he wrote back: "It sums it up, wot you say bout 'abit o not being interested 'speshly wen its cuppled wif much natral 'gaucherie' wot as never been strove against." The two may never have spoken openly to one another. Their child, Alistair, might serve to hold the marriage together, but only by becoming a terrible victim of his parents' separate wishes for him. Grahame's financial security was hard to enjoy since he felt hemmed in, unable to up and leave his family as his father had done, unable to stay and be the husband and father at least a part of him wished to be. It is not pleasant to think of *The Wind in the Willows* as the work of a man becoming increasingly miserable, but such seems to have been the case; he began the work as stories told in letters to Alistair to placate him and his mother for Grahame's spending so much time away from them.

Since *The Wind in the Willows* did begin in this fashion, it superficially resembles Milne's Pooh books and J. R. R. Tolkien's *The Hobbit*, all being stories fathers told their sons, written by men who never thought of themselves as authors of children's books. The resemblance, however, may be one reason people have been mistaken about *The Wind in the Willows*. Ostensibly Grahame is inventing a world to enchant his son of six or seven, but actually he is describing a world he himself had lived in so completely that it seems false to say he invented it; he had been Rat, Mole, Badger, and Toad. Somewhat nervous about its reception, Grahame himself wrote on the dust jacket that the book is "perhaps chiefly for youth," but it was really written for himself and it usually fails to please a child who has just been delighted by the Pooh books and *The Hobbit*. But thereby lies the reason for its superiority to these other books: it has none of the superior tone that mars Milne's book or the smugness that hurts Tolkien's. It is *about* coziness, but it never seeks an uncomfortably cozy relation with its reader or listener. Its best audience is certain children, or adolescents, or adults, people of a particular sort or in a particular mood. If there is a "good age" to give a "child" *The Wind in the Willows*, it is not the age of Alistair Grahame when he first heard it, but twelve- or thirteen-year-olds, boys especially, who need to be told or reassured that the demands of adult life—work, sex, family, aging—which loom so frighteningly for them are in fact capable of frightening everyone. If one is rather doubtful about one's suitableness as an adult, one can be enthralled by *The Wind in the Willows,* and in this as in a number of other interesting respects it resembles two books that have never been thought of as fit reading for children, John Cleland's *Fanny Hill* and Hemingway's *The Sun Also Rises.* Like the *Alice* books, it is too personal, too signed by the needs of its author, to be a children's book as the Pooh or Oz books are.

By the time Grahame wrote *The Wind in the Willows* he was almost fifty and able to see that he was, in certain important respects, never going to "grow up." He also could see the ways in which the demands of maturing could no longer levy on him as strongly as they once had. He was what he was, he loved what he loved, which is why this book is much less self-conscious and satiric than the earlier ones. "I love these little people, be kind to them," he told Ernest H. Shepard when Shepard came to see him near the end of his life to ask permission to illustrate *The Wind in the Willows,* illustrations, incidentally, so good they seem to belong to the book as much as Tenniel's of Alice or John R. Neill's of Oz. In one particular way, it seems a ripe book, mature: it has an unerring sense of season and of the effect certain seasons can have on us irrespective of the demands of work or school. "The River Bank" in early spring, "Wayfarers All" in October, "Dulce Domum" at Christmas, are perfect expressions of a seasonal mood. If for no other reason, *The Wind in the Willows* is part of the ongoing emotional equipment of those who love it; there are many times and situations that recall its characters and scenes with vividness and fondness. Its sense of fun carries with it a sense of belonging, of the deep rightness of this kind of pleasure.

In his biography of Grahame Peter Green plausibly reconstructs the order in which the chapters of *The Wind in the Willows* were written. First came the adventures of Mr. Toad, which were the letters sent to Alistair, chapters 2, 6, 8, 10–12, or about half the book. Next came the chapters dominated by the friendship of Rat and Mole, 1 and 3–5, which for me are the heart of the book. Last came chapters 7 and 9, "The Piper at the Gates of Dawn" and "Wayfarers All," written most frankly out of personal compulsions of Grahame's and quite unreflective of any desire to tell stories to Alistair or to write a book "perhaps chiefly for youth." But in the book as Grahame finally assembled it, the divisions I have named are not as evident as the division into something like two halves. Up to chapter 7, "The Piper," everything is of a very high order, and the early Toad episodes blend splendidly with those centered on Rat and Mole. After "The Piper," Grahame seems less certain, more forced into letting Toad dominate and into letting plot play an unwontedly large role. Ask any lover of the book to name the most memorable parts, and the answer will invariably be scenes from the first half, even though the halves were never constructed as such by Grahame.

The special and enduring pleasure of *The Wind in the Willows* is an invitation into an enclosed space, and from its first pages Rat is the essential inviter, and Mole the essential enterer:

> "Lean on that!" he said. "Now then, step lively!" and the Mole to his surprise and rapture found himself actually seated in the stern of a real boat.
>
> "This has been a wonderful day!" said he, as the Rat shoved off and took to the sculls again. "Do you know, I've never been in a boat before in all my life!"

The day has kept opening up wonderfully for Mole: he has reneged on his spring housecleaning and come above ground, chaffed some rabbits and discovered the river, and now he has stepped into a real boat. Something close to this could easily have happened to Grahame with F. J. Furnivall. "Lean on that!" and "Step lively!" mean Mole has become an initiate, and Mole is only delighted as Rat keeps making it clear he is only on an outer threshold " 'What?' cried the Rat, open-mouthed: 'Never been in a—you never—well, I—what have you been doing then?' " Rat's consternation is strong enough to dissolve his usual simple politeness, and Mole is so impressed by the consternation he does not notice Rat's insult of his way of life:

> "Is it so nice as all that?" asked the Mole shyly, though he was quite prepared to believe it as he leant back in his seat and surveyed the cushions, the oars, the row-locks, and all the fascinating fittings, and felt the boat sway lightly under him.
>
> "Nice? It's the *only* thing," said the Water Rat solemnly, as he leant forward for his stroke. "Believe me, my young

friend, there is *nothing*—absolutely nothing—half so much worth doing as simply messing about in boats."

As an insider it is not Rat's task to persuade, advertise, or inventory activities. He gestures only, and it is Grahame's task to make the gestures seem sufficient: " 'Whether you get away or whether you don't; whether you arrive at your destination or whether you reach somewhere else, or whether you never get anywhere at all, you're always busy, and you never do anything in particular.' " This does not describe messing about in boats. It says, rather, why there is no need for such a description, because messing about in boats abolishes destination, time, and purpose, and that is the point of doing it.

Nature does not quite create such rivers, but the Thames as Grahame knew it was just such a place, a warren of streams, weirs, locks, and marshes that had been created to make purposeful navigation possible and that also made purposeless navigation delightful. Given such possibilities, "nice" is an inadequate word, and activity is just a series of doings connected with "or": on the river one does this or that or the other, and it does not matter which. There is nothing essentially boyish about Rat and his pleasures here, and certainly nothing childish or childlike. The boyishness, the childlikeness, is all in Mole:

> The Mole waggled his toes from sheer happiness, spread his chest with a sigh of full contentment, and leaned back blissfully into the soft cushions. *"What* a day I'm having!" he said. "Let us start at once!"

It is hard to praise Mole enough here. The river and Rat are so inviting that anyone might feel delight in their company, but to admit one's delight, to share it without shame—that is hard, and rare, and completing.

So Rat packs lunch:

> "What's inside it?" asked the Mole, wiggling with curiosity.
>
> "There's cold chicken inside it," replied Rat briefly; "coldtonguecoldhamcoldbeefpickledgherkinssaladfrenchrollscresssandwidgespottedmeatgingerbeerlemonadesodawater—"

> "O stop, stop," cried the Mole in ecstasies: "This is too much!"

Come inside the charmed circle and there is everything, including the longest of words. Mole, an outsider but no stranger to English buffet lunches, cannot contain his delight at being continually asked to step over the line Rat keeps drawing. This is freedom, newness, springtime, friendship, and all Mole needs for his passport is his own modesty upon being asked. How wonderful, one feels, to be Mole, to be thus invited and thus accepting; the joining and sharing in things makes one feel, for once, fully alive.

What difference does it make that these characters are a rat and a mole? They speak, wear clothes, scull, pack cold lunches, and wish they could afford black velvet smoking jackets. They are much more like human beings, and individual human types, than Beatrix Potter's animals. Yet it will not do to say they are human beings, because Grahame's fantasy depends on his being able to give them so much because they are not human, because he does not have to give them an age, a biography, a past for which they might have to feel guilty, or a future they must anticipate. These are the basic freedoms which then create the possibility of those other freedoms we have just seen: messing about in boats, enjoying a full larder, making a new life, for oneself, for someone else.

So Rat and Mole are not human, for all their human apparatus. They are also, in a dimmer sense, animals, as Rat reveals when he begins to describe what lies outside the charmed circle, starting with some residents of the Wild Wood, on the opposite side of the river from Mole's house:

> "Well, of course—there—are—others," explained the Rat in a hesitating sort of way. "Weasels—and—stoats—and foxes—and so on. They're all right in a way—I'm very good friends with them—pass the time of day when we meet and all that—but they break out sometimes, there's no denying it, and then—well, you can't really trust them, and that's the fact."

Rat here resembles an Englishman describing French and Germans, but what he says is also based on the natural fact that weasels, stoats, and foxes all kill rats, so that when Rat says these others "break out sometimes," he is being English, politely understating the nasty truth, but without any taint of English insularity or prejudice. Mole then remembers "it is quite against animal etiquette to dwell on possible trouble ahead, or even to allude to it." Grahame here is touching on precisely the point Potter raises when Peter and Benjamin find the rabbit bones and skulls outside Mr. Tod's house, but his way is almost the opposite of hers. Where Potter wants to voice a horror and to find a limit to that horror, Grahame wants to have it both ways, to elevate both animal and human possibility. It is fun, but irresponsible, for human beings to ignore the future, especially the natural fact of death. Animals have, on the other hand, only the most instinctive sense of any future, nothing more than a pregnant female preparing a home, or birds migrating. Grahame's animal etiquette resembles English manners in insisting on the virtue of understatement, but it carries with it something much more important to Grahame than that: the freedom to ignore the future by not speaking of it, so that if this weekend must end, or if weasels kill rats, it is best we not even think of it. The abolition of worry about the future without abolishing the knowledge that day will break, or that summer will follow spring, encloses Grahame's animals in a secure present where all time is rhythmic time, and rhythmic time brings all the changes one needs.

Freed from the future just as Mole has been freed from his past, the two can go on so Rat can draw another boundary and secure another enclosed space:

> "Beyond the Wild Wood comes the Wide World," said the Rat. "And that's something that doesn't matter, either to you or me. I've never been there, and I'm never going, nor you either if you've got any sense at all. Don't ever refer to it again, please. Now then! Here's our backwater at last, where we're going to have lunch."

The backwater in question has such human-made objects as a weir and a mill wheel, but they, clearly, are all right, because they are far from the Wide World, London, and the Bank of England. It is possible to stand next to the Thames, near Grahame's childhood home in Cookham Dean or his last home in Pangbourne, and feel the scale reduce itself just as Rat dictates: a weir or a canal creates a back-water, and there are woods beyond. Not far off are Maidenhead, and Windsor Castle, and the Great Western Railway, but as one stares at the quiet water, and the reeds, and the willows lining the bank, one feels the pleasure not just of quiet beauty but of being able to say: "I know you're there, nearby even, but I'm here, and staying here."

Such pleasures, lived on such a small scale, must be active to be fully felt, so that stepping inside the charmed circle and seeing the boundary drawn can feel liberating rather than confining, at which point the unwanted is excluded and the circle can be explored. In the opening chapter, one of the finest openings to any book, Grahame keeps inviting, drawing a boundary, making those pleasures into relief and release. After sculling, lunch; and after lunch, meeting the society of the river—Otter appears and disappears with graceful lack of announcement, news comes of Toad out sculling, Badger appears briefly, then departs, and Rat must explain that Badger, a denizen of the Wild Wood, "hates society." All the while we understand, as Mole does, that we are learning about the limits of enclosed space without ever arriving at a definition of what belongs inside it. But we understand more than Mole does about all this. This is the greatest day of Mole's life, and "The River Bank" is also one of the great opening chapters of any reader's reading life. But what is to follow? We know that the great failing of invented ideal worlds is not in their opening chapters but in what follows, in their tendency to become dull once we have become accustomed to their ways and means. All too often, we know, the original sensation of release—how wonderful to be free to do this, to leave all that behind —is followed by other feelings—that the space is too narrow, the blessed activity too repetitive, such that we long to return to uncertainty, hope, doubt, and despair, the future even. If Grahame's opening chapter is exhilarating, he succeeds in it in ways others have succeeded too.

Sensing his situation and its problem, Grahame introduces us to the perpetually outside insider, Mr. Toad. We know, of course, that Grahame began with Toad when writing to Alistair, but when he made a book that could embody his own deepest longings, he rightly shifted Mr. Toad from the center of attention and placed him to one side. We hear of him first from Otter's announcement that he is out on the river: "Such a good fellow, too, but no stability—especially in a boat." The phrase "good fellow" reads like a code word here, an insider's phrase, such that neither we nor Mole expect to understand it fully the first time around. We do gather, though, that "no stability" is a pun, of Grahame's and perhaps of Otter's, because not only is Mr. Toad liable to tip over in a boat, but he also is always searching for new things to do. He has sailed and houseboated in the past, and the other animals expect he will soon tire of sculling, and before he learns to manage the oars. To reinforce his point about the virtues of stability, Grahame has Mole suddenly imagine he has become a master of the oars after only one afternoon; he soon tips the boat over, and Rat has to haul him out. But Mole is a "good fellow," and learns his lessons quickly. Mastery comes through repetition, and repeated actions are the best because they teach you how to live in your landscape.

But with Toad we are not immediately clear where to stand. In the second chapter Mole says he would like to be introduced to Toad, having heard so much about him. Of course, Rat answers:

> "It's never the wrong time to call on Toad. Early or late he's always the same fellow. Always good-tempered, always glad to see you, always sorry when you go . . . He is indeed the best of animals . . . So simple, so good-natured, and so affectionate. Perhaps he's not very clever—we can't all be geniuses; and it may be he is both boastful and conceited. But he has got some great qualities, has Toady."

When Rat described the stoats and weasels he drew a boundary— "They're all right in a way" but they "break out"—and we and Mole could see where and why the line is drawn so stoats and weasels will be on the other side. But it is different with Toad. "Simple" may mean "so good-natured, and so affectionate," but it is not clear how "best of animals" equals "not very clever" and "boastful and conceited." Rat is inside the circle, but we cannot see if Toad is inside or outside it. So we need to go see him, and for at least two chapters Grahame does marvelously at placing and re-placing Toad for us.

Toad is "Mr. Toad," he lives in magnificent Toad Hall, but no one ever condemns him for being rich and living ostentatiously; anyone might enjoy such splendor at least some of the time. It is the instability that is bothersome; when Rat and Mole first visit Toad Hall the boathouse has "an unused and a deserted air," because Toad has given up boats altogether. But Toad greets his visitors like "the best of animals," gives them lunch, and exultantly shows them his new toy, a gypsy caravan:

> "There's real life for you, embodied in that little cart. The open road, the dusty highway, the heath, the common, the hedgerows, the rolling downs! Camps, villages, towns, cities! Here today, up and off somewhere else tomorrow!"

The life of the open road might seem to embody instability as a principle, but clearly, also, it resembles messing about in boats; you go, and it doesn't matter where you get to because there is so much to see and do all the time. Mole, always eager to be invited, longs for the open road as he longed for the life on the river, but Rat, who knows more than Mole about this best of animals, has to be coaxed into going. For two days the open road is delightful; the animals ride, and tramp, and greet other animals, and delight in the fresh air. On the first night out, as they are going to sleep, Toad exults:

> "Well, good night, you fellows! This is the real life for a gentleman! Talk about your old river!"
>
> "I *don't* talk about my river," replied the patient Rat. "You *know* I don't, Toad. But I *think* about it," he added pathetically, in a lower tone: "I think about it—all the time!"

Toad's search, we see, is for "real life," while Rat's is not a search at all. Presumably he does not talk about the river because that would make him boastful, like Toad, a possessor of activities and places; presumably, too, he does not think about the river *all* the time, but it is always there, inside him, defining him.

On the third day out the animals hear a loud "Poop-poop," and the caravan is suddenly upset by a speeding automobile. Rat and Mole look at the wrecked caravan and see it is time to return home, but Toad is not the least dismayed as he sprawls on the dusty highway:

> "I've done with carts forever. I never want to see the cart, or to hear of it, again. O Ratty! You can't think how obliged I am to you for consenting to come on this trip! I

wouldn't have gone without you, and then I might never have seen that—that swan, that sunbeam, that thunderbolt! I might never have heard that entrancing sound, or smelt that bewitching smell! I owe it all to you, my best of friends!"

Now "boastful and conceited," "always happy to see you," and "best of friends" all fall into place. Toad's conceit lies in his being unable to consider anyone but himself, his pleasure lies in his easy willingness to share his joy, even to give Rat credit for it. Unstable he is, so hedgerows and downs give way to swans, sunbeams, and thunderbolts, but constant he is too, in the innocent friendliness with which he conveys and shares his passions.

It is easy, we now see, to exclude the Wide World; one just messes about in boats or has lunch and all thought of it is gone. It is not difficult, apparently, to exclude weasels and stoats, because their natural instinct is to be predators, and to "break out," water rats being their prey. If all animals were simply to obey their instincts, however, then Rat and Mole would never meet, and there would be no holiday. To enjoy their lives the animals must not just professionally do as they are naturally fitted to do; they must also be amateurs, more "human," and lead life as a series of charmed possibilities. For precisely these reasons Toad cannot be easily excluded. He cares nothing for the Wide World, he is a gentleman, an amateur above all, fully enjoying what he does. He shares easily, he goes his own way, he never pries into the private concerns of others. Grahame presents him so that in a great many ways he resembles Rat. To rule him out would be most unfriendly, since it would in effect be insisting that everyone be like everyone else.

Yet Toad is dangerous. We may think at first that his defect is flightiness and faddishness as he goes from one exciting activity to the next, always scorning everything he did previously. But after Toad discovers automobiles he never develops another interest, because Grahame wants to define the problem involved here more precisely. Toad buys cars, he wrecks them, he is a menace on the highway, but he is constant to his love. His dangerousness lies in the source and the uncontrollableness of his passion. He has no natural instinct to guide him, and he has a profound and pathetic inability to resist what he mistakenly assumes are his greatest inner needs. Thus, in chapter 6, "Mr. Toad," after Badger, Rat, and Mole incarcerate him in Toad Hall, and after Toad himself seems willing to admit he has been victimized by a terrible malady, his passion leads him to escape from the others and then to become a car thief:

> Next moment, hardly knowing how it came about, he found he had hold of the handle and was turning it. As the familiar sound broke forth, the old passion seized on Toad and completely mastered him, body and soul. As if in a dream he found himself, somehow, seated in the driver's seat; as if in a dream he pulled the lever and swung the car round the yard and out through the archway; and, as if in a dream, all sense of right and wrong, all fear of obvious consequences, seemed temporarily suspended. He increased his pace, and as the car devoured the street and leapt forth on the high road through the open country, he was only conscious that he was Toad once more, Toad at his best and highest, Toad the terror, the traffic-queller, the Lord of the lone trail, before whom all must give way or be smitten into nothingness and everlasting night.

It is one of the best moments in the book, Grahame's version of hell. Like all well-conceived hells, it closely resembles heaven. Every gesture here invites, draws a boundary, and excludes the unwanted outside world, so that the grammar of hell and heaven are precisely the same. Thus Toad can never be excluded from the society of the other animals. What differentiates heaven from hell is what is excluded and included. Inside Toad's passion there is only Toad. In this passage we focus first on the car, the handle, the driver's seat, the ignition; but gradually the car disappears, having succeeded in obliterating everything else in the world: "he was Toad once more, Toad at his best and highest, Toad the terror." Perhaps the most deceiving aspect of such passions is that they convince us we are most alive, most ourselves, when we are in fact most mastered, most not ourselves. "The car responded with sonorous drone, the miles were eaten up under him as he sped he knew not whither"; that *seems* like "whether you arrive at your destination or whether you reach somewhere else . . . you're always busy and never do anything in particular," and Grahame never once implies Rat is better because he does not play with complicated twentieth-century machines. But Rat is always looking outward, keeping his windows clean and his ears waxed, delighting in whatever the river and its banks happen to show him, which is why it is possible for him to say "I think about it—all the time!" Toad is concerned with his own pulse rate and delights only in whatever can raise it to new heights; he is bored and twitchy all the rest of the time, since now he has found his "real life." Passion, the great excluder, is thus for Grahame the great enemy, because its dangers lie within us and can never be ruled out just by drawing a boundary or evolving an etiquette that agrees not to discuss the future. To be free, to be released, to live in the present—these are crucial for both Rat and Toad. Toad's is a perversion of a way of life of which Rat is the deepest embodiment.

But here, in this passage, Grahame reaches one of his limits. It is the nature of passions that, once their temptations have been given in to, little good can result for very long, so Toad soon ends up in the dock. It is also the nature of passions to become repetitive, so that once Toad has become "Toad at his best and highest," neither Toad nor Grahame can do more than to try to climb the mountain again and again, so the adventures of Mr. Toad must become the further adventures of Mr. Toad, and these must consist mostly of the frustrations and miseries of Toad as he is kept from getting into cars. When such passions are the subject of works whose scale is larger than Grahame's they are the stuff of high tragedy; we can watch for the length of an entire work the fatal consequences of the initial passions of Faustus or Macbeth. Of course none of that is wanted here, since Toad's passion is designed to seem only the serpent in the garden of Grahame's paradise. The trouble is that after this moment of Toad's fulfillment all we can have is Toad in jail, Toad making a car out of a railroad, Toad with the barge woman, Toad regaining Toad Hall from the weasels and stoats. Perhaps he is chastened at last, but the book must end lamely since a chastened Toad is of no interest; and the unchastened Toad has had too many tales told of him already. In *The Sun Also Rises* Hemingway handles his outside insider, Robert Cohn, with greater tact and never allows Cohn to occupy the center of the stage, as Grahame does let Toad do in the later chapters. He belongs, to repeat, over to one side, and Rat and Mole belong at the center.

We have hardly done enough thus far, however, to celebrate Rat and Mole. If *The Wind in the Willows* were only the stunning opening chapter, and the two chapters with Toad before he reaches the height of his passion, the book would not be the irreplaceable work I think it is. But this is not all, and in the other non-Toad chapters Grahame tries to find ways to keep his animals inside their boundaries and, at the same time, describe their responses to impulses as powerful in their way as Toad's. Of the five chapters involved at least three seem totally successful: "The Wild Wood," "Mr. Badger," and "Dulce Domum." The other two, "The Piper at the Gates of Dawn" and "Wayfarers All," are very attractive in part, but in them Grahame is trying to do what is really beyond his capacities. Let us look at an example of each. First "Dulce Domum," the gem of the book, Grahame's wonderful story of Rat's success at the apparently impossible task of inviting Mole into his own home.

Caught in the "rapid nightfall of mid-December," far from their river home, Rat and Mole trudge through a village where a canary in a cage reminds them of how snug and warm it is to be indoors. As they go on, Rat in the lead, Mole is struck and then overwhelmed by a series of scents that come over him. He soon interprets them to mean home, his home, his old home in the ground: "Poor Mole stood alone in the road, his heart torn asunder, and a big sob gathering, gathering, somewhere low down inside him, to leap up to the surface presently, he knew, in passionate escape." This designedly resembles Toad's response when he first hears the "poop-poop" of the automobile, but it is noteworthy that Mole is not so much excited as made miserable: "But even under such a test as this his loyalty to his friend stood firm. Never for a moment did he dream of abandoning him. Meanwhile, the wafts from his old home pleaded, whispered, conjured, and finally claimed him imperiously. He dared not tarry longer within their magic circle." The word "imperiously" is an important one for Grahame. He uses it in the opening pages to describe the way Mole is commanded by the spring to leave his housecleaning and come above ground and go to the river. There, as here, the power that does the commanding is every bit as great as the passion of Toad, but it is located outside the characters, in the world, as part of the great creation of nature. The imperious command to return to one's natural habitat is made stronger here because it is December, and cold, and all living things are seeking home as their refuge.

Mole breaks away from the magic circle of the imperious smells, catches up with Rat, but then breaks down:

> "I know it's a—shabby, dingy little place," he sobbed forth at last, brokenly: "not like—your cozy quarters—or Toad's beautiful hall—or Badger's great house—but it was my own little home—and I was fond of it—and I went away and forgot all about it—and then I smelt it suddenly—on the road, when I called and you wouldn't listen, Rat—and everything came back to me with a rush—and I *wanted* it!"

This is the perfect speech to contrast with Toad's triumphant conversion to the automobile. Mole is not in heaven here, but he is a candidate for admission. What shames Mole is a power strong enough to break down his duty as Rat's friend to keep up and not to bother anyone else with his private troubles. The network of pleasures and loyalties the animals work so hard to build cannot resist such power, which is why Mole is so miserable. But Rat, best of animals, knows the crucial difference between seeking passion as a form of excitement and giving into imperial powers naturally greater than oneself. The opposite of the amateur pleasures is not anything professional, but a power essentially religious. So, insisting that Mole blow his nose to keep it keen so it can guide them, Rat takes over, himself having only to obey the need to be loyal to his friend.

When they arrive at Mole's house Mole must go on being ashamed, because all he can see is a "poor, cold little place." Rat, however, kind beyond thanks, dissolves Mole's shame, not by cheering him up but by discovering the pleasures of Mole End: "So compact! So well planned! Everything here and everything in its place!" He sets out to build a fire, gets Mole to dust the furniture, but Mole discovers a new shame: there is no food. Rat, having just seen an opener for a sardine can, insists there must be sardines somewhere. Indeed, after "hunting through every cupboard . . . the result was not so very depressing after all, though of course it might have been better." Not "coldhamcoldtonguecoldbeefpickledgherkins," and all the rest of Rat's picnic, but sardines, a box of biscuits, and a German sausage. Rat keeps on drawing the circles, inviting Mole across his own threshold, recreating the splendors of home and thereby recreating the purpose and possibility of friendship:

> "No bread!" groaned the Mole dolorously; "no butter, no—"
>
> "No *pâté de fois gras,* no champagne!" continued the Rat, grinning. "Ah, that reminds me—what's that little door at the end of the passage? Your cellar, of course! Every luxury in this house! Just you wait a minute."

Down Rat goes, and back he comes, a bottle of beer in each hand, and one under each arm:

> "Self-indulgent beggar you seem to be, Mole," he observed. "Deny yourself nothing. This is really the jolliest place I ever was in. Now wherever did you pick up those prints. Make the place so home-like, they do. No wonder you're so fond of it, Mole. Tell us all about it, and how you came to make it what it is."

In these pages Grahame makes home both richly nostalgic and actively alive in the present. One wants to keep cheering Rat on to find more things to love, and one wants also to weep, as one's gratitude for Rat reveals the knowledge that no homecoming, no friendship, could ever quite be this good.

Then, at the end, it is the Christmas season. A group of field mice appear outside, singing carols, and Mole and Rat are delighted to see them until Mole remembers how bare his larder is and how little he can give the mice. Again Rat leaps to the occasion: "Here, you with the lantern! Come over this way. I want to talk to you. Now, tell me, are there any shops open at this hour of the night?' " The English are famous for shutting their shops at the slightest hint of a customary excuse or a holiday, but Grahame, self-indulgent beggar himself, concedes everything: " 'Why certainly, sir,' replied the field-mouse respectfully. 'At this time of year our shops keep open to all sorts of hours.' " No enchantment in a fairy tale, no magic picture in Oz, is more magical or enchanting than this discovery that the shops are open: "Here much muttered conversation ensued, and the Mole only heard bits of it, such as 'Fresh, mind!—no, a pound of that will do—see you get Buggins's, for I won't have any other—no, only the best—if you can't get it there, try somewhere else—yes, of course, home-made, no tinned stuff—well then, do the best you can!' " This is the triumph of snugness; the shops are all the shops in the world. They are good sturdy village shops where one can expect to find something homemade, not tinned, a meat pie perhaps. They are also market-town shops and can be expected to cater to the gentry and keep Buggins's in stock; Buggins's makes marmalade, maybe, or chutney. They are also as grand as Fortnum and Mason's and can be expected to have fresh food in the dead of winter, not just bread or apples, but tomatoes or lettuce. Only by having his scale so small can Grahame make such pleasures seem to mean everything. Only by longing for such pleasures himself could he have wanted them at all, as a last magical Christmas present, from Rat to Mole: all the dreams of home. What begins as the summons of an imperial power ends as the relaxed intense excitement of giving to a friend what he could not, were he the mightiest or most wealthy, give to himself.

But this sense of imperious powers in nature haunted Grahame, and he could not rest content with having that power be whatever drove Mole up out of his hole and then drove him back down into it. Grahame came to his world of the river and the woods with thanksgiving, he entered its courts with praise, and so he wanted to name its god. Thus, after the splendid burrowings into the houses of Mr. Badger and Mole, he makes an attempt to soar, in "The Piper at the Gates of Dawn," as high above the earth as the other chapters go beneath it. This chapter divides the book; before it we have Grahame at his very best, in all the ways we have seen thus far, and after it we have the later and less interesting Toad stories. In "The Piper" Grahame rather self-consciously tries to justify his excursions into cozy fantasy when, in fact, no such justification was needed.

It is a summer evening, and it feels, even late at night, as though the sun has never quite left this spot of earth. Rat and Mole hear that Otter's son Portly is lost, and, worried and unable to sleep, they set out to try to find him. As they row up the river, it begins to get light in the east, and Rat hears a noise, a bird maybe, the wind in the reeds: " 'Now it passes on and I begin to lose it,' he said presently. 'O Mole! the beauty of it! The merry bubble and joy, the thin, clear, happy call of the distant piping! Such music I never dreamed of, and the call in it is stronger even than the music is sweet!' " Once again, the imperious power. Mole, who only smells his powerful callers, hears only "the wind playing in the reeds and rushes and osiers," but Rat needs more, a religious summons. This is a strain in Rat that has been there all along—in his dreaming off at the very beginning while telling Mole about messing about in boats, in his writing poetry when the fit seizes him—but it seems more a part of Grahame himself than something he can make actively a part of Rat's character. We can concede Rat's "I think about it—all the time!" certainly, but this more ethereal propensity seems just not to belong. Thus, when Rat and Mole, following the piping music only Rat hears, arrive at their destination, it does not sound like Rat who is speaking: " 'This is the place of my song-dream, the place the music played to me,' whispered the Rat, as if in a trance. 'Here, in this holy place, here if anywhere, surely we shall find Him.' " We hardly seem to be in *The Wind in the Willows* at all.

It would be easy enough to explain it away. We could go back to Grahame's first book, *Pagan Papers*, and to quite a few other *fin de siècle* writers who seem to lapse into a soft religion that was not quite nature, not quite out of this world, but an aestheticism about nature; Water Pater's hard gemlike flame is very much akin to Grahame here. Yet we should trace it a little further in "The Piper" before making such a dismissal. As Rat and Mole come to the island to which they have been summoned, they see "the very eyes of the Friend and Helper," complete with horns and rippling muscles and shaggy limbs. Then:

> . . . last of all, nestling between his very hooves, sleeping soundly in entire peace and contentment, the little, round, podgy, childish form of the baby otter. All this he saw, for one moment breathless and intense, vivid on the morning sky; and still, as he looked, he lived; and still, as he lived, he wondered.
>
> "Rat!" he found breath to whisper, shaking. "Are you afraid?"

"Afraid?" murmured the Rat, his eyes shining with unutterable love. "Afraid! Of *Him?* O never, never! And yet—
and yet—O Mole, I am afraid!"

No one not already a worshipper of Pan would actually prefer this
Rat, this Mole, this writing, to "The River Bank" or "Dulce
Domum." The adjectives—"very," "entire," "unutterable"—all
show a straining toward a feeling that by its thrilled vagueness makes
us remember how much, elsewhere in the book, Grahame can convey with language only slightly more pinned down. Grahame may
say Mole and Rat are afraid, but he himself is not; he is only thrilled
at the possibility of feeling such fear.

The trouble is the context, or, in this case, the feebleness of the
context. When, in the opening pages, Mole says, "So this—is—a—
River!" and Rat answers, "*The* River," we have already enough of
Mole's life underground, and we soon will have enough of Rat's life
on the river, so that this language, which out of context is no clearer
than that in the passage above, can remain gesture and still seem
precise enough to describe the relation of Rat to Mole and the de-
sirability of that relation's developing. Surprisingly little of the book,
as it evolves, is actually about life on the river, but that does not
matter seriously, since we have also evolving alongside the relation
of Rat and Mole. But here, because the experience is religious, that
relation necessarily matters less, and so we must try to look at Pan
himself to see what Grahame is caring about, and of course Pan
himself is, and probably must be, vague. The young otter is there,
protected by Pan the Friend and Helper, but even he, the most clearly
seen figure in the scene, is only putative; we know nothing of him,
and Rat and Mole are looking for him mostly because it is a restless
summer night, not because they know where or how to look for
him. In other words, the imperious command does not arise out of
anything, or, really, lead to anything beyond a rescued Porky. Pan
simply is, and we must take him or leave him. Even the relation of
Pan to the dawn is more suggested than carefully realized.

I don't for a minute think that in any serious way Grahame believed in Pan or in any other deity. What he knew was the intensity
of his own longings to live life as an escape, as holiday, as Rat
and Mole can live it and Toad cannot. He was not ashamed either

of the feelings or of the intensity. Still, one of the secrets of the power of the release was some sense that grown people are not supposed to yearn that much for something that many other grown people see as the yearnings of a child. If everyone in Grahame's England had been like F. J. Furnivall, Grahame would never have been driven to become an author, or at least not the author of *The Wind in the Willows*. But everyone wasn't like Furnivall; other people took and gave orders, accepted work as a sacred duty, and expected others to agree with them. Grahame did all these things, too, and part of him believed in doing so, but the greater part of him felt himself to be an exile from a world, a childhood, a Thames life, he had never quite lived in. Lonely and unhappy, possessed by longings, he was driven to justify them. The first six chapters of *The Wind in the Willows* were the only justification he needed, but he was driven to insist on more than this. There is no radical defect involved here, only a reminder that books like this one are often written by huddled, self-protective people who can be driven toward a definition of a vaguely understood "higher experience."

How odd, thus, that someone whose writing was so personal should ever have been thought of essentially as a writer for children. If Grahame "understood children," it was not because he liked them, enjoyed their presence, or even thought about them. Rather, because he was deprived of much that goes into the usual experiences of a childhood, he remained something of a child throughout his life, perceptibly more so than the rest of us. This can be said of Lewis Carroll, too, but he was too powerful and too quirky a writer to settle for trying to create in his books a world he actually wanted to live in. Generally, it is a diminishing thing in a writer to seek to do this, because it allows the edges of the imagination to go soft and remain untested, and it is usually very difficult to tell stories that take place in ideal worlds. But Grahame did just this, and in its finest moments *The Wind in the Willows* creates and sustains a genuine ideal, one that is going to continue to appeal strongly to many people, for centuries perhaps. To be rid of the cares of personality and responsibility, to forget or never know yesterday's wrongdoings or tomorrow's needs—it is a great wish, close to universal perhaps. Later, in L. Frank Baum, we will encounter another writer who wrote in obedience to this wish, though in a different way from Grahame's entirely. Most writers and most people find that when they have tossed off adult tasks and human curses they have, left over, only a rather empty space. But Grahame could fill that space and invite us into the charmed circle he thereby created. He could make little sounds seem like bustle, make gestures of invitation seem like love, make food and fire feel like home.

(8) Kipling's Boys

> Now this is the Law of the Jungle—as old and as true as
>   the sky;
> And the Wolf that shall keep it may prosper, but the Wolf
>   that shall break it must die.
> As the creeper that girdles the tree-trunk the Law runneth
>   forward and back—
> For the strength of the Pack is the Wolf, and the strength
>   of the Wolf is the Pack.

These loose, thrilling, and easily memorized couplets, so quickly recognizable as Kipling's, intone values they do not explain and imply that no explanation is necessary. They, and many other snips of poetry, excited two generations with passion, even reverence. It was Kipling's magic that one could thrill to his words, learn and repeat them, without ever seriously asking what they meant. When I saw a movie of *The Jungle Book* in the mid-1940s, full fifty years after the book had been published, advertisements still assumed that the word "Kipling" could be used like the words "Shakespeare" or "Dickens" as a mark of classic greatness. A few years later, my mother told me that my uncle and the father of my best friend had stayed up late the night before reciting Kipling, and I assumed that was a magical way to spend an evening. I had read neither of the *Jungle Books,* not even *Just-So Stories,* but I attributed that to a flaw in myself, and I assumed that most others had read these books, themselves as old and as true as the sky, committed to memory. Just recently, when I mumbled some demurring remarks about the *Just-So Stories,* I was answered on one side with long phrases about the Elephant Child's " 'satiable curtiousity' " and about Tegumai and his daughter on the other.

Everyone I knew when growing up did not, of course, know Kipling's famous books for children, though I'm sure many did, and not many derived, as I now see my best friend did, their vocabulary from *Stalky & Co.* My guess is that for most Americans now he is what he was for me, a rumble of distant thunder. He is of course better known in the countries that once made up the British Empire than he is in the United States, but even there his fame seems to be passing as those who knew the Empire itself also pass away. Writers on Kipling used to begin by saying people either adored or hated him, but there are few real adorers now and almost no passionate haters. He has become an academic subject, alas, a figure of uncertain status, better known than H. G. Wells, not as well known as George Bernard Shaw, certainly not as much admired as Hardy or Conrad.

But the implied equation of Kipling with the British Empire is unfortunate, because it is only the lesser Kipling that can be made to stand in that equation. Kipling is rightly best known as a writer about India, but he was never an ardent apologist for the British presence there, and his really unpleasant jingoistic work comes in the years when he was concerned with Africa. The fact that the British in Africa were more truly imperial than they ever were in India made their cause less easy to defend, which made defenders like Kipling more defensive, more shrill and harsh. But the Empire was never more than a manifestation of what really absorbed Kipling, which was not politics and power but authority, systems of order, of which the Law of the Jungle is the most famous and the Great Game and the lama's Way in *Kim* the most interesting; most interesting of all was the India that defied all systems of order by having and obeying so bewilderingly many.

The point can be stated more precisely. Kipling at his best is a writer about the relations between order, and laws, and youthful boyish energies. Like Kenneth Grahame, who was his almost exact contemporary, Kipling never outgrew boyish impulses and desires. Unlike Grahame, Kipling wanted to grow up and indeed thought he had, so he never offers his stories and poems frankly as the literature of escape. The loose, thrilling, and easily memorized couplets in which the Law of the Jungle is stated are in form escapist, because they imply one can learn a formula and thereby forget life with it. The law they announce, however, is offered seriously, as a grim, wise statement of the sort that Grahame would never have written. He wanted to run from such statements.

Fortunately for us the Kipling that seeks status as adult literature need not concern us here. Even at its best, it seems to me, the adult Kipling is minor stuff, clever and polished, memorable for a few exciting gestures and scenes, but narrow and thin. Kipling's poems, for instance, have lots of lines one remembers when one needs a formulaic way to state a mood or an argument:

> From down to Gaehenna and up to the throne,
> He travels the fastest who travels alone.

> If you can make one heap of all your winnings, and bet it
> on one turn of pitch and toss—
> And lose, and start again at your beginnings, and never
> breathe a word about your loss.

> For the sin that ye do by two and two ye must pay for one
> by one.

> When you get to a man in the case
> They're as like as a row of pins,
> And the Colonel's Lady and Judy O'Grady
> Are sisters under their skins.

> Each for the joy of the working, and each, in his separate
> star,
> Shall draw the Thing as he sees It, for the God of Things as
> They Are!

I quote these easily from memory, as anyone can who has once fallen under their spell. For just that reason Kipling's poetry won't ever die, though fewer and fewer will stay up late at night reciting it. George Orwell calls it very good bad poetry; T. S. Eliot says it isn't poetry at all, but verse; no matter the best definition. As for the stories, it seems enough to say that only at his best does he earn the title of being the British de Maupassant; the tales are neatly turned, pathetic or shocking, situationally precise but humanly shallow, innocent of what Chekhov or D. H. Lawrence could make short fiction be.

The Kipling that has always been the most popular, and that will last longer than any of the rest, is the work done for children and growing boys. There is a good deal of this, all written in Kipling's so-called middle period, between 1890 and 1910. Let me arrange it along a scale of its audience, from its youngest to its oldest readers: *Just-So Stories* (1902), *The Jungle Books* (1894 and 1895), *Puck of Pook's Hill* (1906), *Rewards and Fairies* (1910), *Stalky & Co.* (1899), *Kim* (1901). Some of these need not concern us, since they are more useful for trying to decipher Kipling than as lasting literature; some of the others we can use as we did Grahame's early books, as foil for the better ones. The stress must fall on *The Jungle Books* and especially on *Kim*, which, though it is barely a children's book, is the finest expression of the impulses at work in all Kipling's stories for children. There the relation of the boyish impulse to be free and the boyish desire to obey receives its most interesting and fullest treatment, and there India is so densely realized it does not seem a playground at all.

Kingsley Amis has said of the Mowgli stories that they are paraded wisdom, the sort of stories adults like to give children more than children really enjoy reading. The judgment seems at best partly true of the *Jungle Books*, but perfect for the *Just-So Stories*. Unlike the *Jungle Books* or *Kim*, they were not written out of the need to satisfy anything deep or personal for Kipling, but out of the desire to tell stories to his eldest daughter Josephine, and as we have seen more than once, when an adult works hard to satisfy a child, the results are seldom that adult's best stories. What makes the situation especially sad is that Josephine died before these tales could be collected and published, which accounts for the elegiac tone in many of the verses late in the book:

> Far far—oh, very far behind,
>   So far she cannot call to him,
> Comes Tegumai alone to find,
>   The daughter that was all to him.

Since parents and children of Kipling's time and class were often kept apart from each other, his need to try to establish a close relation with his daughter is especially touching. The stories about the making of the first letters and the first alphabet offer an image of a close, loving relation between Kipling and Josephine, and everyone who ever heard him read these stories speaks of being entranced by him and them.

What made the *Just-So Stories* successful in their original telling may be just what makes them, with one exception, seem mostly cute, in the bad sense, seventy-odd years later. Kipling's idea is to tell timeless stories about how animals came to be as they are—how the camel gets his hump*f*, or hump, because he would only say "Hump*f*" when asked to help out; how the elephant gets his trunk because the Elephant Child has his nose stretched in the jaws of a crocodile; how the kangaroo hops because he was chased ever so long by the Yellow-Dog Dingo. The stories ring false for two related reasons: first, there is little necessary relation between the animal and its behavior, for the elephant is not known for being greatly curious or the kangaroo for wanting to be different; second, the close, or cozy, relation between the storyteller and the child audience is achieved by means of a shared condescension toward the animals.

For instance, in one of the most famous of the stories, "How the Leopard Got His Spots," the leopard is losing his prey because the giraffes, zebras, and elands have moved from the veldt to the forest and have grown disguising colors. The confused leopard goes to see the wise Baavian, who tells him: "My advice to you, Leopard, is to go into other spots as soon as you can." A joke. The leopard interprets the Baavian to mean "places" when he says "spots," while an Ethiopian tells him "spots" means black blotches on the leopard's tawny skin. The leopard, too stupid to know it doesn't matter who is right, obeys the Ethiopian, himself a "nigger" and not very bright. Thus he eventually gets to the forest and grows his spots. Thus too we have created a hierarchy that goes from teller to child audience to Baavian to Ethiopian to leopard that is very similar in its smugness to the hierarchy of teller–male doll–female doll–young girl we saw in Grahame's "Sawdust and Sin." Since the accompanying illustrations are often filled with jokes no child can be expected to get, the hierarchy shows that the only figure worth being is the one at the top, the adult storyteller. Though the *Just-So Stories* are sometimes praised for their mythic qualities, they are very far removed from any inquiry into the nature of either human beings or other animals such as a myth must make. The camel, the leopard, the kangaroo, the elephant, and the rhinoceros all gain their distinctive qualities in spite of themselves, and the crab, Pau Amma, must shed its shell as a reminder to all crabs that the real boss is a surrogate for the storyteller, the Elder Magician. Beatrix Potter shows more genuine attentiveness and mythic power in almost any one of her stories than Kipling does in all but one of these.

That exception, "The Cat That Walked by Itself," shows clearly what Kipling could do when he stopped, however briefly, to think hard about his subject. He starts with simple observable facts—the man hunts, the woman stays by the fire, the dog is man's friend, the horse is man's servant, the cow is man's source of food, and the cat is distinctively independent. He then creates a story that explains how the animals in the tale came to act as they do. The cat, clever and intelligent, can bargain with the woman without giving up anything, so the cat ends up by the fire, drinking milk three times a day, behaving kindly to children as long as children are good, yet he walks by himself, "all places alike to him." This is no great story, and the pieces are all being fitted into prearranged slots, but at least they are doing that, and Kipling succeeds because he really respects the qualities he sees in cats, which is just what he does not do, here at least, with wild animals.

Nor does it matter that Kipling had to make his stories simple because his daughter was very young. The point is not that the stories are simple but that they are careless, nasty even. We have seen already, with de Brunhoff and Potter, that writing and drawing "for" young children can yield great things in which anyone can take intense and renewable pleasure. One could extract from de Brunhoff's work at least an implicit racism, and Potter has, should one wish to stress them, a number of unpleasant qualities. But what they touch, they touch with respect, what they do centrally they do with care, and they establish good relations with their audience by seeming almost to ignore the fact that they have an audience. Kipling's central subjects in these stories, the animals, are kept down by being made to seem stupid, and this has the effect of keeping the children in Kipling's audience down: they are "bought off," persuaded to keep the friendly relation with the storyteller in exchange for being allowed to adopt superior attitudes toward the animals.

The Jungle Books reveal no such crippling concern with audience. They were written when Josephine was too young to hear them, they were not told with anyone in particular in mind, and they are also and perhaps therefore much better. One sees what Kingsley Amis means when he accuses them of offering paraded wisdom, but that does not really get to the heart of the matter. Let me quote again the lines with which I began—they come at the end of "How Fear Came":

> Now this is the Law of the Jungle—as old and as true as the sky;
> And the Wolf that shall keep it may prosper, but the Wolf that shall break it must die.
> As the creeper that girdles the tree-trunk the Law runneth forward and back—
> For the strength of the Pack is the Wolf, and the strength of the Wolf is the Pack.

I take these lines out of context, as many others have done, and the effect is to make this one law into The Law, when actually the poem that follows lists all kinds of rules for wolves, and the story which precedes the poem is not much concerned with wolves but with the one night in which man fears the tiger. But even if the lines are taken from context and even if they are then given to Wolf Cub Scouts, aged nine, as though they spoke the only law, even then they seem to me thrilling and harmless, paraded wisdom, but much truer concerning wolves and nine-year-olds than the *Just-So Stories* are about leopards and kangaroos. Kipling's wolves are not Ernest

Thompson Seton's, or Farley Mowat's, but neither are they terrible distortions. Lone wolves, almost unknown in Kipling, are also almost unknown in the wild. The law which demands mutual dependence among wolves is also the law which makes them what they are usually called in *The Jungle Books,* the Free People. The wolves are anthropomorphic, and the wisdom is paraded, but it isn't ignorant or patronizing.

The basic texture of *The Jungle Books* is like these couplets, and the result is a happy but not complacent picture of the jungle as a place that is obedient to a wide range of laws, habits, and instincts, so that it becomes humanly habitable, as most jungles are not. Kaa, Baloo, Bagheera, Akela, the Bander-log, and Hahti are all easily described because each has only one or two salient qualities, each derived from stereotyped but observable qualities in pythons, bears, panthers, wolves, monkeys, and elephants. They make excellent background figures because, once typed, their traits become as laws, and this takes them out of the category of creatures that can be turned into a hero or a villain. The Bander-log are annoying, but not bad or evil. Even in the non-Mowgli story of Rikki-Tikki-Tavi, where we are intended to want Rikki to win, the antagonists, the cobras, are only being obedient to their natures. There is nothing profound in Kipling's rendering of any of these characters, but nothing is distorted either, except perhaps for those who might wish to complain that Kipling's jungle is not a real jungle.

Far from being real, Kipling's jungle is an ideal as much as Grahame's river and woods, and a brief glance at Kipling in his early years can show how it came to be. He was born and spent his first six years in India, lovingly surrounded by servants with whom he could have relations that were at once secure and dynamic. The servants could treat young Ruddy as an inferior, because he was a child; as an equal because servants and children both lived apart from adults; as a superior because he was British and they were native. At six he was abruptly removed from India and sent to England, where no such surroundings existed. Worse, his foster parents were vengeful and narrow-minded Methodists who, out of duty and desire, made life miserable for young Kipling. In his strongly worded autobiographical story, "Baa Baa Black Sheep," Kipling says near the end: "When young lips have drunk deep of the bitter waters of Hate, Suspicion, and Despair, all the Love in the world will not wholly take away that knowledge, though it may turn darkened eyes for a while to the light, and teach Faith where no Faith was." A terrible and pathetic utterance, surely. Furthermore, after he left his foster family and went to public school, he was given anything but "all the love in the world." If he achieved "Faith where no Faith was," it was what Philip Mason has tellingly called faith in the higher power of the headmaster at the expense of subordinate house-masters (see *Stalky & Co.*).

Then, at seventeen, Kipling returned to India where he found himself "moving among sights and smells that made me deliver in the vernacular sentences whose meaning I knew not." Had this been Kipling's first stay in India, he might have done as he did, work seven years as a reporter, editor, and contributor of stories to provincial newspapers, which laid the groundwork for the literary success that was to follow him back to England when he returned there at age twenty-four. *Plain Tales from the Hills, Departmental Ditties,* and *Soldiers Three* would all be exactly as they are, the work of a young man trying to act more knowing and adult than he feels or is, eagerly and excitedly observing the whole Indian scene, from beggar to half-caste, from native prince to British viceroy, from Mohammedan mistress to memsahib. But *this* India Kipling left for good when he left India for the second and last time, and very little of his "adult" writing after he left reveals distinctive traces that he had ever gone.

But that leaves *The Jungle Books* and, a few years later, *Kim,* and these differ from the rest of Kipling's work, for adults or children, about India or elsewhere. They are happy books about ideal worlds, worlds that are not so much versions of the India Kipling knew between seventeen and twenty-four as derived from the world of his first five years. Mowgli and Kim are not Kipling, of course, but versions of the boy he might have been, or imagined he could have become, had he stayed in India. Each is thrust out of the nursery and into the world when very young, and each finds in the world versions of those servants who had surrounded Kipling when he was very young.

Of course Kaa, Baloo, Bagheera, Akela, Hahti, and the others are not Mowgli's servants, because both they and he are better than that name implies, but Mowgli is never alone, either. Even at the end of "Tiger! Tiger!" when Mowgli ends up saying, "Man-Pack and Wolf-Pack have cast me out . . . Now I will hunt alone in the Jungle," the next line is " 'And we will hunt with thee,' said the four cubs." Mowgli is never more than a few sentences away from the animals who mean most to him. Yet what Mowgli forms with Kaa, Baloo, Bagheera, and Akela is not a pack relation either. For the nameless wolf it may be true and enough that his strength is in the pack and its strength is in him, but Mowgli's relation with those animals closest to him is better, and different from anything the Law of the Jungle could say. It is what C. S. Lewis rightly sees as an essential feature in Kipling, the Inner Ring, the group banded together by ties not of blood but of comradeship, mutual dependence, and higher wisdom. Being distinctly different in kind one from another, Mowgli and his comrades often pursue separate ways, but given a challenge, especially from the outside, suddenly they are all together.

It is, of course, understood without its ever being said that Mowgli is at the center of the stories. "We'll play Jungle Book, and I shall be Mowgli," says Oswald Bastable at the opening of Edith Nesbit's *The Wouldbegoods*, written just five years after the first *Jungle Book*. Of course he wanted to be Mowgli, who is able to be free, to understand wild animals, to sleep by day and hunt by night, to be competent in the jungle, to enact punishment but never recrimination, to be indifferent to the value of money or treasure. These are undoubtedly the major ingredients in the fantasy, but fortunately Kipling needed Mowgli to be more than a boy at one with the jungle, a younger Tarzan. He also had to enact the varied relations Kipling had had with the servants. Thus, being a boy, Mowgli had to be taught, and so we have "Kaa's Hunting," where Mowgli foolishly goes off with the Bander-log because his teacher, Baloo, has been hard on him and the monkeys have been kind to him, or so he thinks. The result is a story of the fun of being wrong when the teachers of the lesson are wise and kind.

A much more important element in the best stories derives from Mowgli's special status as a human being. Kipling's servants had had to treat him as something special too, because one day he would be taken away since he was, finally, not of their world. Kipling learned in England what Mowgli learns in his brief stay in the village: there is nothing happy about this specialness. If there is a law that says he must leave the wolf pack and live among human beings, the law must be obeyed, but with doubt as to its goodness and regret as to its power. Thus Kipling spends little time describing Mowgli in the village, but what he does more often, and with excellent results, is to tug Mowgli between the various laws he must obey and the various roles his relations with animals and people thrust upon him. There is no finer moment in either *Jungle Book* than the scene at the Council Rock in "Mowgli's Brothers," where the wolves, Baloo, Bagheera, and Mowgli all struggle to say who they think Mowgli is.

The crisis in this scene arises because Akela and the other wolves who originally agreed to let Mowgli grow up with the pack, and who have kept Shere Khan the tiger from attacking him, have all grown old. The younger wolves do not want Mowgli living with them. Bagheera gives Mowgli the law: you are a man; Mowgli protests: " 'I was born in the Jungle. I have obeyed the Law of the Jungle, and there is no wolf of ours from whose paws I have not pulled a thorn. Surely they are my brothers.' " But no, and Mowgli's ability to pull thorns from paws shows he is not a wolf, as Bagheera tells him. Also, none of the animals can look Mowgli in the eye, and "the others they hate thee because their eyes cannot meet thine." Heredity is stronger than environment; get human weapons before you fight Shere Khan, get fire.

Shere Khan comes to claim Mowgli as his rightful prey, and in the debate that follows the various laws keep pulling various animals in different ways. Some wolves argue they must protect Mowgli because he has kept their law, others that he is a man cub; Shere Khan insists he became his prey years ago; Bagheera answers he paid the price of a killed bull to save Mowgli's life. Mowgli, having been told he is unredeemably a man, rises to the challenge: " 'Ye have told me so often tonight that I am a man (and indeed I would have been a wolf with you to my life's end) that I feel your words are true. So I do not call ye my brothers any more, but *sags* (dogs), as a man should. What ye will do, and what ye will not do, is not yours to say. That matter is with *me*; and that we may see the matter more plainly I have brought here a little of the Red Flower which ye, dogs, fear.' " This is what Ruddy Kipling, aged six, could not imagine saying when he was cast out of his pack and sent off to England. Yet it wasn't the servants he wanted to punish, and we can notice that the wolves he attacks remain nameless, while a loyal group remains: "At least there were Akela, Bagheera, and perhaps ten wolves that had taken Mowgli's part." That would be enough, except Mowgli must leave them all: "Then something began to hurt Mowgli inside him, as he had never been hurt in his life before, and he caught his breath and sobbed, and the tears ran down his face. 'What is it? What is it?' he said. 'I do not wish to leave the Jungle, and I do not know what this is. Am I dying, Bagheera?' " "No," says Bagheera, it is only tears, "such as men use." Mowgli has set himself apart from the wolves and has managed to become the Mowgli that young Kipling or Oswald Bastable wanted to be, but in his revenge on the wolves he also seems a rather unpleasant *übermensch*. That leads only to this, though; animals are not given to revenge, and they do not cry either. Mowgli, obeying the laws that make him human, is softer and more pathetic than any of the others.

Mowgli, in this and in the other stories, is seldom allowed to be king of the castle for very long, because he had to be etched with deeper longings than the simple desire for power and mastery. He had to belong somewhere, but the place where he belonged could not be, like Grahame's river and woods, created simply by ruling out all that Kipling disliked. He could belong only when he could feel all those tugs that Kipling felt with his servants because he was their inferior, their equal, and their superior. In a different writer, these tugs could have been made to come into conflict with each other, so that Mowgli could have become doubtful, confused, tormented. Kipling wanted none of that—that was what he had been in England —and so he lets the tugs pull one after the other, but none is so strong that another cannot just pull back. After Mowgli learns his tears are human, he dries them quickly and leaves the jungle. But then comes another story, about his life before he left, and another, in which he kills Shere Khan and comes back to the jungle. The fantasy is rich but not complex. The young lips that had drunk deeply of the bitter waters of hate, suspicion, and despair are not

Mowgli's, and Kipling had to protect him from whatever might lead in that direction.

On the other hand, Mowgli's ambivalent status in the forest keeps him unsettled, and this keeps him and Kipling from the smugness of the *Just-So Stories*. The great longings that animated the *Jungle Books* were too strong for Kipling to want to blemish them with easy nostalgia or the easier desire for revenge. The flaw in these books lies elsewhere: the stories are not very good stories. When Mowgli is being tugged to stay or to leave or to return to the jungle, as in "Mowgli's Brothers," "Tiger! Tiger;," and "Spring Running," all is well. But when Mowgli's role is more settled, the result tends to be a simple adventure story. In this respect Kipling here resembles a contemporary of his, Arthur Conan Doyle. Mowgli and Sherlock Holmes are fantasy figures of such richness that they become quasi-mythical and seem able to exist almost independently of the stories told about them. But the stories themselves tend to be casually done, as if by someone who does not know it is difficult to sustain a good tale. By Kipling's own statement, the killing of Shere Khan, the climax of "Tiger! Tiger!," is accomplished with absurd ease. "Red Dog," a story that has been lavishly praised, is good as long as Kaa is using the bees to attack the dogs, but the dogs themselves, like the tiger, are too gullible to be challenging enemies. "How Fear Came" is like a good Just-So story, neatly enough told but with nothing to mottle or densify its paraded wisdom. "Letting in the Jungle" starts out very well, but Mowgli's plan for the evacuation of the village takes so long that the punishment seems much in excess of the crime. As with the Sherlock Holmes stories, these failings are not strong enough to destroy our sense of the power of the central figure, but strong enough so that the stories are more powerful as a residue in the memory than they are when reread.

Kipling was not yet done with India. After the *Jungle Books* came *Stalky & Co.*, the first of a spate of books about pranksters in public schools—Owen Johnson's Lawrenceville stories are the best known of the others—which employ a good deal of Kipling's cleverness; but even Kipling's admirers speak of Stalky apologetically, and his detractors rightly use it to locate what was most deficient and distorted in him. Then came the *Just-So Stories*, which may reflect how far Kipling had gotten away from places where he paid attention to undomesticated animals. After Josephine Kipling's death, as if in recognition that he needed to do something therapeutic, he returned to a book about India he had been planning and postponing for years, and the result was *Kim*. It is a very well-known book, but students of the novel never seem to have known how to pay it the attention it deserves, and so perhaps it is best claimed here, as a kind of children's literature. Certainly it is a book about which it is easy to make mistakes, and it can be best understood in the context of Kipling's other books for and about children and adolescents.

In "The Kipling That Nobody Read," Edmund Wilson shows the kind of mistake one can make about *Kim*. "Now what the reader comes to expect," Wilson says as he describes Kim's involvement in the Great Game of British espionage, "is that Kim will eventually come to realize that he is delivering into bondage to the British invaders those whom he has always considered to be his own people, and that a struggle between allegiances will result." The mistake here at first glance seems political or ideological, because Kipling shows that India, in every breath the book takes, is the country the British could never truly invade, never deliver up in bondage. The deeper mistake is more literary; Wilson expects the book to work as a novelistic fiction, in which external conflicts lead to conflicts within the hero. The book succeeds because it does not do the novelistic thing, the grown-up thing, Wilson wants. I would like to quote four passages to show that those that are apparently most useful for the commentator are in fact the least important, and that when *Kim* is being least consequential in the novelistic sense it is being most itself.

The first comes while Kim and the lama are on the Great Trunk Road that will take them from Lahore to Umballa and then to Benares. The lama is looking for a river of truth, but does not know where to find it or how to look except by wandering. Kim is looking for a red bull on a green field "and the Colonel riding on his tall horse, yes, and . . . nine hundred devils," or so his father told the woman who tried to raise Kim. One night they stop by the road, and an old soldier asks Kim if he will accept his hospitality for the night, and a priest, who has been asking lots of questions about the lama, "insisted that the honour of entertaining the lama belonged to the temple." The lama smiles guilelessly:

> Kim glanced from one face to the other, and drew his own conclusions.
>
> "Where is the money?" he whispered, beckoning the old man off into the darkness.
>
> "In my bosom. Where else?"
>
> "Give it me. Quietly and swiftly give it me."
>
> "But why? Here is no ticket to buy."
>
> "Am I thy *chela,* or am I not? Do I not safeguard thy old feet about the ways? Give me the money and at dawn I will return it." He slipped his hand above the lama's girdle and brought away the purse.
>
> "Be it so—be it so." The old man nodded his head. "This is a great and terrible world. I never knew there were so many men alive in it."
>
> Next morning the priest was in a very bad temper, but the lama was quite happy . . .
>
> "Certainly the air of this country is good," said the lama. "I sleep lightly, as do all old men; but last night I slept unwaking till broad day. Even now I am heavy."
>
> "Drink a draught of hot milk," said Kim, who had carried not a few such remedies to opium-smokers of his acquaintance. "It is time to take the road again."

Next, here is Kipling's description of Kim's classmates after Kim has found the red bull and been sent to St. Xavier's by Father Victor:

> They were sons of subordinate officials in the Railway, Telegraph, and Canal services; of warrant-officers, sometimes retired and sometimes acting as commanders-in-chief to a feudatory Rajah's army; of captains of the Indian Marine, Government pensioners, planters, Presidency shopkeepers, and missionaries. A few were cadets of the old Eurasian houses that have taken strong root in Dhurrumtollah—Pereiras, De Souzas, and D'Silvas. Their parents

could well have educated them in England, but they loved the school that had served their own youth and generation followed sallow-hued generation at St. Xavier's. Their homes ranged from Howrah of the railway people to abandoned cantonments like Monghyr and Chunar; lost tea-gardens Shillong-way; villages where their fathers were large landholders in Oudh or the Deccan; Mission-stations a week from the nearest railway line; seaports a thousand miles south, facing the brazen Indian surf; and cinchona-plantations south of all.

Next is Mahbub Ali's speech to Kim as he sends him off to Lurgan Sahib's during Kim's first summer vacation:

> "What talk is this of *us,* Sahib?" Mahbub Ali returned, in the tone he used towards Europeans. "I am a Pathan; thou art a Sahib and the son of a Sahib. Lurgan Sahib has a shop among the European shops. All Simla knows it. Ask there . . . and, Friend of all the World, he is one to be obeyed to the last wink of his eyelashes. Men say he does magic, but that should not touch thee. Go up the hill and ask. Here begins the Great Game."

Finally, here is the third of three passages in which Kim repeats the same question:

> All that while he felt, though he could not put it into words, that his soul was out of gear with its surroundings—a cog-wheel unconnected with any machinery, just like the idle cog-wheel of a cheap Beheea sugar-crusher laid by in a corner. The breezes fanned over him, the parrots shrieked at him, the noises of the populated house behind—squabbles, orders, and reproofs—hit on dead ears.
>
> "I am Kim. I am Kim. And what is Kim?" His soul repeated it again and again.

The last of these is the one Edmund Wilson, and most other commentators, quote.

The fourth passage is not so much the least important of the four as it is the one whose importance it is easiest to exaggerate. It implies a crisis in Kim's identity, and thereby that the book has reached a structural or thematic junction. The third passage also does this; it comes at the end of a chapter, and "Here begins the Great Game" implies a turning point. But it really is the first two passages, and especially the first, that most need comment if we are to describe *Kim* adequately. In the first Kim is only saving the lama, financially at least, from the wiles of a priest who does not appear again; in the second we hear about people who don't even appear elsewhere in the book. Both passages are display pieces. In one Kipling is showing off Kim's ability to spot thieves even among the priestly caste, and in the other Kipling is showing off his own knowledge of India. They are the stuff of the book.

Kipling himself said *Kim* is plotless, which it certainly is not, but it is profligate, a huge mural of all Kipling has known and cared about in India. Kim himself, likewise, bobs in and out, making himself at home in a myriad of strange conditions, delighting in his ability to be like a chameleon, or like India itself, cursing with Hindustani and Pathans, playing in the British-run Great Game, following his holy lama. In the first passage above we are meant to stand slightly on the outside of the scene; "Kim glanced from one face to the other, and drew his own conclusions," and we do not know what conclusions he has drawn. He gets the lama's money, the priest wakes up unhappy, the lama has been drugged with opium. What we figure out as the episode ends Kim has known from the beginning, "but one does not know Lahore city, and least of all the *faquirs* by the Taksali Gate, for thirteen years without also knowing human nature." Kim knows, we find out. It is easy to imagine Kipling coming to the Taksali Gate when he was twenty, seeing the faquirs, spotting their occasional fraudulence, feeling glad he can do that much, but wishing he had never left India, so he could be Kim, and truly a part of it. Kipling may have felt he knew India better than all but a few Britishers, but he could long to be more than that, a white boy who also was an Indian. It is a fantasy as rich as that which went into the making of Huck Finn, Kim's only rival among the vast array of sexless and orphaned boy heroes. Nowhere is the richness so lovingly displayed as in the early episodic, pointless chapters on the road: Kim getting on the train and then cadging the money for his ticket, Kim delivering Mahbub Ali's message to Creighton Sahib, Kim chaffing the hillmen and swearing in their tongue, Kim loving the squish of the mud because it tells him he is free and India is vast.

Given all that Kim tries to be and do, of course he must stop now and then to ask who he is. "Thou art a Sahib and the son of a Sahib," says Mahbub Ali in the third passage above, as though saying something important; but it does not define Kim, though it does force him to spend three years being a student at St. Xavier's. It does not keep him from rejoining the crowds whenever he can get free, and it does not make him like the drummer boy, who is also a Sahib and the son of a Sahib, and who calls all the natives "niggers." It does not mean he will not be able to rejoin the holy lama and become his chela. Yet it is a pull on Kim, and there certainly is the suggestion that he is such a prize apprentice in the Great Game because he is the only known Sahib who also can move with perfect accommodating ease among all Indians. But the pull is not really more than a momentary puzzle to Kim, and being a Sahib never limits his character. Nor does the pull of the lama, which is in precisely the opposite direction. The lama keeps his face to the ground while Kim is wide-eyed and fascinated at the panorama of the Great Trunk Road; the lama denounces as mere worldly temptation all desire to gain an edge, be on the inside, play Great Games. Yet from the moment Kim is aghast to see the curator of the museum in Lahore act deferentially to the lama in the book's opening scene he is fascinated by the lama and by the possibilities of adventure represented in becoming his chela. "He is mad—many times mad. There is nothing else," Kim says at one point, and three pages later he says, "But he *is* a holy man . . . In truth, and in talk and act, holy." But this pull, which is perhaps the strongest in the book, never is so strong that Kim seeks to follow the Middle Way of the lama or to care about whatever can be found at the lama's sacred river.

Kim, like Mowgli, always boyishly runs toward the more liberating of his possible fates and away from the more confining of them. His great advantage over Mowgli is not a matter of personality or ability, for in these respects they are almost identical, but a matter of his world: India in *Kim* is so much more crowded and challenging a place than in Mowgli's Jungle. Kim's freedom is a way of living, whereas by comparison Mowgli's seems only an attractive principle. If we think first of young Ruddy Kipling and the servants, then of Mowgli talking to Shere Khan, then of Kim manipulating the scene with the priest and the lama, we can see that all three might be alleged to be saying: "You are bigger and more experienced than I, but I am quick and eager and love to learn, which makes me just about your equal now and your superior in the long run." That statement becomes more assured, more interesting, less snobbish, more truly liberating, as we move from young Kipling to Mowgli to Kim.

Having stressed that the important thing about *Kim* is the grand variety of India and the grand variety of Kims we are offered in response to it, we can now look at the book's central structural struts, which are the initiation of Kim into the Great Game and the lama's search for the River with the Arrow. They serve a rather extraordinary purpose, actually, since they achieve the opposite of what they seem designed to do. We see them, at least after the Great Game comes fully into view, as being not only different but at least potentially opposed to each other, and presumably we can entertain the possibility that they will eventually conflict and that Kim will be forced to say who he is and choose which way he will go. This, of course, would put Kipling in the position of choosing between the Game, for which Kim is suited by temperament and talent, and the Search, which is much less brilliant and brittle but in which Kim has no great interest. But Kipling never had any intention of forcing this conflict or this choice.

When Mahbub Ali says the Great Game begins when Kim goes to Lurgan Sahib's, he is misleading because the Game has been going on all along, ever since Mahbub Ali gave Kim a message to deliver in Umballa. The Game gives proof to Kim of the mystery and excitement of India, of the need to improvise and to be flexible enough to play any part, and of Kim's own status as a wonderfully promising polo pony. At several key moments Kim demonstrates his great ability, only to have someone else appear to show him how much he still cannot do. There is the Hindu lad at Lurgan Sahib's who keeps beating Kim at the Jewel Game even after Kim demonstrates his self-command by refusing to be crushed by Lurgan Sahib's magical illusions. There is, in one of the most impressive such displays in the book, E. 23, who encounters Kim in great distress, and Kim delightedly changes him from a Mahratta to a Saddhu before the eyes of a small group, thereby saving Kim's life. Kim then sees E. 23 give a message to a District Superintendent of Police who is also a player of the Game and is abashed to realize he does this simply by cursing him:

> He blundered out almost into the Englishman's arms, and was bad-worded in clumsy Urdu.
>
> *"Tum mut?* You drunk? You mustn't bang about as though Delhi station belonged to you, my friend."
>
> E. 23, not moving a muscle of his countenance, answered with a stream of the filthiest abuse, at which Kim naturally rejoiced. It reminded him of the drummer-boys and the barrack-sweepers at Umballa in the terrible time of his first schooling.
>
> "My good fool," the Englishman drawled. *"Nickle-jao!* Go back to your carriage."
>
> Step by step, withdrawing deferentially, and dropping his voice, the yellow Saddhu clomb back to the carriage, cursing the D.S.P. to remotest posterity by—here Kim almost jumped—by the curse of the Queen's Stone, by the writing under the Queen's Stone, and by an assortment of Gods with wholly new names.
>
> "I don't know what you're saying,"—the Englishman flushed angrily—"but it's some piece of blasted impertinence. Come out of that!"
>
> E. 23, affecting to misunderstand, gravely produced his ticket, which the Englishman wrenched angrily from his hand.

Thus the message is delivered, and the policeman is as adept at playing his part as E. 23 is at his. In the scene quoted earlier between the lama and the priest, Kim discovers the truth some time before we do, but we can spot when he does, and Kipling can then give us the clues so we will see before the lama. Here Kim jumps, for reasons not explained, when the Saddhu swears by the Queen's Stone, but he seems not to catch on until later, when he remembers having seen the Delhi policeman playing a different Sahib role in Umballa three years earlier. We, trailing long after, almost have to be told by E. 23 what has happened, and even when we then reread the scene we cannot tell when or how the two gamesters recognize each other.

What makes the Game more than spy intrigue is that it can be played and won only by those who know and care enough about the multiplicity of India to be able to take on some of its coloration, to identify tones and customs and necessities in an instant. The Russian agents in the mountains fail because they have not bothered to understand the coolies who are their bearers and have not learned that whatever else one might do in India, one never hits a holy man. So too with the lama and his quest, though of course they must be portrayed very differently. If the lama denounces the temptations of the Great Game, and of all other forms of human life, he does not scorn it. All are caught on the Wheel of Life, but the victims are to be pitied and forgiven, and the lama carefully draws the ways of the Wheel on his scroll. The lama knows Kim's quest and his own are not the same, and he never asks that they should be. He encourages Kim to learn the wisdom of the Sahibs even though he knows that wisdom may deceive the boy in its worldly gaudiness. His love is the great religious love that does not seek to change the beloved, often though it may wish to. He doesn't keep an eye on Kim as the players in the Game do, but he is there, waiting, when Kim leaves school, and the two can then head out again. In other words Kipling presents no conflict here, because on the one hand the Great Game has little in the way of its own system of values, and very diverse people among its players, and because on the other the lama is truly "in talk and act, holy," denouncing but always forgiving, never offering his search as something Kim must learn to undertake: "I am an old man—pleased with shows as are children. To those who follow the Way there is neither black nor white, Hind nor Bhotiyal. We be all souls seeking escape."

For most of the book Kipling moves the story along simply by making sure that the passing years and Kim's increasing mastery of the Game do not allow him to grow up or to settle down, secure in his knowledge. Kim is always a boy, a fascinated beginner, and Kipling's task is to keep him fascinated. Because this is not easy to do, a lesser writer would have been tempted to raise the stakes, to make the

Game turn into an "important international intrigue" or to make the lama decide that, like Jesus, his is the only way, truth, and life. Loose plots have a way of getting thus distorted in their later stages. When Kipling moves the story to the mountains, it certainly feels as though the book is reaching some kind of resolution or climax. The lama is from the mountains and rejoices in his return, and it is natural to assume he may be able to find his River there. The Great Gamester, Hurree Babu, appears in the mountains too, to find the Russian agents who have been surveying and bribing local kings while disguised as animal hunters. We know better by now than to ask about the details of the espionage; the eight thousand redcoats of Mahbub Ali's first message to Kim never went to war, and the "crucial letter" E. 23 left in Mhow has nothing in it as far as we are concerned. Nonetheless, the game is afoot, and the lama is eager and excited, and something, clearly, must happen.

One evening the two agents, one Russian and one French, accompanied by Hurree Babu, who has managed to ingratiate himself as their guide, come on the lama and Kim. The lama is expounding the figures on his scroll of the Wheel, and the agents sit down to listen as their coolies prepare camp; Hurree tells Kim the papers he wants are in a large red packet:

> "See here the Hell appointed for avarice and greed. Flanked upon the one side by Desire and on the other by Weariness." The lama warmed to his work, and one of the strangers sketched him in the quick-fading light.
>
> "That is enough," the man said at last brusquely. "I can not understand him, but I want that picture. He is a better artist than I. Ask him if he will sell it."

To think of the lama as an artist is not only not to understand his words, but his life; "the lama, of course, would no more have parted with his chart to a casual wayfarer than an archbishop would pawn the holy vessels of a cathedral." When refused, the agent takes out some money, then snatches at the chart, which tears, and the lama rises:

> *"Chela!* He has defiled the Written Word."
>
> It was too late. Before Kim could ward him off, the Rus-

sian struck the old man full on the face. Next instant he was rolling over and over down hill with Kim at his throat . . . the coolies under their loads fled up the hill as fast as plainsmen run across the level. They had seen sacrilege unspeakable, and it behove them to get away before the Gods and devils of the hill took vengeance.

It would be very easy for the action at this point to move away from the lama and onto a battle between Kim and Hurree and the agents. But Kipling knows that the whole balance of his book depends on that kind of action not taking over:

> For a moment, for just so long as it needs to stuff a cartridge into a breech-loader, the lama hesitated. Then he rose to his feet, and laid a finger on the man's shoulder.
> "Hast thou heard? *I* say there shall be no killing—I who was Abbot of Such-zen. Is it any lust of thine to be re-born as a rat, or a snake under the eaves—a worm in the belly of the most mean beast? Is it thy wish to—"
> The man from Ao-chung fell on his knees, for the voice boomed like a Tibetan devil-gong.
> "Ai! ai!" cried the Spiti men. "Do not curse us—do not curse him. It was but his zeal, Holy One! . . . Put down the rifle, fool!"
> "Anger on anger! Evil on evil! There will be no killing. Let the priest bearers go in bondage to their own acts. Just and sure is the Wheel, not swerving a hair! They will be born many times—in torment!" His head drooped, and he leaned heavily on Kim's shoulder.

This is the lama's sternest and most worldly moment, the one where he most strongly shows that his values are not irrelevant in the world of the Wheel or to players of the Great Game. We are all in bondage to our own acts, of course, just as the lama is here, just as he will later realize he is here. Kim jumps at the Russian agent because he is a lad of action and his lama has been attacked; Hurree Babu is thinking throughout this scene of the best way to get hold of the red packet; the man from Ao-chung can only think of revenge. All are on the Wheel, and caught, and the lama's language is not set against that of anyone else, but governs it.

Yet this superb moment is not, and cannot be, the end either of the Game or of the lama's quest. The strands of the tale have gone together in a knot, but they must unwind and disengage, because to put the story together here would be like trying to put India together. Hurree Babu's neatest trick is to see how to turn the lama's prohibition against killing into a gamester's triumph. He commandeers his captive agents down out of the mountains and turns them over to nameless higher authorities in Simla, all without the captives' knowing they are captive or knowing who he is. They even write Hurree a testimonial to any future employer of his, attesting to his care and skill. The lama also moves back out of the mountains, injured, fading, and insisting he had fallen victim to vanity and had adored his own renewed strength and expertise. Kim, himself weary and ill, follows, and Kim then collapses into a long sleep. When he awakens, of course he feels strange, a cog wheel unconnected with any machinery, as in the fourth of my passages above, and he asks who he is. But the source of the lama's river was not to be found in the mountains, and the Great Game goes on after Hurree has the Russian agents arrested, and this illness does not end with Kim's sudden cure or with his maturity. He must ask who he is, but we know all along.

This is perhaps another way of saying why *Kim* belongs in this book about children's literature. It is not a *bildungsroman,* a novel of growing up, a book with an interior life for its hero. A child just over the age of ten might find it difficult reading, especially near the beginning, because in all the bustle Kipling does not make it easy for us to gain our bearings and insists, as some of the passages above show, on keeping us as outsiders in this world. But anyone who enjoys reading a long book can decipher all this easily, and then the high romance of the rest opens up like the Great Trunk Road itself. Kim is a boyish boy throughout, the most attractive such creature I know, energetic, resourceful, eager, curious, resilient. Thus, near the end, there is nothing much Kipling can do with him, and, quite tactfully, he realizes this and ends the book with Kim barely there. The lama finds his River at last, and, in a nice touch, it is Hurree Babu who hauls him out of the river after he goes in. And so the lama can die, fulfilled, and have a conversation with Mahbub Ali about Kim just before he finally closes his eyes, and we need neither a change nor a great triumph for Kim to bring the book to a close.

Especially because *Kim* has always been popular, people have had to ask whether its India is the "real" India. Part of Kipling felt he had been truer and wiser about India than any other English writer had been, and one can agree with that without having assented to very much. It is such a seductive book because every detail is real, authentic, yet its aim is romance, excitement, adventure, a view of life so boyish that it sees nothing ugly, mean, or dull. Kipling's investment in an exciting present, to be followed by a possibly even brighter tomorrow, makes *Kim* resemble *The Wind in the Willows* and the best of the Oz books more than it does E. M. Forster's *A Passage to India* or J. G. Farrell's *The Siege of Krishnapore* or, for that matter, *Stalky & Co.* All the sources of authority, power, and wisdom in *Kim* are made evanescent by Kim's fascination with them, and this may make the book unrealistic, but it is the source of its great alertness, its life always feeling fresh, so that the question of whether its India is the real India isn't important. Presumably one should not, in 1901 or now, go to India expecting to see what Kipling shows and Kim sees.

We might, for a final comparison, place *Kim* on a spectrum of other books that are boyish about boys. At one end we can place *Peter Pan,* which is about the desire to remain always a boy and having fun. *Kim,* in this comparison, is never limp, sentimental, or wan, never nostalgic or precious in the bad sense. At the other end we might place a book that is all slam-bang action, like Dumas' *The Three Musketeers,* or Stevenson's *kidnapped,* or, if the England of the Empire is in question, Rider Haggard's *King Solomon's Mines.* In this comparison *Kim* seems less theatrical, less filled with cutouts, more resonant, more wise. At least at the present time, only a special sort of person would actually want to be Peter Pan, and the desire to be d'Artagnan or Alan Quatermain is a relatively passing desire, a mood. But it is easy to want to be Kim, in his India, and find excitements day after day, delighted to be a perpetual beginner. Peter Pan embodies a longing, Alan Quatermain offers a splendid role. By comparison Kim comes closer to expressing life "as a whole," in the sense that while

Kim never sets up house, goes to bed with a woman, or prays, we intuit how he would do these things even as we know why Kipling would never have Kim do them. It is this sense of life's wonder and variety, not seen as in a panorama but lived as in an adventure, which makes *Kim* so wonderful:

> Each long, perfect day rose behind Kim for a barrier to cut him off from his race and his mother-tongue. He slipped back to thinking and dreaming in the vernacular, and mechanically followed the lama's ceremonial observances at eating, drinking and the like. The old man's mind turned more and more to his monastery as his eyes turned to the steadfast snows. His River troubled him nothing. Now and again, indeed, he would gaze long and long at a tuft or a twig, expecting, he said, the earth to cleave and deliver its blessing; but he was content to be with his disciple, at ease in the temperate wind that comes down from the Doon. This was not Ceylon, nor Buddh Gaya, nor Bombay, nor some grass-tangled ruins that he seemed to have stumbled upon two years ago. He spoke of those places as a scholar removed from vanity, as a Seeker walking in humility, as an old man, wise and temperate, illumining knowledge with brilliant insight. Bit by bit, disconnectedly, each tale called up by some wayside thing, he spoke of all his wanderings up and down Hind; till Kim, who had loved him without reason, now loved him for fifty good reasons.

It is good to be a scholar removed from vanity, a Seeker walking in humility; better still to be that, which Kim is, and still be young, and to feel life unfold ahead, with gratitude for everything one learns.

Never a day when the outside world does not call, direct, and set up its authority as something for Kim to confront, and obey, seek liberation from in the challenge of a more enticing authority; never a day when the energies do not well up from within to love the challenge, to test and see and explore the fun of disobeying and the deeper delight of obeying, to know the joy of acting, doing, being the center of the stage, and the deeper joy of listening; "Kim, who had loved him without reason, now loved him for fifty good reasons." Oh, to be that young and that good at once. *Kim* is the apotheosis of the Victorian cult of childhood, but it shines now as bright as ever, long after the Empire's collapse, because it is intensely romantic about the facts of daily life. Of what it offers, no book offers either more or better.

(9) L. Frank Baum and Oz

In the introduction to *The Wonderful Wizard of Oz* (1900), L. Frank Baum writes: "For the time has come for a series of newer 'wonder tales' in which the stereotyped genie, dwarf and fairy are eliminated, together with all the horrible and blood-curdling incidents devised by their authors to point a fearsome moral to each tale. Modern education includes morality; therefore the modern child seeks only entertainment in its wonder-tales and gladly dispenses with all disagreeable incidents." The old "wonder-tales" Baum is speaking of here haven't been mentioned in this book since we considered Countess d'Aulnoy, but Baum is not speaking so much about old and new as he is about European and American. He wants an American children's literature that is free of morality and of disagreeable incident as well. In *Studies in Classic American Literature* D. H. Lawrence says we must always beware an American author who announces a casting off of an old and a taking on of a new; the cry of freedom is only another rattle of chains, he adds; beneath the exterior of a blue-eyed darling Nathaniel Hawthorne is an interior man obsessed with guilt, sin, and death.

But if there is one distinctive quality about Baum's works, and about American children's literature in general, it is a sunny air of naïveté which, more often than not, does not try to hide a gloomy or obsessed concern. It is not realistic literature for the most part, but it tends to include or to accommodate the real with an ease, even an optimism, that is generally not found in European children's books. Take a perennially popular book like Virginia Lee Burton's *Mike Mulligan and His Steam Shovel,* a charming tale indeed, in which Mike Mulligan agrees to dig a hole for the foundation of a new school in just one day. Impossible, surely, but the steam shovel huffs and puffs and does it all, in just one day. The only trouble is, at the end of the day the steam shovel is left at the bottom of the hole, which would ruin everything, except that a small boy appears to suggest that the steam shovel be turned into a furnace, Mike Mulligan into a janitor, so the schoolhouse can be built up all around them. Nothing easier, and the ease of the solution, as well as the confident faith in "solutions," especially technological ones, is characteristic of many similar American children's books. Here is a problem, how can we face it? Someone whispers something to someone else, or someone puffs for awhile on a pipe, or the smallest person at the gathering speaks up, and all is well. It happens frequently in the Oz books, in Walter R. Brooks's Freddy books, in Dr. Seuss. In Robert McCloskey's *Make Way for Ducklings* the ostensible problem is to find a place for the ducks to raise a family away from the pond in the Boston Public Garden, and then at the end, after Jack, Kack, Lack, Mack, Nack, Ouack, Pack, and Quack wander around Boston with their mother, the group ends up at the pond anyway. Here there is no explanation, and hardly a solution, but the same insouciance nonetheless. It should not be surprising that American children's literature remained predominantly rural long after the country itself became predominantly urban, and often without strain, or nostalgia, or self-conscious pastoralism. If very little of it is great, it is often surprising to rediscover how delightful a great deal of it is.

America is an enchanted land, and a great deal of commentary on American literature has sought to determine the terms of the spell it lies under. It is one thing, though, to learn the "Sesame" that seems to unlock the enchantment; it is quite another thing to respond to the enchantment in a way that is itself enchanting. *Walden* is perhaps our one major example of an enchanting book, a work in which we can begin to believe in possibilities we ordinarily deny, and that life could be more inventive, gay, and delightful than it usually is. Thoreau does this not by talking about America after the fashion of Whitman, or of D. H. Lawrence and his critical successors, but by being immersed in where he is, by crying up the glories of the morning, or of how much he can do without, or of how much he has within him. The part of Thoreau that was concerned and despairing about the United States is not enchanting in this way at all. A good deal of the best American children's literature is like this; it enchants by its ease, its unselfconsciousness, its naïveté. And the first to achieve this, and still the best, is Baum.

In 1900 Lyman Frank Baum was forty-four. Before this he had kept himself busy with a large range of jobs and hobbies: editor and printer of an amateur magazine, *Rose Lawn Home Journal*, Rose Lawn being his parents' home in Chittenango, New York; reporter for the *New York World*; printer for *New Era*, in Bradford, Pennsylvania; manager of a string of vaudeville houses in New York and Pennsylvania; author, writer, composer, and director of Irish musical comedies and melodramas; operator of a variety store and editor of a weekly newspaper in Aberdeen, South Dakota; traveling salesman in the midwest for a Chicago firm importing china and glassware; editor of *Shop Window*, a monthly for window trimmers; author of a number of children's books, *Mother Goose in Prose, Father Goose His Book*, and *A New Wonderland*, and of two technical books, *The Book of the Hamburgs* and *The Art of Decorating Dry Goods Windows and Interiors.*

It is all pure and splendid Horatio Alger America, or so it seems a century later. Baum enjoyed almost total mobility of body and spirit, and whatever made him a success or failure at any one thing seems to have had little bearing on what he did next. Not rootless, not a gypsy, he was a man with a large family that he loved, a man apparently at home anywhere, or as much in one place as in another. Baum had a knack for both making and losing money and—a probable explanation for this knack—of gaining and losing interest quickly. Almost all reports speak of his charm, pleasantness, energy, and easy ability to get along with others. In short, Baum was like Arthur Miller's Willy Loman; inventive and, given the type, hugely talented, but Willy Loman nonetheless. One is as much at a loss to explain his successes as his failures; the real task is to catch both in a single focus.

In 1900, as one of four books Baum published that year, came *The Wonderful Wizard of Oz.* Unlike some of his apparently unpromising ventures, this one had difficulty finding a publisher, even though *Father Goose His Book* had enjoyed a considerable success. The *Wizard of Oz* was published by a small Chicago firm, George W. Hill, only after Baum and his illustrator, W. W. Denslow, agreed to absorb the printing costs. From the beginning it was a great success; Martin Gardner, Baum's biographer, says that "before the end of the year it had become the fastest selling children's book in America." That, if we follow one set of notions about Horatio Alger's America, should have been that. Baum should have realized he had discovered a way to make him rich forever. He had always thought along lines of what would sell, and all he had to do was to keep repackaging the formula of Dorothy Gale and the Land of Oz. Part of him did just that. When *The Wizard of Oz* was turned into a musical show two years later, the producer, Julian Mitchell, changed the book and lyrics Baum had written for him; Dorothy's pet dog became a cow, and she was given a prince to fall in love with. At first Baum was angry, but he subsided when the show succeeded: "The people will have what pleases them," he said, according to Gardner, "and not what the author happens to favor, and I believe that one of the reasons why Julian Mitchell is recognized as a great producer is that he faithfully tries to serve the great mass of playgoers."

But Baum was too restless, too little able to calculate or care about the future, to be Horatio Alger or Julian Mitchell. Regardless of the clamor for more Oz books, Baum was not eager to go on writing them. He did give up editing the window dresser's magazine in 1902 to devote full time to writing, but he wrote *Dot and Tot in Merryland, The Master Key* (science fiction about electricity), *Baum's American Fairy Tales, The Life and Adventures of Santa Claus,* and *The Enchanted Isle of Yew* before he consented to do another Oz book, *The Marvelous Land of Oz,* in 1904, and it was three years and half a dozen books later before he did a third, *Ozma of Oz* (1907). Three years after that, at the end of the sixth Oz book, *The Emerald City,* Baum tried to get out of writing any more by announcing that communication between Oz and the outside world had been cut off permanently. By that time, however, the pressure of the success of the Oz books was too strong for him, and he had to invent a fancy wireless set-up between Oz and America so news of Oz could be given him by Dorothy and tapped out by the Shaggy Man. He then resigned himself to doing an Oz book a year, though in fact he ended up doing more than that. The seventh in the series, *The Patchwork Girl*, came out in 1913, and the fourteenth, *Glinda*, was published in 1920, shortly after he died.

Even after agreeing to be saddled with the Oz books permanently, however, Baum had no interest in relying on their income to sustain him. He wrote other fantasies—*John Dough and the Cherub, Sky Island, Sea Fairies, Queen Zixi of Ix;* he wrote three adult romances under the name of Schuyler Staunton, two boy's books as Captain Hugh Fitzgerald, six more as Floyd Akers, seventeen girl's books as Edith Van Dyne, and a novel about some friends as John Estes Cooke. So, on the one hand Baum is known as the author of the Oz books, and most of the rest of his output should remain known only to collectors. On the other hand, Baum would never settle into a single role, and until we understand the way he loved and hated writing Oz books we will not be able to account for the careless, slapdash writing that mars and even destroys some of the Oz books, and, more important, we will not understand why, despite all that is wrong, the Oz books have rightly gained for Baum a permanent place in the minds of those who love him.

We might begin with a look at the figures who provide the easy and pleasant solutions that I mentioned earlier as being part of the standard furniture of American children's literature. The most famous of these is the Wizard himself, but there are also the Shaggy Man and Cap'n Bill; they are all older men, dry and sexless, and they accompany Dorothy and other young heroines on their journeys to Oz. They seem types of Baum himself, and the rule about these figures is that the less one sees of them the better they appear. The humbug wizard in the first book, mild, squat, and pathetic, is rather memorable because he only appears in a few chapters, and exists mainly as the focus of others' discoveries about him. In later books he appears more frequently, mostly as Dorothy's companion on journeys, and gradually he becomes more prissy and less interesting, an adjunct to the kindly, strong magic wielded by Glinda and Ozma. Cap'n Bill has a wooden leg, but otherwise he is hard to tell from the Wizard. The Shaggy Man is occasionally better when he is embodying the shrewd restlessness of Baum himself that was responsible for getting the Wizard up in his balloon in the first place. The truth expressed by these men is that solutions are easy if you know how—how to lie to Dorothy about where the Love Magnet came from, how to catch the heads of Scoodlers as though they were baseballs, how to whistle along that portion of the Yellow Brick Road where plants will lean over and capture you if you don't. But since their effectiveness depends on their ability to do such tricks, they are good only in short bursts, and, as a result, much the best of this type is Johnny Dooit, who appears only in six pages of one book, *The Road to Oz* (1909), when the Shaggy Man has run out of solutions and calls on him to convey his party across the Deadly Desert:

> Johnny Dooit puffed his pipe and looked carefully at the dreadful desert in front of them—stretching so far away they could not see its end.
> "You must ride," he said briskly.
> "What in?" asked the shaggy man.
> "In a sand-boat."

It is as simple as that if you have whiskers and a pipe and puff a little:

> "But where is the sand-boat?" asked the shaggy man, looking all around him.
> "I'll make you one," said Johnny Dooit.

On the opposite page is one of those John R. Neill drawings you have to look at twice just to know what's being drawn. It is Johnny Dooit, but only his very slim posterior, slim legs, and one arm carrying a hammer appear above his copper chest, into which he has plunged to find what he needs to make the sand boat. Two trees provide all the wood he needs, and, working miraculously fast, he assembles boat, mast, and sail: " 'It ought to be painted,' said Johnny Dooit, tossing his tools back into the chest, 'for that would make it look prettier. But 'though I can paint it for you in three seconds, it would take an hour to dry, and that's a waste of time.' " With a typical

American bow at aesthetics, Johnny sees no reason to waste time. Then comes the question of how the thing works:

> "Did you ever sail a ship?"
> "I've seen one sailed," said the shaggy man.
> "Good. Sail this boat the way you've seen a ship sailed, and you'll be across the sands before you know it."
> With this he slammed down the lid of the chest, and the noise made them all wink. While they were winking the workman disappeared, tools and all.

Johnny Dooit, not Oz the Great and Terrible, is the true American wizard—just sail this boat the way you've seen one sailed. That's all it takes, and it is what Baum's American men aspire to, and it is impressive. It does help, though, that he then disappears.

These men can for a moment or two fill up a scene as though it were all there was, as though there were no impinging past or future, and it is that which makes them impressive, more than their practical know-how. That it is the presence and not the expertise that counts is what the consistently enchanting Oz figures, Dorothy and Tip and the other children, show us. They cannot build boats in two minutes, or know when or how to whistle their way past the encircling trees. They must rely on their native sense of themselves and let that be enough. The fact that what is magical about them is their spirit and their presence and not their knowledge gives us the clue to Baum's achievement. They do not fuss, they immerse themselves in the present, which makes them children, to be sure, but it also makes them important. We are inclined to think Baum works better with girls than with boys, but Baum in fact is an almost totally sexless author and our impression is created by Dorothy alone. The other girls, Betsy Bobbin and Trot, have nothing like Dorothy's stature, and three of the boys, Tip, Inga, and Ervic, have some very fine moments. But it is nonetheless Dorothy who is most impressive, so we need to look at one of her magical journeys closely to describe what is most enchanting about Baum.

At the opening of *Ozma*, Dorothy and her Uncle Henry are on a ship bound for Australia, and a storm comes up. The captain is not alarmed but advises everyone to stay below. Dorothy has been dozing, however, while this message is being delivered, and so, when she wakes and does not find her uncle, she goes on deck. She sees a man who might be Uncle Henry clinging to a mast and rushes toward him, but she gets no closer than a chicken coop lying on the deck when the storm doubles its force and she is hurled from the ship, holding onto the coop: "She kept tight hold of the stout slats and as soon as she could get the water out of her eyes she saw that the wind had ripped the cover from the coop, and the poor chickens were fluttering away in every direction, being blown by the wind until they looked like feather dusters without handles." The storm is not so much a threat as an event that creates situations, problems, and oddities. A moment later Dorothy climbs into the coop: " 'Well, I declare,' she exclaimed with a laugh. 'You're in a pretty fix, Dorothy Gale, I can tell you! and I haven't the least idea how you're going to get out of it.' " If you go off for Australia you can get caught in a storm, and if you get caught in a storm you are liable to be blown over and end up in a pretty fix. We might think of Kim, who also is totally devoted to facing the present situation, but where Kim seeks mastery and is excited by anything he does not understand, Dorothy exclaims with a laugh, is not excited, and accepts.

When the wind dies down, Dorothy sleeps on the floor of the chicken coop, and in the morning she discovers one remaining hen at the far end. The hen has just laid an egg, and she and Dorothy start a conversation. After a minute or two, Dorothy says to herself: "If we were in the land of Oz, I wouldn't think it so queer, because many of the animals can talk in that fairy country. But out here in the ocean must be a good long way from Oz." Indeed, the ocean is a long way from Oz, and a long way from Kansas, too, where Dorothy started from. Just as one expects talking animals in Oz, but not in Kansas, one isn't sure what to expect on the ocean. So the two discuss the hen's grammar, which turns out to be rather like Dorothy's, and after a while the coop lands on a sandy beach. They find a key and an admonitory inscription in the sand to *BEWARE THE WHEELERS*. Both are hungry, and they have a long conversation about whether it is better to eat live things, like bugs, or cooked dead things, like chickens who have eaten bugs. The hen seems to get the better of this, and she gets her bugs too, but Dorothy does even better when she finds a grove of trees on which grow lunch and dinner pails, all filled with food. The Wheelers appear, gaudily dressed and a little frightening, claiming to own the pails, and so Dorothy and the hen flee to a hill of rocks on which the Wheelers cannot wheel. Wandering around, she finds a door with a keyhole, so she tries the key she found on the beach, and it works. Inside is a mechanical man named Tik-Tok, and although he turns out to be magic, his makers are Johnny Dooits named Smith and Tinker, American mechanical geniuses.

At night people go to sleep, in the dark they look for light, in the morning they search for food, when a door appears in a rock they look for a key, when they find a disused mechanical man they wind him up. Baum moves totally without self-consciousness from a real world to an improbable world to a magic world. The sentences come easily and imply they were no harder to write than it would be to take the journey they describe. Dorothy commands a presence just by responding to and accepting each detail with the same equipoise and easy curiosity with which she faced the last. It is precisely the atmosphere of Baum's writing not to be atmospheric, or faerie, or invoking, or mysterious; his "new wonder-tale," free of morals and disagreeable incident, is free of all that as well. He genuinely accepts Dorothy and never tries to create a storyteller's manner that is any different from hers. That way he can imply what is obviously true: he could do no better at taking these journeys than she does.

Some time after they meet Tik-Tok, Dorothy and the hen meet Princess Langwidere of the Land of Ev. She turns out to be the real owner of the lunch and dinner pails claimed by the Wheelers. She also has a collection of thirty heads she can put on or take off as she pleases. The conversation that ensues between the Princess and Dorothy shows Baum at close to his best:

> "You are rather attractive," said the lady, presently. "Not at all beautiful, you understand, but you have a certain style of prettiness that is different from any of my thirty heads. So I believe I'll take your head and give you No. 26 for it."
>
> "Well, I b'lieve you won't!" exclaimed Dorothy.
>
> "It will do you no good to refuse," continued the Princess, "for I need your head for my collection, and in the land of

Ev my will is law. I have never cared much for No. 26, and
you will find that it is very little worn. Besides, it will do
you just as well as the one you're wearing, for all practical
purposes."

"I don't know anything about your No. 26, and I don't
want to," said Dorothy firmly. "I'm not used to cast-off
things, so I'll just keep my own head."

As Dorothy rejects Langwidere's No. 26 head, she is accepting something far more important: the fact that she has such a head, and
twenty-nine others too. Dorothy is totally inside the situation, not
interested in how heads might get on or off, or even in how best to
deal with this imperious princess. She wants only to express her
indignity, and what she is and is not used to, in Kansas or in Ev.
The extraordinary freshness of the writing lies in Dorothy's never
thinking about how she got where she is, or how she is going to
get away, or how she might have done differently or have avoided
danger.

To be able to go, without meaning to, into a strange and magical
land, and to be able to accept each moment there as it comes and
for what it brings—it is like having it always be morning, to be
always setting out, and that is one of the most enchanting and
elusive of life's possibilities. In Thoreau's terms, Dorothy is fully
awake. She does not worry or fret or plan, and so everything can be
fully itself. The smallest details can be memorable, even though
Baum seldom offers full descriptions. The surest sign of this is in
the illustrations. Neither W. W. Denslow, who did the pictures for
The Wizard, nor John R. Neill, who did all the others, is close to
being a great artist, but Baum gave them chances to do wonderful
things, and they did not fail. Baum did not describe with the kind of
meticulousness that might tie an illustrator's hands, yet Baum's way
of being engaged in the present tense provided an audience eager
to have illustrations that could reveal the outlines, shapes, and
expressions that embody the freshness and vividness that Baum
makes important.

Baum, furthermore, seems to have enchanted Denslow and Neill
so that when he is at his best, so are they, and when he is not, they
are not. For instance, Dorothy and the Wizard is an unpleasant book,

and Neill's pictures are equally so: Dorothy is wooden and the Wizard is grotesque, red-faced, hook-nosed, assertively bald, often as frightening as the monsters he faces. In the book just before this, *Ozma*, Dorothy is pudgy and is usually twisting her head or her shoulders in some splendidly confident way; in the book just after, *The Road*, Dorothy is thinner, more of a lady, prettier, less animated, but all that fits in very nicely with the almost dangerless situations of the book, as do Neill's intricate and decorative drawings of the Shaggy Man, and the lovely statues of Dorothy, the Tin Woodman, and the Scarecrow, all done in admiring imitation of the plain, wooden, and beautifully naïve drawings and paintings Denslow did for *The Wizard*. As a result, there are no books except perhaps Lewis Carroll's in which it is as important to find those editions with good, clear reproductions of the illustrations. Most of the later impressions that Reilly & Lee, Baum's publishers, have done of the old plates have smudgy and even unrecognizable pictures, but older impressions can still be found, as they can of Tenniel's illustrations, if one is willing to hunt.

This sense of situation I have been speaking of, and Dorothy's ability to accept her presence in some strikingly strange ones, is and must be closely related to Baum's sense of plot or story. Few of the works discussed in this book have a strong sense of narrative lasting much longer than an episode, and it may well be that the kind of brightness and vividness in authors otherwise as diverse as Lewis Carroll, Potter, Grahame, and Kipling is inimical to a strong sense of story, where pace and plot often gain the author's major attention rather than vividness of separate characters and situations. Alexandre Dumas and Robert Louis Stevenson, for instance, had a stronger narrative sense than any of the writers considered here, but their characters and situations are often standard and even uninteresting as a result. Lewis Carroll and Grahame were content with episodes for the most part, and Potter's spinning out of a tale usually involved little more than examining the implications of a single situation. In Kipling, though, we saw how skillfully and tactfully he employed a loose plot in *Kim* so as to hold a large book together without sacrificing his investment in the immediate situations. So too with Baum. After one moment we have another, and we move without feeling we are going deeper or farther into some mystery; in a strong narrative we are always remembering the past and anticipating the future, and Baum works against those feelings. To feel one is getting deeper into something, getting closer to the heart of a mystery, is to diminish the desire to live totally now. Thus what Baum lacks is also the source of his way of being enchanting. Dorothy talks to the hen, flees from the Wheelers, rescues Tik-Tok from his cave, defies Langwidere and is imprisoned, is herself rescued by Ozma. Each event is complete in itself, and what holds the sequence together is only a very loose sense of narrative, one that does not impinge on Dorothy's allowing every action to be entered into for itself alone and not for what it allows one to go from or toward. The young son of a friend of mine complains that the Oz books are "too cinchy," because Baum's storytelling is transparent and naïve; one can easily find tales that are less "cinchy," but they cannot do what Baum's can.

Not long ago I received a happy confirmation of just the kind of enchantment I am trying to describe here. A friend wrote describing a journey he had taken, "We crossed Lake Champlain on the nicest ferry in the world, a regular Oz ferry." A "regular Oz ferry" is not, as one might think, like a ferry one can find in the land of Oz. As it happens, there is a ferry in Oz, in *The Lost Princess*, but it is only a large rowboat and the journey it takes across a river is described in two uninteresting sentences. But a regular Oz ferry is one that enchants by making its passengers feel locked into the present, oblivious of life on either bank, past or future. On the ferry life is magical because one can accept the present without feeling one is leaving or going toward anything. It is the child's journey to a magic country that Baum does best, because this gives us both the enchanting present and just the right amount of narrative sequence. He does occasionally try to link events causally and tightly in some of his books, and thus create suspense and strong narrative motion, but he does not usually do this well. He more often falls into a fully disparate series of events, a journey from this to that to the other place without any narrative tissue, and the results can be unfortunate because the emphasis is taken away from the child making the journey and put onto the odd things she meets, and so we feel we are wandering around in a zoo, locked into the present all right, but without the central presence to enchant us. But the trip to the magical country offers just the right sense that we are going somewhere, but without cause or guide or map, so that Dorothy or some other child must respond freshly, with the sense that each moment is different, and a challenge, and itself.

Let me offer one final example, one that I mentioned in the introduction as a classic instance of the blend of realism and magic that is the hallmark of so much of the best children's literature. At the opening of *The Road to Oz*, Dorothy meets the Shaggy Man, who asks her the road to Butterfield, but when she sets out to show him she finds that not far from her house there is a host of roads she has never seen before. Finding she doesn't know the way home, Dorothy agrees to follow one of the roads with the Shaggy Man, and so, very quickly, we are in Kansas but also in a magic country as well. A little way down the road they meet a boy digging:

> Dorothy watched the boy dig.
> "Where do you live?" she asked.
> "Don't know," was the reply.
> "How did you come here?"
> "Don't know," he said again.
> "Don't you know where you came from?"
> "No," said he.
> "Why, he must be lost," she said to the shaggy man. She turned to the boy once more.
> "What are you going to do?" she inquired.
> "Dig," said he.
> "But you can't dig forever; and what are you going to do then?" she persisted.
> "Don't know," said the boy.
> "But you *must* know *something*," declared Dorothy, getting provoked.
> "Must I?" he asked, looking up in surprise.

Even the accepting Dorothy is being outdone:

> "What must I know?"

"What's going to become of you, for one thing," she answered.

"Do *you* know what's going to become of me?" he asked.

"Not—not 'zactly," she admitted.

"Do you know what's going to become of *you?*" he continued, earnestly.

"I can't say I do," replied Dorothy, remembering her present difficulties.

This is perfect, one of my favorite moments in all children's literature. The boy himself, Button-Bright, is fine here, but equally fine in his placement in the story. By means of his ignorance he can expose Dorothy's ignorance about the relation of "lost" to "found" and of "real" to "magic." Had Baum introduced him before Dorothy and the Shaggy Man reached the cluster of roads, he would seem only a piquant stupid lad; and had Baum waited to bring him in after the visits to the fox and the donkey kingdoms, after we and Dorothy became clearer about the kind of magic we are dealing with, he would have seemed only one more new thing, part of the zoo. The journey forces careful timing, if only of an instinctive sort, on Baum, and the events need not be arranged causally for their sequential relations to be important. What Baum achieves here with Button-Bright he achieves with other characters met early on his best magic journeys: with the hen in *Ozma*, with the Scarecrow in *The Wizard*, with Jack Pumpkinhead in *The Marvelous Land*, and to a lesser extent with the Patchwork Girl in the book named after her, and with the Ork in *The Scarecrow*.

As one might expect, it is in the early Oz books, when there are still fresh journeys to Oz to be taken, that Baum is at his very best. After Dorothy moves to Oz permanently as part of Baum's strategy for writing no more Oz books, she loses a good deal of her sparkle and becomes like most of the other residents of the Emerald City. Baum tried with Betsy Bobbin and Trot to find substitutes for Dorothy, but his heart wasn't in such journeys any more; he knew too completely how they went and where they would end up before he started. For this reason some of his admirers wish he had been able to stop after *The Emerald City*, when he first said he wanted to be done with Oz. The later books often do, indeed, show a marked falling off in quality. *Tik-Tok* is almost entirely a reworking of old materials; *The Patchwork Girl* has Ojo, the least interesting of Baum's children, and is constantly marred by some of Baum's worst punning and horseplay; *The Scarecrow* begins well with Trot and Cap'n Bill getting to Oz but then dwindles into wooden romance; *The Tin Woodman* and *The Magic* are almost grotesquely tired; the last book, *Glinda*, had to be padded with census taking of all the old Oz characters in order to be made into one of the shortest books in the series. Furthermore, nothing in these books matches the great opening journeys in *The Land, Ozma,* and *The Road.*

This way of arguing the case, however, distorts Baum's talents and achievements even if it does isolate his very best things. Baum wrote quickly and never seems to have worried if he could sustain his interest for the length of a whole book. He seems to have known when he began a book how he wanted it to start, and perhaps where he wanted it to end, but he left the middle to be contrived as he went along. Rereading *The Wizard,* for instance, is always a strange experience for anyone who has come to know Victor Fleming's movie. Book and movie each begin wonderfully and in different ways; the movie has its spectacular cyclone and shift from brown-and-white to color, and Baum's matter-of-factness about Kansas, cyclones, and the Munchkins is winning. From then on, though, the advantages seem to belong to the movie. Baum's admirers may complain about having the whole thing be a dream, but the movie makes the dream create its own kind of sense, by emphasizing two characters, the Wizard and the Wicked Witch of the West, whom Baum uses only as part of his zoo. The second Oz book, *The Land,* and the fifth, *The Road,* are wonderful for a hundred or more pages, but then fade, while the fourth, *Dorothy and the Wizard,* and the sixth, *The Emerald City,* are among the weakest in the series. We can't, thus, imagine Baum doing wonderfully well with Oz until he lost interest because he was always capable of losing interest, of falling into slapdash writing, easy satire, or trivial zoo-keeping inventiveness. Furthermore, two of the later books, *Rinkitink* and *The Lost Princess,* though they take no journey to magic lands and therefore lack some of the moment-to-moment sparkle of some of the early books, are very good at sustaining their narrative propositions through to the end; and the last book, *Glinda,* has a fine central situation and, as we will see, one spectacular stretch.

The essence of Baum is his restless, careless ease, his indifference to the complexities of life, his eagerness to describe what enchanted him without ever exploring or understanding it. Such people often become entertainers of one sort or another, but they seldom become writers. It might be said he had a knack for writing the way some people have a knack for singing or dancing or hitting a baseball. He obviously enjoyed writing, but his view of himself as a pleaser of audiences and his indifference to any disciplining of his genius meant he often wrote a good deal he didn't want to write. He wanted above all, as we have seen, to avoid the "horrible and blood-curdling incident" he found in European fairy tales, and yet, more than once, he fell into writing such incidents almost as if without knowing he was doing so. At the time he began writing the fourth Oz book, for instance, *Dorothy and the Wizard,* he had three commercial and two artistic successes behind him. He begins by dropping Dorothy and a friend of hers into the earth—having gotten her out of Kansas by air and water, an earthquake was the next obvious step. But something about being under or inside the earth must have upset Baum in ways he did not anticipate, and so he drops Dorothy into an extremely unpleasant place, and not even dropping the Wizard in helps. The Wizard finds himself matching wits and tricks with the Sorcerer of the Mangaboos, who are vegetable people. Since the Wizard and the Sorcerer are mostly humbug, all should be well, but Baum gets careless with his tone and mistakenly tries to make the icy Prince of the Mangaboos into an arbitrator, thereby taking the whole thing out of the Wizard's power and very far from anything in Dorothy's power. The Prince decides the tourney in favor of the Wizard, the Sorcerer tries to stop the Wizard's breath, the Wizard makes a sword out of a series of knives and slices the Sorcerer in two. Each step gets Baum inadvertently closer to uncontrollable violence, and when the Prince announces that all the strangers must be destroyed, the tone has become so grim that Baum is lost. All the responses Dorothy can make, or even that the Wizard can make in a pinch, are no longer possible, so Baum has to haul them out of this whole situation, which takes him forty uninteresting pages, and by this point the book has stumbled on for so long Baum has no interest in recovering it. So, once set wrong, Baum found it hard to do more than plunge ahead, which seldom worked well; conversely, however, once set right, he tended to be able to invent and plot with ease and grace. But his attention span, if that is the right word for it, seems to have been no longer than that of an intelligent child. As a result there is no one Oz book to which one can point as clearly the best, the one for skeptics to begin with; *Ozma of Oz* for me does more good things for the whole stretch of the book than any other, but it would be unfair to it, and to the series as a whole, to call it Baum's masterpiece. He wrote too much, too quickly, and too restlessly to have a single book as his masterpiece. He tired of many individual books before they were ended, and he tired of the series as a whole before it was ended, yet he kept on with it, and some of the characters and incidents his admirers remember best come in odd places in otherwise not very good books.

This is especially true of the last books in the series, where there are signs that Baum is almost pleading to be able to give up, and at least twice these signs are given in interesting, even moving ways. *The Tin Woodman* (1918) is, on the whole, a wretched affair, but it has in it Mrs. Yoop and Nimmie Aimee, both of whom seem to be figures of Baum himself, and very different too from the other Baum figures, like the Wizard or the Shaggy Man. The Tin Woodman, the Scarecrow, and Woot the Wanderer set out to find the girl the Tin Woodman lost when he rusted in the forest before Dorothy found him in *The Wizard,* and they come on the castle of the giant Mrs. Yoop. She has been sitting for years, keeping herself amused by doing transformations, but mostly she is lonely and bored, and for the first time in the Oz books we sense the possible curse of living forever. Mrs. Yoop wants to be left alone, but if others are foolish enough to enter her valley, then she will transform them: "The woman was not unpleasant to look at; her face was not cruel; her voice was big, but gracious in tone; but her words showed that she possessed a merciless heart and no pleadings would alter her wicked purpose." We can tell here, as we could with the Prince of the Mangaboos, that Baum is getting out of his depths, but what is more interesting is his insistence that we do not see Mrs. Yoop simply as a monster. She is heartless, but not really cruel; she seeks neither friends nor enemies; she has no insatiable appetites and wants to be left alone to try to amuse herself as best she can. This is not Baum we are seeing here, perhaps, but she is expressing some feelings that Baum felt by 1918, when he had written a dozen Oz books and dozens more of other kinds and was "retired" to Catalina Island in California. Part of him, clearly, wanted to be left alone to amuse himself with his transformations.

All this is a little too dark and scary to be developed, but it proved too powerful to be dropped. At the climax of the book the Tin Woodman finds Nimmie Aimee, and she is, as it were, Mrs. Yoop transformed. She lives behind an invisible wall that was built to keep strangers out, and with a man who was assembled from the meat parts of Nick Chopper and another man now made of tin. About her husband she sounds the same note Mrs. Yoop sounds about her pets; he isn't much, she says, but "a new husband would have to be scolded—and gently chided—until he learns my ways." Baum disliked feminists, and never thought husbands were creatures you brought to heel, but here he is clearly on Nimmie Aimee's side:

> "I advise you to go back to your own homes and forget me, as I have forgotten you."
>
> . . . "Are you happy?" asked the Tin Soldier.
>
> "Of course I am," said Nimmie Aimee; "I'm the mistress of all I survey—the queen of my little domain."
>
> "Wouldn't you like to be Empress of the Winkies?" asked the Tin Woodman.
>
> "Mercy, no," she answered. "That would be a lot of bother. I don't care for society, or pomp, or posing. All I ask is to be left alone and not to be annoyed by visitors."

The Tin Woodman and the others claim to be happy to hear this, but it is a forlorn group that leaves her house, and it is of course a weary climax to the whole story. But against the plea to be left alone, against the wan acknowledgment that what one has isn't much but can be made to serve, there is no pleading, and no magic. There was even no way Baum could expect others to hear him crying out from inside his book.

There was to be one last transformation of this figure, in *Glinda,* and wonderfully it was not into a feebler cry for peace and quiet, but into a sequence of two chapters as good as any Baum ever wrote. A young Skeezer named Ervic has come into possession of a kettle of water in which float three fishes who have been transformed from three young ladies, adepts of magic. The fishes tell Ervic that the only one who can transform them to their true shape is Red Reera, a Yookoohoo: "What her real form may be we do not know. This strange creature cannot be bribed with treasure, or coaxed through friendship, or won by pity. She has never assisted anyone, or done wrong to anyone, that we know of. All her wonderful powers are used for her own selfish amusement." By now we can easily recognize Red Reera as Baum's fantasy figure of himself, a recluse who is a good person strangely beyond the touch of the needs of others. Ervic, clearly, is one last version of Dorothy, Tip, and the other children. As the two meet it is as though Baum is testing himself, his desire to withdraw, by using his own best creation, the child taking a magic journey, as his challenger:

> "I'm told you are the only real Yookoohoo in all Oz. Why won't you amuse others as well as yourself?"
> "What right have you to question my actions?"
> "None at all."
> "And you say you are not here to demand favors of me?"
> "For myself I want nothing from you."
> "You are wise in that. I never grant favors."
> "That doesn't worry me," declared Ervic.
> "But you are curious? You hope to witness some of my magic transformations?"
> "If you wish to perform any magic, go ahead," said Ervic. "It may interest me and it may not. If you'd rather go on with your knitting, it's all the same to me. I am in no hurry at all."

Baum is the old magician, leery of any new claims to be made on him, determined to do no one else any favors. Yet he is fascinated as always by the child who instinctively lives where he is, and he will do one last trick if the child is clever enough to charm him into forgetting his resolve. Ervic is at once bold and cautious, playing on Reera's curiosity about his apparent indifference to her, trying to fix her attention on the fishes so that she will think he does not want them transformed. Reera, bored unless she is doing some magic, falls into his trap:

"Why not let me transform them?"

"Well," said Ervic, as if hesitating, "ask the fishes. If they consent why—why then, I'll think it over."

Reera bent over the kettle and asked:

"Can you hear me, little fishes?"

All three popped their heads above the water.

"We can hear you," said the bronze fish.

"I want to give you other forms, such as rabbits, or turtles, or girls, or something; but your master, the surly Skeezer, does not wish me to. However, he has agreed to the plan if you will consent."

"We'd like to be girls," said the silver fish.

"No, no," exclaimed Ervic.

Ervic offers Baum's plea—no more girls—as a ruse. Reera responds with Baum's final bargain with the same girls—I'll do it one last time your way if you'll let me believe I'm having my own way:

"Will you agree to go away and leave me alone in my cottage, whenever I command you to do so?" asked Reera.

"We promise that," cried the three fishes.

"Don't do it! Don't consent to the transformation," urged Ervic.

Reera, like Baum, had succumbed long before. The child, grave and playful, had to be himself, and when he is that, he is also magic and transforming, and so Reera is transformed into someone helpful, and the fishes become girls once again.

It is as close, I think, as Baum ever came to understanding his art, this late scene between Ervic and the Yookoohoo. The conditions demanded that the child in this scene be more calculating, less simply accepting and responding, than the children in earlier enchanting moments in other books, because the cry to be left alone is harder to challenge, accept, or defy than the demand to leave the lunch pails alone or to have one's own head exchanged for another. Baum's usual definition of "evil" was only a presumed adult who acts childishly and is preemptory or has temper tantrums, but Reera is not evil, any more than Nimmie Aimee, or even Mrs. Yoop. In *Ozma* the Nome King actively seeks to destroy the Ev and Oz people by transforming them so that he can become more powerful; Reera stays home, surrounds herself with magic, and wants the Oz people to go somewhere else. All Baum seems to have known is that he was indeed a Yookoohoo, one who could do transformations, and that the world refused to tire of his magic. In the end he saw himself having to accept this fact about himself, just as Dorothy has to accept Langwidere's threat as a real one, preposterous though it is. Of course Baum is not as good as Dorothy at accepting, but he was old and tired and she is young and living in the morning. So, sweet as it is, splendidly and freshly written though it is, this scene can never be the one we remember most quickly when we think of Oz.

Baum's was such a rare gift that it seems almost impertinent to ask how good he is, or how much he achieved, or to try to assess his books with great soberness. He was careless of his art and he seldom wrote as well as he could; he never thought hard about life or grasped its complexities; he could not, even at his best, convey sadness or fear or deep joy. He has always been scorned, or guardedly admired, by the traditional custodians of children's literature, so he has had to find his audience in spite of teachers and librarians, for the most part. Yet his audience is still extremely large long after he and his naïve view of life have departed. The virtues of which these many apparently crushing limitations are only the defects are virtues of the sort we believe to exist in life far more than we ever expect to see in literature, and so Baum is rightly treasured more than many who seem to have a better claim on our respect and on our imagination. Neither we nor Ervic need ask why it is important to have the fishes transformed, or what difference it will make if they are, which is another way of saying that the magic itself, the transformation performed by Yookoohoos, is not the important quality in the Oz books; it exists mostly as validation of that other magic that is the child's wonderful acceptance of situation, self, and journey. That validation is total, and so the child and Baum's readers are never deceived, never shown anything they cannot trust or whose motives are ulterior; they need never be suspicious or mistrustful, never be grown up, and the readers can envy the child without folly or other penalty.

As a guide to life it is as naïve as it is essential. To be free of self and of the nagging necessities of maturity is usually to be irresponsible and wasteful, but on the roads to Oz it is truly liberating and enchanting, the challenge and promise of the morning.

(10)   Two Pigs

The first pig is Freddy, the central figure in a series of twenty-five books, the "Freddy books," written by Walter R. Brooks between the late 1920s and the early 1960s. If L. Frank Baum has a successor, it is Brooks, though there is no evidence that Brooks or anyone else ever thought of him that way. Brooks also is a rural American given to extolling the virtues of innocence, resourcefulness, and shrewdness, and to pleasantly and loosely plotted books in which combinations of these virtues can be put on display; Brooks's air is also that of an entertainer who just happens to have turned his hand to writing. To be sure, Baum's rural America is apt to be a bleak place, while Brooks's barnyard and small town world is standard American idyllic, and, to be sure, by the time Brooks was writing, this version of the American countryside had to seem almost as fantastic as Oz. But Brooks shares with Baum a kind of imperviousness, a sense that such discrepancies cannot really matter much when one's native good humor and capacity to be fascinated are strong. The Bean farmyard and Centerboro are pretty much the same when housing a baseball team from Mars in the fifties as when Freddy first solved a mystery and proved Simon the rat guilty back in the early thirties; it's a rather interesting place, still, isn't it, seems to be Brooks's tone, and no one ever thought it was a real place, actually, did they? Yet it is *like* a real place, too, and Brooks's amused playing with the facts of life in a blandly unreal way offers one of the most original handlings of the possibilities of talking animals in the annals of latterday children's literature.

Freddy and Mr. Camphor, the eleventh in the series, was published in 1944, in the closing years of World War II. About halfway through the book, Freddy is walking home from Mr. Camphor's in disgrace because he has been accused of being a thief and he cannot prove his innocence. He meets his best friend, Jinx the cat, who shows him a sign woven by two spiders, Mr. and Mrs. Webb, announcing a "Patriotic Mass Meeting" that same evening. The meeting is just for spiders and insects, and the animals are asked to stay away so they won't step on members of the audience. Freddy, though, is asked to come if he can bring Mr. Webb a megaphone so he can be heard by everyone. That night Mr. Webb gives his speech:

> "I see here tonight representatives from every walk of insect life. I am glad of that, for you all can help. Some, of course, more than others. I refer to the potato bugs, squash bugs, cabbage worms, cut worms, leaf hoppers, grasshoppers, caterpillars, and others whose main diet is garden vegetables. Now in ordinary times Mr. Bean does not grudge you what little you eat. It's only when there are too many of you and you begin to destroy his whole crop that he tries to drive you away. But this year I don't think you should destroy any of the crop. Mr. Bean is rationed in what he eats, and if you are patriotic bugs, you won't object to being rationed too. And I believe that you *are* patriotic bugs. And so I am going to ask you to agree not to eat any vegetables at all this year."

A potato bug stands up and says this is all well and good for Webb, who does not eat vegetables anyway, but what are the others to eat? "There's nightshade vines, for instance," answers Mr. Webb, "I know you potato bugs like nightshade, for I've seen you eatin' it." He then recommends milkweed for the caterpillars, not as good as garden vegetables, to be sure, but "for the duration," "for your country's sake. How about it, bugs?"

It is a delicious scene, totally unexpected in its context, and typical of what is best in all the Freddy books. Underlying everything is Brooks's piquant way of handling the facts of animal life: insects can get crushed if animals attend their meeting, a spider making a speech will need a megaphone. One imagines Beatrix Potter staring at a potato bug until it seems, in her copying of it, alive and wearing a human face; one imagines Walter Brooks having trouble with insects as he grows his victory garden, and thinking it would be wonderful if insects were patriotic, and he remembers once seeing a potato bug eat a deadly nightshade. It is the intensity of Potter's stare that makes her animals seem like human beings; it is Brooks's imagining that we are all in this together—in the business of staying alive, talking, upholding values in a diverse world, fighting a war—that gives his animals their most distinct coloring. In this case, what makes Brooks's patriotism piquant as well as appealing is an extension of a community he has been creating all along, because patriotism for him is only the voluntary cooperation of creatures who by nature would not cooperate. Mr. Bean is rationed, isn't he, and he thinks bugs and he can live together just fine until they start to kill his whole crop; why can't we be rationed too, then? How about it, bugs?

The reality of Brooks's animals is only the convenient reality they offer so they can then present pleasing problems. Wouldn't it be a grand circus if the animals got together with the owner to plan the acts? Yes, of course, but if the audience got used to talking and clever animals, wouldn't that take away the thrilling fear they feel when they see caged wild animals? Did you ever wish you had a rhinoceros on your side in a fight? No, but they would be good, wouldn't they; yet, since they see so poorly, they would be good only at charging fixed targets. Do animals like money? No, of course not, but they do find lots of coins and other valuable things people lose, so maybe it would be good if animals had a bank to keep these things safe, especially if they are trying to prove to Mr. Bean they are responsible enough to run the farm by themselves so he will agree to take Mrs. Bean to Europe. If Martians were only three feet tall but had four arms, would they not make great baseball pitchers? Yes, but being so small they could not throw very fast, and would have to rely on the batters' not knowing which arm they were going to throw with. If it would be nice if the animals could have just one winter in

Florida, who is going to wake the Beans up if Charles the rooster goes along, and it would not be right for all three cows to go because then the Beans would have no milk. If all the animals, including the big ones, use the duck pond to cool off during the summer, there is not going to be much room left for the ducks, is there? Even the mild-mannered ducks want then to know why it is called a duck pond.

The result is not beast fables, because Brooks raises these questions not to make some point but simply to ask how the animals, or the people, are going to answer or solve them. Animal natures and human nature are not imagined to be very different, and no one is in any persistent way superior to anyone else. What distinguishes creatures from each other is their size, or their activities; the actual goings-on of a barnyard, the planting and sowing and giving of milk, are seldom described in and for themselves, and they become interesting for Brooks only when they raise these funny little problems. Let us start with the pleasures of a peaceable community, as in the speech of Mr. Boomschmidt, the circus owner, in *The Story of Freginald:* " 'I've always tried to be good to my animals,' he said. 'I find it pays in the long run to let 'em do about as they please. It's nice for them to have friends in all the towns we visit, and nothing pleases me better when we're putting up the tents in a town we haven't visited in a year than to see a farmer and his wife rush up and shake hands with the hippopotamus and tell him how glad they are to see him, and how they've missed him while he's been away.' " Since anyone might miss, say, players on a team when one does not see them in the off-season, it is not hard to imagine friendly talking animals from a circus being missed while they're playing other towns. But, and this is always the characteristic Brooks turn, this presents problems: " 'But, on the other hand, I expect it isn't a good thing for the show. Nobody's going to pay twenty-five cents in the afternoon to see a panther they've entertained at their own home in the morning. Friends are one thing and a menagerie's another, though sometimes there isn't much difference. But who wants to pay to see his friends? The most important thing is to make this show a success.' " There's the problem, and so then the solution: " 'So I'm going to ask you, Louise, since you're our principal attraction, not to get too friendly with the neighborhood people. I hate to ask it of you —it seems kind of mean. But you see how it is. If we don't do it we'll fail to draw the crowds, just as the other animals have failed, and the show'll have to disband. Then we won't any of us have any more fun.' " The appeal for voluntary cooperation again. And the solution, as can easily be imagined, is one that in itself will lead to more problems.

Some of the problems, like this one, are so short-lived as to run their careers in just a speech or a page, some are given a whole chapter, like the appeal to the patriotism of the potato bugs, and one or two in each book are usually allowed to become the plot of the book, such as it is. Brooks's skill rests on his ability to calculate how much each of his piquancies is worth. The Bean farm is going to have unwanted visitors, and, after a long debate, the animals devise a plan. "It wasn't a very good plan though," Brooks adds, and so a page or two is probably enough to see how a not-very-good plan does not work. This is in *The Clockwork Twin,* and the twin himself is worth more than a few pages. A lad named Adoniram is living on the farm, and he needs a companion. Mr. Bean's brother, Uncle Ben, tinkers around with machines and comes up with a Tik-Tok-like creature. Jinx paints his face to look like Adoniram's, and he looks perfect as he first mechanically strides into the barnyard. But nothing has been devised to make him stop, and so he strides right into the duck pond. Unlike Tok-Tok the clockwork twin cannot think or speak; "No engineer," says Uncle Ben. Can a place be provided in the back of the twin for such an engineer? Ben thinks so. Who, then, will be the engineer? How about Ronald, a rooster recently arrived from England? Ronald is delighted: " 'It'll be just like having an automobile,' he said. 'I can drive him to Centerboro—go anywhere I want to—' 'The idea is to have a playmate for Adoniram,' said Freddy." Ronald agrees, of course, but here we can see that a clockwork twin with a rooster engineer, and a sound system whose voice can be heard for six miles, is going to be good for offering problems as well as being much too good just to serve as a companion for Adoniram. The plots that result are low-keyed, episodic, ramshackle, but, in another way, crucial.

In the first two Freddy books, *To and Again* and *More To and Again,* later retitled *Freddy Goes to Florida* and *Freddy Goes to the North Pole,* the journeys are the only plot there is, and the results are disappointing. Brooks has none of Baum's feel for the magic of traveling into the magical unknown. Florida is not Oz for him, is not even a particularly interesting destination, so that after some problem-solving involving a group of alligators, Brooks can only say the animals had a good winter and hope he can find a few things for them to do on the way home. The books are too episodic, spineless; the problems never blend or meld into other problems, but stay discrete and contained. They read, indeed, as though Brooks had invented a barnyard of talking animals to tell stories to a child or children, and then, when asked for more, he was pressed to invent things for his animals to do. This is a fate that overtakes E. B. White's *Stuart Little,* and, to a lesser extent, Tolkien's *The Hobbit,* because those authors are not as good as Walter Brooks or A. A. Milne at moment-to-moment inventiveness, which is essential for good episodic storytelling.

In the next four books, though, *Freddy the Detective, The Story of Freginald, The Clockwork Twin,* and *Wiggins for President,* Brooks really hits his stride, and these remain, on the whole, the most satisfying of the entire series. In each book problems arise which cannot be settled in a single episode, but no one problem is allowed to dominate the book, even though each has a big scene at the end that serves as climax and completion. In the first decade of the series, Freddy is not always or even usually the central figure. He is barely distinguishable among the others in the journey in the first two books, known only as the animal who writes poems and songs. But in the third book, *Freddy the Detective,* Freddy stumbles onto the fact that he can figure out who stole a toy train and then, at the climax, he makes his first of many exposures of the villainy of Simon the rat. The appeal of using Freddy as a central figure may have been clear to Brooks this early, because a pig has no "natural" activity on a farm other than geting fat, so he can become available to be the resident amateur, the central solver of problems. But Freddy did not assume this major role until later in the series, and when he did, when the books became the "Freddy books," when a number of the earlier books were retitled, something tended to go out of many of the books. In order to keep on finding new things for Freddy to do, Brooks had to resort to more controlled and dominating plots, and when he did this, certain of his best qualities were lost or muffled. All this is something that evolved so slowly that it seems unlikely that Brooks ever made a decision about these matters; like Baum,

Brooks seems to have had only an instinctive awareness of his best talents, so that he could develop his best form in the books of the thirties and then, under the pressure of having to write more books, he could evolve another, somewhat less satisfactory form perhaps without knowing it.

The reason Brooks works less well with a predesignated central figure and controlled plots lies in the nature of the solutions Brooks finds to the problems he poses. I spoke earlier, when discussing the patriotic potato bugs and the friendly circus animals, of the way in which certain problems are solved as the result of voluntary co-operation: a community is created when one animal or more is willing to act against the grain of his or her natural self; the coopera-tion is a willed triumph of sorts, and it often involves an expulsion if someone remains recalcitrant. The villains in Brooks's books, thus, are different from the others mostly in being obedient to their na-tures, in being obdurate when it is not, as Brooks sees it, altogether necessary. The human villains tend, thus, to be a rather standard and often scruffy lot, a man or groups of men whose nature is to be dirty, scheming, mistrustful; they also tend to be uninteresting. In some books, such dull villains might prove a near fatal defect— imagine *Treasure Island,* say, without Long John Silver, or *Othello* without Iago—but in the Freddy books this is usually no more than a blemish, since it is the way the others work together that is most interesting anyway. Still, the books with the animal villains usually work best, especially when the barnyard is the central stage for the action. All this is perhaps most clearly seen in *Wiggins for President,* which, if not the outstanding book in the series, is close enough to it to show off Brooks's major virtues and to conceal his shortcomings.

The Beans, as mentioned before, will go for a holiday to Europe if Mr. Bean can be convinced that the animals can be responsible and run the farm by themselves. Someone suggests that they need a president, someone who can run the barnyard as if it were a republic; someone else suggests starting a bank. Then a visitor comes, a wood-pecker named John Quincy Adams, whose life has been lived in Washington, D.C., and he looks upon coming to live in rural New York state as a grand lark. A perfect figure to run a bank, and though he knows nothing about banking and quickly admits this, he knows a lot about appearances:

"The quickest way to convince him is to start your bank."

"Well, why can't we do both right away?" asked Jinx.

"Because it will take longer to get the bank going," said the woodpecker. "Anybody can start a republic in five minutes. But a bank—well, you haven't even got any safe-deposit vaults yet."

As always, you solve a problem by creating another. Since safe-deposit vaults are the prime requisite of banks, Jinx hires some woodchucks to dig a twenty-five-foot tunnel and two rooms, for money and valuables, at the end of it. The animals flock to the bank, $21.03 is deposited the first day, and the valuables room fills up quickly; some must be rejected because the tunnel is small, and John Quincy will not let in foodstuffs, because "What kind of a bank is that to be president of—one that has its vaults full of nuts." Mr. Bean is much taken with the bank, especially when the woodpecker refuses a loan to a horse because he has no security, so he guarantees the loan himself and deposits a hundred dollars as well. When Mr. Weezer, of the human bank, objects that the First Animal Bank will cut into his business, Mr. Bean does just that and draws out all his savings, just under five thousand dollars, and deposits it in the First Animal.

In the earlier chapter on "Animals," I discussed problems of narrative expectation raised by an author's way of handling the humanness of animals; if the handling becomes fixed or settled too soon, a kind of paralyzed storytelling can result. At this moment in *Wiggins for President* Walter Brooks has set no clear limit on what his animals can or cannot do, but he has also seemed to bring his story to a halt, since if the opening problem was to gain Mr. Bean's confidence in the animals' sense of responsibility, that problem is now solved. But banks do generate their own problems, and we next have Freddy talking John the fox into building proper quarters for the bank, since it has so quickly outgrown what the woodchucks dug for it, and though he accepts John offers some doubts:

"Well," said John, "I wouldn't take too much woodpecker advice, if I were you. I don't trust those boys, and that's a fact. Don't ask me why. It's just a feeling. Don't you have those feelings?"

> "Why, now you mention it," said Freddy, "I guess I do. Weasels, now. I don't trust weasels. And yet I haven't any reason not to, really."

If we remember Rat's explanations to Mole about weasels in *The Wind in the Willows,* we can sense what Brooks is up to here. Rat's dubiousness about weasels is based on the fact that weasels "break out" and catch and eat rats. But foxes have no need to mistrust woodpeckers; Freddy has no need to mistrust weasels either. In Freddy's case it is, we notice, an unexplainable quirk, but in John's it is not woodpeckers as a group but "those boys" that he mistrusts. It is not clear why he mistrusts them, but Freddy agrees to keep this in mind, and the moment he gets back to the bank, he finds Jinx and John Quincy falling out because Jinx is not showing up for work at the bank, and Jinx is not showing up because there is never work enough for John Quincy, Freddy, and Jinx. John Quincy insists banks must have treasurers—"What kind of a bank is that? We've had quite enough of this, Jinx"—and Jinx quits:

> "I'm sorry, J.Q.," said Freddy as the woodpecker picked himself up and smoothed down his feathers, "but you asked for it. That's no way to handle Jinx. He's a good fellow, but—"
> "There's only one way to handle animals like him," said John Quincy, "and that's with a firm hand."

Slowly Brooks begins to make it clear why he thinks an animal bank might offer problems more interesting than gaining Mr. Bean's confidence. John Quincy's question—"What kind of a bank is that?"—is still up for grabs, but the question now is how human, as it were, it is to be. Jinx wants to take the sensible animal line and not have to show up for work when there is no work; John Quincy wants to insist banks must have officers and then to add that the unruly must always be handled with an iron fist, all of which marks him as one who has learned his rules in the human world. Finally, since banks must have treasurers, John Quincy says he will go off and recruit his father—"I think perhaps I could persuade him to come up and take charge"—and with that "take charge," we hear another ominous note.

It all begins to look a little like George Orwell's *Animal Farm,* though *Wiggins for President* not only preceded Orwell's work, but is a good deal more careful with its materials and, for that matter, shrewder about its politics. Orwell wanted to assume that the lock-step of a Communist takeover could be paralleled in a beast fable without making the fable's action seem mechanical, too; Brooks wants only to assume that the easygoing cooperative spirit of the Bean barnyard is susceptible to coercion. But since his subject is still the barnyard, the political actions take place within its yielding and varied contexts, so that the actions emerge much less mechanically than do Orwell's. In the next chapter Freddy finds himself voting that future bank board meetings be held in a new room dug out by John the fox, only to discover he is too big to get through the tunnel, so he cannot attend meetings or vote. John Quincy's father, Grover, takes Jinx's place on the board. Freddy blusters, says the woodpeckers better not try to fool him a second time. But he knows he is blustering and must shift his attention away from the bank and onto the election of the president of the new animal republic.

Freddy assumes that if the main animals of the barnyard stick together, they can name their candidate and win. But "there are a lot of animals living on this farm that we don't ever have much to do with. Field mice, woodchucks, squirrels, chipmunks—and the birds. I dare say there are a hundred birds, and they all have votes." If all these have votes, what about the insects? Exclude them, some-one says. What about Mr. and Mrs. Webb, the spiders—"They went with us all the way to Florida." Fortunately the Webbs decline to press the issue, and the thousands of bugs are to remain unen-franchised. Meanwhile, though, the rats have returned, Simon in the lead, and they can vote, and the woodpeckers have been out hustling votes too. So who will be the candidate for the Farmer's Party? Freddy declines—too much work. Charles the rooster volun-teers, but his wife declines for him. Hank the horse says he'd like to remain anonymous. So Mrs. Wiggins the cow is proposed; she's big, she can speak in public, she has common sense: " 'Well,' she said at last, 'all right. I'll do my best. If you'll all get behind me, as Freddy says, maybe we'll get somewhere. But,' she added with her booming laugh, 'if you shove good and hard it'll be better. A cow's awful hard to move.' " Problems, then solutions that create more problems, and all the time Brooks is making his problems by asking what in effect are political questions: Who votes? How to pick a candidate? Why can't we all just be for ourselves?

Especially, what does one do in the face of determined opposition? At the mass meeting to nominate candidates everyone turns out, even old Whibley the owl, whom no one has seen for years. The rats and the woodpeckers have combined to nominate Grover, and birds, more birds than anyone has seen, cheer wildly, so Mrs. Wiggins lets out a loud laugh: "And believe me, when a cow laughs as loud as she can, you sit up and listen. Lions aren't in it." This infuriates Grover, who in turn infuriates Whibley, and the threatened stampede is off:

> "And you say you're not clever!" said Freddy to Mrs. Wiggins, under cover of the excited buzz of conversation that went round the hall.
>
> "Thought it might stir 'em up," said the cow. "But old Whibley was just a piece of luck. Anyway, it's always safe to laugh and not explain, if the other side seems to be getting the best of an argument. Makes 'em think maybe they've said something foolish and don't know it."

Which is both precise and wonderful, not just laughter but great cow laughter employed as the solution to a problem that is political but not just political, so that it can be employed by anyone faced with an obdurate opposition. Whibley finds another such solution a little later when Grover demands an apology for Whibley's having insulted him at the meeting:

> "All right. I apologize."
>
> "You apologize?" said Grover.
>
> "Certainly. You *are* a stuffed shirt, and you *do* talk balderdash, but I apologize for saying so."

A friend of mine tells me she received her first and wisest initiation into political action when she read *Wiggins for President* before she was ten. One sees why. Instead of a lockstep fable, broad human action, all done by cows and owls.

The woodpeckers are not through yet, of course. Grover goes around the farm making promises—if elected, he will build a revolving door in the henhouse, have a special vegetable garden for the rabbits, make cat-proof apartments for the rats, and, Whibley guesses, intends to pay for all this by commandeering Mr. Bean's large deposit in the First Animal Bank. "What's Mr. Bean going to do? Go to law with a woodpecker?" But would it help Freddy to suggest that when John the fox dug the hole for the new bank rooms he must have made two entrances, since no fox would ever be content with just one? It does indeed. Freddy gets Peter the bear to enlarge the tunnel to the second entrance so he can crawl through, and he then tells the woodpeckers, who have demoted him to sixteenth vice-president, he wants to be president of the bank. They laugh, but when they arrive at the board meeting their entrance is blocked up, Freddy is serving as self-elected president in Grover's behalf: "When you play a mean trick on anybody, you want to go the whole way. You want to be as mean as you can. You should have thrown me out of the bank entirely, not left me in. That was your mistake. And now I think you'd better go. People not connected with the bank are not allowed in the vaults." At this point there are still a hundred pages to go, but Brooks has snaked and woven his way among his problems and solutions, and he still has many of both remaining, all of which have grown out of solutions to previous problems. Grover is far from finished as the candidate for president, the clockwork twin is renovated as a dangerous political toy, and even Mr. Wheezer, the president of the rival First National Bank, wants to get his revenge for having been thwarted when he first objected to the animals' bank, and each side finds ways to use the means employed against it to exploit the other side. But it never is a plot in any usual sense of the term; it is, rather, an elaborate unfolding of a long set of related problems and solutions that work almost like a chain reaction.

As can be easily imagined, there is no such thing as a final solution. Of course Grover is defeated and exiled, but Brooks's imagination is too shrewd to pretend that the point of it all is that John the fox is right and that one cannot trust woodpeckers. Nor does he imagine that the vast array of political wisdom he has offered will immediately be permanently learned by all the animals. One reason, indeed, that Brooks's solutions are so satisfying is that he does not imagine one solves all that much with them. The genius is comic and situational, not thoughtful or doctrinal. It may not always work to laugh without apparent reason at one's opponents; it certainly will not always work to tell someone they are what you claimed they are and then to apologize for saying so, or to advise players of mean tricks to go in for no halfway measures. In Brooks's barnyard there is no heroic upholder of democracy in the face of organized would-be tyrants, though the kinds of difficulties democracies can get into have seldom been more clearly shown. Freddy himself is mostly just an activist in *Wiggins for President*, much in need of the foresight of John, the widom of Whibley, the laughter of Mrs. Wiggins. Nor are the results peace and love so much as comic triumph and a momentarily achieved community that recognizes how temporary such achievements must be when conversion and changes of heart are not possible and voluntary cooperation is all one can hope for.

When our children were young, and sick or home from school, my wife would read them Freddy books aloud, and the house would be filled with giggles and cackles from all three. I had read some Freddy books when young, but had never responded that way, and I did not join in the laughter later on. I doubt if an adult, reading even the best of these books silently, would do much giggling and cackling, but one can easily and even constantly be tickled by them, by Brooks's clear sense of his own limits and possibilities. Kenneth Grahame moved his comic fantasies toward the religious, and if that got him into trouble, it also allowed him to warm and move the heart. Brooks's genius is altogether more secular than that and less enchanted than Baum's, but perhaps for that reason he could write many books where Grahame could only write one, and the general level of his series is closer to his best books than is true of Baum's. Because there is neither magic nor mystery in Brooks, he probably can never be as popular a writer as most of the others discussed in this book. He is, though, a winning author, one that anyone can carry around through one's days, because one's days have many situations in them very much like Brooks's. There is so little verbal magic in him that one can barely remember lines—though I've grown quite fond of "Lions aren't in it"—but one can easily be in Alice's and Emma's situation when the other animals are taking over "their" duck pond, or Hank's when he is asked if he'd like being president—"If I could just be president on the good days, I dunno's I'd mind. But every day for a year ain't my choice." It would be lovely, too, if Brooks's piquant solutions worked as well in life as they do in his books, as he tempts us to believe they might. He is our real Johnny Dooit. Life, alas, is something else again.

The second pig is Wilbur, the central figure of E.B. White's *Charlotte's Web*, which is probably *the* classic American children's book of the last thirty years. White's is rather an odd case. On the one hand he is the one author considered here who has made a full and lasting reputation as a writer of other kinds of literature, the essays and sketches that for so many years distinguished the pages of *Harper's* and the *New Yorker*. On the other he is the author of three children's books—*Stuart Little* and *The Trumpet of the Swan* are the other two—and neither, it seems to me, is even good enough to be called a distinguished or considerable failure. One might conclude that White is just not a writer of books, except that *Charlotte's Web* is full, sustained, serene, a *book* in ways that perhaps only the great Potters and *Kim* rival or exceed among all those discussed in these essays. One surmises that he seldom tried to think of himself as a writer of whole books, which is perhaps just as well, given his talents. But with *Charlotte's Web* he worked hard to get it to come right, and he did not let himself be satisfied until he had. *Stuart Little*, by comparison, is terribly bored during many of its episodes, and *The Trumpet of the Swan* seems explainable as a book that White wrote for personal reasons that he never could get to square articulately with his materials. But *Charlotte's Web* is a gem, the perfect book with which to end this one.

White calls *Charlotte's Web* a "hymn to the barn," and it is the word "hymn," and the sense of celebration and praise, that is important here, though the way the book is a hymn is not clear at the outset. Brooks's way with his barn is from the beginning detached, amused, and dedicated to the proposition that the barnyard has problems, that problems have solutions, and that nothing essentially ever changes. There are no seasons in the Freddy books, the barnyard activities are assumed rather than described, and no one ever grows a day older. White's way is different; with him process and change are all, because only buildings and tools are unchanging, and the essential celebration is of the beautiful things change brings or can bring. But the key change, the one upon which our sense of all the others hangs, comes early, before we are fully aware of White's way with realism and with animals. By the third chapter, by the twentieth page, White has played his one magical trick, because of which he can show in a nonrealistic way what the life of a barn is really like.

The opening pages are all realism. A sow has littered, and one of her piglets is a runt, and Mr. Arable is going to kill it "because it would probably die anyway." His daughter Fern is outraged:

> "But it's unfair," cried Fern. "The pig couldn't help being born small, could it? If I had been very small at birth, would you have killed *me*?"
>
> Mr. Arable smiled. "Certainly not," he said, looking down at his daughter with love. "But this is different. A little girl is one thing, a little runty pig is another."

This is a variation that none of our books so far has faced: human beings value animals less than they do human beings, and farmers tend to treat animals as conveniences and necessities rather than as fellow creatures. White next does all he can to make his reversal of Lewis Carroll's "Pig and Pepper" seem a joke at Fern's expense. Her father agrees to let Fern keep the runt, and Fern gives it a bottle, names it Wilbur, puts it in a baby carriage, and we are told "he liked this." But the moment Wilbur's appetite begins to increase, Fern's father insists he must be sold, and Fern's efforts at motherhood come to an end: pigs are not human, and they mature much faster too. The best that can be done for Wilbur is to sell him to Uncle Homer Zuckerman, whose farm is not far off.

So first we thwart the "natural human" tendency to want to treat animals like people. Next we put Wilbur into Zuckerman's barn and make Fern into nothing more than an occasional bystander; Uncle Homer won't allow Fern into Wilbur's pen, but she comes every afternoon: "Here she sat quietly during the long afternoons, thinking and listening and watching Wilbur. The sheep soon got to know her and trust her. So did the geese, who lived with the sheep. All the animals trusted her, she was so quiet and friendly." The sentences are all peaceful, but they are building a bridge. Wilbur "liked" being in Fern's baby carriage, and now the animals "trusted" Fern.

If it will not work to deny the possibility of animals' liking and trusting, then it can make "Wilbur happy to know that she was sitting there, right outside his pen," and in the context of that trusting happiness, we learn "But he never had any fun—no walks, no rides, no swims." Are we over the line yet, the one we usually draw between thoughts and feelings we easily imagine intelligent animals having, and those we seriously doubt them having? Can Wilbur remember his treatment as an infant by Fern? Can he stand "in the sun feeling lonely and bored"? Can he say "I'm less than two months old and I'm tired of living"? He can, of course, and he does, but White has also moved across his bridge to the unrealistic quietly and without fuss, as though Wilbur's thoughts and speaking were available to him and us because Fern has sat watching him in ways more patient than the rest of us offer animals.

Once Wilbur can speak and know he is two months old, then the gander can tell him about a loose board in his pen, and he can seek the outside world. From this point on White never shifts his bearings; having given himself this much magic on page 16, he uses it to sing his otherwise realistic hymn to the barn. This is Selma Lagerlöf's way too, and White's intentions are similar, if softer. Both want to imagine it is only human egotism and busyness that prevents us from seeing the lives of animals that are lived all around us, lives that could, they say, be understood in human terms. Wilbur can be bored and lonely, plan out his day in advance, and be disappointed when that day comes up raining. As I write this I watch my cat, staring out the window on a rainy morning. Usually he goes outside and sniffs about in the yard at this time, but he hates rain. Is he lonely, bored, disappointed? Randall Jarrell's mermaid would say no, and certainly if he feels something like these feelings, he does not respond to them with the same impatience or mournfulness that I would. But when I read about Wilbur's loneliness I think I don't understand my cat very clearly because my patience and imagination are weak. Think what a long day it would be—"I have no real friend here in the barn, it's going to rain all morning and all afternoon, and Fern won't come in such bad weather" (p. 27). The goose can't play because she is sitting on her nest, the lamb won't play because she is not interested in pigs, Templeton the rat won't play because he hardly knows the meaning of the word: "I prefer to spend my time eating, gnawing, spying, and hiding" (p. 29). So the same circumstances concerning the lives of pigs which amused Walter Brooks into making Freddy an amateur and thus his central figure are those which make time and loneliness so oppressive for Wilbur. Pigs, as he is soon to learn, are given nothing to do except eating and growing fat.

But before he learns that, he finds his friend, a voice from the rafters as he goes asleep one night, Charlotte A. Cavatica as she introduces herself the next morning, a spider about the size of a gumdrop. As if to make sure he realizes what Templeton was telling him the day before—some creatures around here get fed by farmers, and some just have to make their own way—Charlotte first shows Wilbur how she traps flies, then stuns them, then drinks their blood; "I love blood," she says; " 'Don't say that!' groaned Wilbur"; "Why not? It's true." No blood, no spiders; no spiders, no friend for Wilbur. White then drops a stitch, as it were, and ends this chapter with a needless reassuring note about Charlotte's true kind heart, "and she was to prove loyal and true to the very end." It is as though White knows to his own satisfaction why he wants to introduce Charlotte as a lover of blood—to get that over with so he can ignore it—but is nervous his young readers will not see this. As always, when a writer fixes on children as the audience, a mistake is almost sure to follow. Beatrix Potter never makes such mistakes, and White, fortunately, makes very few.

Having established his cast, White is ready to begin singing his hymn:

> The early summer days on a farm are the happiest and fairest days of the year. Lilacs bloom and make the air sweet, and then fade. Apple blossoms come with the lilacs, and the bees visit around among the apple trees. The days grow warm and soft. School ends, and children have time to play and to fish for trouts in the brook. Avery often brought a trout home in his pocket, warm and stiff and ready to be fried for supper.
>
> Now that school was over, Fern visited the barn almost every day, to sit quietly on her stool. The animals treated her as an equal. The sheep lay calmly at her feet.

Then we have the farmers in the field, the bird songs, including the song sparrow, "who knows how brief and lovely life is," and says, "Sweet, sweet, sweet interlude; sweet, sweet, sweet interlude." The interlude is the moment of singing, the early summer days, and all of life, and all three at once. "Everywhere you look is life; even the little ball of spit on the weed stalk, if you poke it apart, has a green worm inside it. And on the under side of the leaf of the potato vine are the bright orange eggs of the potato bug."

White does not imagine the song sparrow understands its song as White asks us to understand it; it takes a human mind to know fully the meaning of "sweet interlude." Nor is it beauty White is concerned with, but the acknowledgment that the love of life, especially the love of early summer days, includes the knowledge of transience and death. For the problem is Wilbur, eating three times a day and getting fat:

> "Well, I don't like to spread bad news," said the sheep, "but they're fattening you up because they're going to kill you, that's why."
>
> "They're going to *what?*" screamed Wilbur. Fern grew rigid on her stool.
>
> "Kill you. Turn you into smoked bacon and ham," continued the old sheep. "Almost all young pigs get murdered by the farmer as soon as the real cold weather sets in."

"Fern grew rigid on her stool," not as though she wants to protest Wilbur's Christmas death, but as though she does not want him to know about it. Though she is fully immersed in the life of the barn, for reasons as yet obscure she is not as she was, and when, in the next chapter, she tells her parents about Templeton taking the goose's runty egg away, and about what Charlotte says and how Wilbur feels about Charlotte, she never once mentions the old sheep's bad news about pigs and Christmas.

Without Fern to help this time, Wilbur runs to Charlotte. She might have told him that just as she needs blood to live, farmers need smoked meat to get them through the winter. Instead she says, "If she says they plan to kill you, I'm sure it's true. It's also the dirtiest trick I ever heard of. What people don't think of!" She then tells Wilbur she will save him, somehow. Charlotte, then, assumes the position Fern took at the opening of the book: she becomes the protester against injustice, though she has no court of appeal. Then, later, after he has had a chance to calm down, Wilbur can offer the real reason, or at least White's real reason, for not wanting to die:

> "Charlotte?" he said softly.
>
> "Yes, Wilbur?"
>
> "I don't want to die."
>
> "Of course you don't," said Charlotte in a comforting voice.
>
> "I just love it here in the barn," said Wilbur. "I love everything about this place."

So White's first hymn, in praise of early summer days, has come to this; the more one loves life, the less one wants to leave it; Wilbur hears the seven goslings whistling, "like a tiny troupe of pipers," and listens "with love in his heart." So he too has taken over part of Fern's position.

One summer afternoon Fern and her brother Avery are playing on a rope swing in Zuckerman's barn when Avery spots Charlotte's web hanging from the rafter next to the swing. He decides to do the human thing and get rid of it, but as he climbs above Wilbur's pig trough he stumbles, falls, and lands on the by-now rotten egg Templeton has been saving. The smell immediately drives him away, and Charlotte and her web are saved. None of this is lost on Wilbur —"It was that rotten goose egg that saved Charlotte's life," he says, and that night he remembers to leave a little extra of his food so Templeton can scavenge it: "Then he remembered that the rat had been useful in saving Charlotte's life, and that Charlotte was trying to save *his* life. So he left a whole noodle, instead of a half." We are back, though by a very different route, to Walter Brooks's sense of the barnyard as a place of mutual cooperation, though White sounds this note in a different key. A whole noodle instead of a half is not a lot, but it is quite a bit. At this point White and Wilbur are ready for Charlotte's "miracle."

Actually, it takes a human perspective to call it a miracle, and White has been urging us for some time to take a somewhat different one. But there it is; Zuckerman's hired man, Lurvy, comes to the barn one morning and sees, distinctly, the words SOME PIG written in Charlotte's web. Clearly, if Wilbur and Charlotte and the others can speak English, it is only a short step to their being able to write it, so there is no reason why we should be surprised at all at the message in Charlotte's web. But of those who first see it, only Mrs. Zuckerman concludes that the extraordinary one is not the pig but the spider. We are to presume Charlotte had counted on that, and there follows some not altogether satisfactory satire about the gullibility of human beings, all of whom think Wilbur is or has become miraculously SOME PIG because Charlotte's web says so. So Charlotte makes another message, the single word TERRIFIC. Wilbur has become Zuckerman's famous pig, and he is to be sent to the county fair for show, and it seems clear that although the people now own the pig and all the publicity attendant upon Charlotte's "miracle," Wilbur is safe.

But if human beings are fools, what of Fern? She has become the one her mother worries about when she talks about the conversations in the barnyard, and White does not want to lose her, though he clearly has, since early in the book, wanted to keep her in the background. One night, after Charlotte sings Wilbur to sleep with a lullaby with its own barnyard lyrics—"Rest from care, my one and only, Deep in the dung and the dark"—White adds, "When the song ended, Fern got up and went home," though he had not said she was even there. In the next chapter Mrs. Arable goes to see the genial and bearded Dr. Dorian, who immediately says it is fine if Fern spends all her time in the barn and asks if anyone has noticed that the ability of a spider to spin a web is itself a miracle, message or no message. What Dr. Dorian is doing in the book at all is, unfortunately, too obvious: he is the wise one who will say that Fern too can expect change, just like Charlotte and Wilbur, because it is only the obdurate adult human beings who truly resist changes and changing. Fern fought to keep Wilbur alive, and then became a silent watcher of the barn; the next step, White and Dr. Dorian assure us, is boys: "Let Fern associate with her friends in the barn if she wants to. I would say, offhand, that spiders and pigs were fully as interesting as Henry Fussy. Yet I predict that the day will come when even Henry will drop some chance remark that catches Fern's attention. It's amazing how children change from year to year." So at the county fair Fern is off with Henry Fussy, while the central drama is played without her, or her attentiveness.

The hymn begins again: "The crickets sang in the grasses. They sang the song of summer's ending, a sad, monotonous song. 'Summer is over and gone,' they sang. 'Over and gone, over and gone. Summer is dying, dying.' " The children know school opens soon, Lurvy knows it's time to dig potatoes, "Charlotte heard it and knew that she hadn't much time left." It's time for her to lay her eggs, and she must build an egg sac, and she tells Wilbur she should not leave her web to go to the county fair. But she decides Wilbur may need her, and she gets Templeton to come along to run errands; in addition, says the old sheep, "a fair is a rat's paradise." So Charlotte and Templeton hide down in the bottom of Wilbur's van and go with him to the fair, where Fern finds Henry Fussy, where Wilbur is not given the blue ribbon but gets a special award anyway because he is SOME PIG, where Templeton gorges himself as he never has before, where Charlotte weaves her last message, HUMBLE, over Wilbur's pen, and also makes her own egg sac, "made of the toughest material I have," where five hundred and fourteen spiders will gestate until the following spring. It is Charlotte's magnum opus, as she says, but partly because she will make only one in her life, and the end of summer means the end of living for her. The hour of Wilbur's triumph comes when he receives his award, but the book's climax comes a little later:

> For a moment Charlotte said nothing. Then she spoke in a voice so low Wilbur could hardly hear the words.
> "I will not be going back to the barn," she said.
> Wilbur leaped to his feet. "Not going back?" he cried. "Charlotte, what are you talking about!"
> "I'm done for," she replied. "In a day or two I'll be dead. I haven't even strength enough to climb down into the crate. I doubt if I have enough silk in my spinnerets to lower me to the ground."

Consciousness, we may often feel, is a debilitating and isolating capacity; it keeps us from having the simple dignity of animals. White gives Charlotte the knowledge that she is dying, but retains the simple dignity of which consciousness usually deprives us. "After all," she tells Wilbur when he asks why she did so much for him, "what's a life, anyway? We're born, we live a little while, we die. A spider's life can't help being something of a mess, with all this trapping and eating flies." The speech is a trifle too pat, but it is hard to know how White might have improved it, because what makes it pat is not so much the words themselves but its being offered as an obviously climactic and concluding attitude. "By helping you," Charlotte goes on, "perhaps I was trying to lift up my life a trifle." That *is* awkwardly said, because White can have Charlotte say "We're born, we live a little while, we die," only if she can add what he has insistently shown: she is SOME SPIDER.

On the one hand White wants us to move into the barn and to imagine the lives of pigs and spiders as being much more interesting than we know. But on the other he wants to tell the story of an extraordinary spider, so that the next time we are tempted to clear out a spider's web we may pause, but know as we do so that that spider is no Charlotte. Charlotte has done more than "lift up" her life "a little." It is a ticklish situation for White, and perhaps one should not mind if he does not handle it as deftly as we could wish. He does much better at the end, after Wilbur has talked Templeton into getting Charlotte's egg sac for him so he can place it under his tongue and bring the spider eggs back to the barn: "She never moved again. Next day, as the Ferris wheel was being taken apart and the race horses were being loaded into vans and the entertainers were packing their belongings and driving away in their trailers, Charlotte died. The Fair Grounds were soon deserted. The sheds and buildings were empty and forlorn. The infield was littered with bottles and trash. Nobody, of the hundreds of people that had visited the Fair, knew that a grey spider had played the most important part of all. No one was with her when she died." The county fair is over just as the summer is over, and it does not matter much if anyone is with Charlotte when she dies. But she did play the most important part of all, she performed the one less than fully natural and heroic act of being Wilbur's friend and saving his life and creating his fame. No need here to insist we should not cry if we feel like crying; it is more important that the simple dignity be Charlotte's than White's, more important that he be dignified than we.

Wilbur, Charlotte's one and only, "came home to his beloved manure pile," deep in the dung and the dark. He has now been guaranteed what, considering the lives of most pigs, is an unnaturally long life. After the autumn comes snow, and Fern and Avery go sledding:

"Coasting is the most fun there is," said Avery.

"The most fun there is," retorted Fern, "is when the Ferris wheel stops and Henry and I are in the top car and Henry makes the car swing and we can see everything for miles and miles and miles."

"Goodness, are you still thinking about that ol' Ferris wheel?" said Avery in disgust. "The Fair was weeks and weeks ago."

"I think about it all the time," said Fern, picking snow from her ear.

Avery has learned one of White's messages: time passes, things change, live with what comes. Fern, sentimental still, cannot think back to her saving Wilbur's life, but she can learn in her own way the other message: remember the best things, treasure them.

Spring comes, a new lamb is born and the goose lays nine new eggs, and Charlotte's tiny spiders crawl from the egg sac. There are dozens and dozens spinning little webs near the sac, but soon most have left, and only three, Joy, Aranea, and Nellie, are left to spin webs in the rafters above Wilbur's pen. At the end White sings his two hymns one last time. First:

> It was the best place to be, thought Wilbur, this warm delicious cellar, with the garrulous geese, the changing seasons, the heat of the sun, the passage of swallows, the nearness of rats, the sameness of sheep, the love of spiders, the smell of manure, the glory of everything.

Then:

> Wilbur never forgot Charlotte. Although he loved her children and grandchildren dearly, none of the new spiders ever quite took her place in his heart. She was in a class by herself. It is not often that someone comes along who is a true friend and a good writer. Charlotte was both.

White may not know here how to sing this hymn as well as the other, but no matter, because he has sung it well enough earlier. It is a sweet interlude of a book.

Notes on Sources

The quotations in Chapter 1 are from Dr. Seuss, *The 500 Hats of Bartholomew Cubbins* (New York, Vanguard, 1938), Jean de Brunhoff, *The Travels of Babar* (New York, Random House, 1934), and A. A. Milne, *The World of Pooh* (New York, Dutton, 1957).

I do not know of any one good all-purpose fairy tale book now in print; the best I have ever seen is *The Fairy Tale Book*, with translations by Marie Ponsot and illustrations by Adrienne Ségur, which Golden Press published twenty years ago. With the increased popularity of children's literature as a course on American campuses, Dover Publications has reprinted some classics: many of the Andrew Lang *Fairy Books*, an 1886 selection of Grimm stories translated by Lucy Crane, and an edition of Perrault's *Contes* translated by A. E. Johnson with illustrations from drawings by Gustave Doré. Iona and Peter Opie, in *The Classic Fairy Tales* (New York, Oxford, 1974), reprint tales from many countries in their earlier English translation, and offer useful commentary. The translations of "The Juniper Tree" and "Snow White" in this chapter are by Lore Segal, *The Juniper Tree and Other Tales from Grimm* (New York, Farrar, Straus and Giroux, 1973, 2 vols., illustrated by Maurice Sendak); that of "The Death of the Hen" is by Lucy Crane from the Dover Publications book mentioned above. Other works quoted in Chapter 2 are Philippe Ariès, *Centuries of Childhood* (New York, Knopf, 1962), p. 411; *The Parental Instructor* in Leonard de Vries, *Flowers of Delight* (New York, Pantheon, 1965), p. 91; Bruno Bettelheim, *The Uses of Enchantment* (New York, Knopf, 1976), pp. 206–211, 212; Harold Bloom's review of Bettelheim's book in *The New York Review of Books*, July 15, 1976; J. R. R. Tolkien, *Tree and Leaf* (Boston, Houghton Mifflin, 1965), pp. 31, 32; Elizabeth Cook, *The Ordinary and the Fabulous* (London, Cambridge University Press, 1965), p. 5.

With the exception of Perrault, the French tellers discussed in "Written Tales" have not been blessed with twentieth-century editions of their works in English, and the older ones are long out of print. The best source I can offer for the quotation from Madame de Murat is the introduction to an edition of Madame d'Aulnoy's *Fairy Tales* (London, Lawrence & Bullen, 1895) by Anne Thackeray Ritchie. The quotations from d'Aulnoy's "Green Snake" are from the translation by J. R. Planché (London, George Rutledge, 1855), except for the final quatrain, which I quote from the much prettier translation of Annie Macdonnell in Ritchie's edition. The quotations from Madame Le Prince de Beaumont's "Beauty and the Beast" are from Marie Ponsot's translation, *The Fairy Tale Book* (New York, Golden Press, 1958); an adaptation of Madame de Villeneuve's version is readily accessible in Lang's *Blue Fairy Book*. The translations from Hans Christian Andersen are by Paul Leyssac, *It's Perfectly True* (New York, Harcourt, Brace, 1938); Karen Blixen's remark about Andersen can be found in Monica Stirling, *The Wild Swan* (New York, Harcourt, Brace & World, 1965), p. 112.

The quotations in the chapter on animals are from Randall Jarrell, *The Animal Family* (New York, Pantheon, 1965), and from Selma Lagerlöf, *The Wonderful Adventures of Nils*, translated by Velma Swanston Howard (New York, Pantheon, 1947). C. S. Lewis, *The Discarded Image* (Cambridge University Press, 1965), offers a good summary description of the "old" universe before the latter days.

Quotations from the Alice books are from *The Annotated Alice*, ed. Martin Gardner (New York, Clarkson N. Potter, 1960); Lewis Carroll's description of the White Queen is from *The Lewis Carroll Picture Book*, ed. Stewart Collingwood (London, T. Fisher Unwin, 1899). All quotations of criticism are from Robert Phillips' excellent *Aspects of Alice* (New York, Vanguard, 1971): from Jan B. Gordon,

p. 94; from Florence Becker Lennon, p. 68; from Roger Lancelyn Green's biography, which cites the passages by Canon Duckworth and Lewis Carroll on the composition of the Alice books, pp. 16, 28, 29; from Roger Holmes, pp. 171, 172–173; from William Empson, p. 371; from W. H. Auden, p. 12.

The Beatrix Potter books are all in print in editions by her original publisher, Frederick Warne, and all quotations are from them. The biographical information comes primarily from Margaret Lane, *The Tale of Beatrix Potter* (London, Frederick Warne, 1968); the quotation from Lane is on p. 45; and the letter by Potter is on p. 78. *The Journal of Beatrix Potter* was decoded and edited by Leslie Linder (London, Frederick Warne, 1966); quotations are from pp. 64, 116, 119, 91, 186, 80, 64, 92, 67, 106. Linder, along with Enid Linder, assembled the beautiful *The Art of Beatrix Potter* (London, Frederick Warne, 1955).

Quotations from Kenneth Grahame are from *"The Golden Age" and "Dream Days"* (London, John Murray, 1962) and from *The Wind in the Willows* (New York, Scribner's, 1933, illustrated by E. H. Shepard). The passage by Jessie Currie about F. J. Furnivall is from *F. J. Furnivall: A Record* (London, H. Froude, 1911), pp. 29–30. The passage from Angus Wilson is from *The Naughty Nineties* (London, Eyre & Methuen, 1976), p. 13. The major biography of Grahame is by Peter Green, *Kenneth Grahame* (London, John Murray, 1959); Grahame's letter to his wife is quoted from p. 211.

All quotations from Kipling are from *The Writings in Prose and Verse of Rudyard Kipling* (New York, Scribner's, 1909–1911). George Orwell's essay on Kipling can be found in *A Collection of Essays* (New York, Doubleday, 1954); T. S. Eliot's in *On Poetry and Poets* (New York, Farrar, Straus, and Cudahy, 1957); Kingsley Amis' remark about *The Jungle Books* can be found in his *Rudyard Kipling and His World* (New York, Scribner's, 1976); Philip Mason's about Kipling's faith in *Kipling: The Glass, The Shadow and the Fire* (New York, Harper & Row, 1975), and I have used Mason for most of my biographical material; Edmund Wilson's about *Kim* in "The Kipling That Nobody Read," *The Wound and the Bow* (New York, Oxford, 1941), p. 123. Kipling's statement about his feelings on returning to India can be found in *Something of Myself* (London, Library Edition, 1951), p. 39.

The Oz books, except for *The Wizard*, were originally published by Reilly & Lee and are still kept in print by Rand McNally; my quotations are from these editions. With the Oz books, more than any others discussed in this book, there is a great difference in the quality of the illustrations between early impressions and those currently available; to see an early impression is to see clearly and beautifully reproduced illustrations, many in color, and printed on colored pages quite often. The biographical information and quotations are from Martin Gardner and Russel B. Nye, *The Wizard of Oz and Who He Was* (East Lansing, Michigan State University Press, 1957). A useful checklist of Baum's writings can be found in Fred Meyer, "Lyman Frank Baum: A Chronological Checklist for his Published Writings," *The Baum Bugle*, X (1966), 15–18.

The editions of the Freddy books cited here are all from the original editions published by Alfred A. Knopf, most still in print; the quotations from *Charlotte's Web* are from the original edition, illustrated by Garth Williams (New York, Harper & Row, 1952).

Illustrations

Chapter 1: Jean de Brunhoff, *Babar the King*, translated by Merle Haas. Copyright 1935 and renewed 1963 by Random House, Inc. Reprinted by permission of the publisher. Chapter 2: *Household Stories from the Collection of the Bros. Grimm*, illustrated by Walter Crane (New York: R. Worthington, 1883). Chapter 3: Walter Crane's Toy Books: *Beauty and the Beast* (London: George Routledge and Sons, 1875). Chapter 4: Beatrix Potter, *The Tale of Peter Rabbit*. Reprinted by permission of the publisher, Frederick Warne & Co., Inc. Chapter 5: Lewis Carroll, *Through the Looking-Glass*, illustrated by John Tenniel (London and New York: Macmillan and Company, 1878). Chapter 6: Beatrix Potter, *The Roly-Poly Pudding*. Reprinted by permission of the publisher, Frederick Warne & Co., Inc. Chapter 7: Kenneth Grahame, *The Wind in the Willows*, illustrated by Ernest H. Shepard. Copyright 1908 by Charles Scribner's Sons; copyright 1961 by Ernest H. Shepard. Reprinted by permission of the publisher. Chapter 8: *Kim*, drawing by Tim Sale, 1978. Chapter 9: L. Frank Baum, *The Wonderful Wizard of Oz*, illustrated by W. W. Denslow (Chicago: George W. Hill, 1900). Chapter 10: E. B. White, *Charlotte's Web*, illustrated by Garth Williams. Copyright 1952 by E. B. White. Reprinted by permission of Harper & Row, Publishers, Inc.

Index